Sam

Sam

A Political Philosophy

WILLIAM JOHN COX

Copyright © 2015 William John Cox

All Rights Reserved.
No part of this publication can be reproduced or
transmitted in any form or by any means,
electronic or mechanical,
without permission in writing from William John Cox,
who asserts his moral right to be identified
as the author of this work.

Mindkind Publications
www.mindkind.info

Portions previously published as articles and electronically as
The Man Who Ate His Fingers: War & Justice.
ISBN 978-0-9857850-6-2
Copyright © 2012 William John Cox

Chapters on Money Matters and Free Enterprise drawn from same
source documents by author as similar chapters in *Transforming America.*

Cover painting by Helen Werner Cox
www.helenwernercox.com

Author photograph by Catherine Diane Frost

ISBN: 0985785071
ISBN 9780985785079

ALSO BY WILLIAM JOHN COX
Hello: We Speak the Truth
You're Not Stupid! Get the Truth: A Brief on the Bush Presidency
Mitt Romney and the Mormon Church: Questions
Target Iran: Drawing Red Lines in the Sand
The Holocaust Case: Defeat of Denial
The Book of Mindkind: A Philosophy for the New Millennium
Transforming America: A Voters' Bill of Rights
An Essential History of China: Why it Matters to Americans
Millennial Math & Physics

Contents

Names xv
Sam's Ordeal 1
    The First Day 7
    The Second Day 8
    The Third Day 9
    The Fourth Day 11
    The Fifth Day 13
    The Weekend 14
    The Sixth Day 15
    The Seventh Day 16
    The Eighth Day 18
    The Ninth Day 19
    The Tenth Day 22
Recovery 25
    Sam's Mental Health 26
    A New Home 28
Sam's Philosophy 31
A Nurturing Society 37
    What Happened to the American Dream? 38
The Way of Women 58
Outlaw War 77
    The Stupidity of War 78
    The War in Iraq 82

    Preemptive War · 88
    Nuclear Weapons · 91
    Military Industrial Complex · 98
    Military Mercenaries · 103
    Outlaw War · 105
A Safe, Just, and Civil Society · 117
    A Government of Laws and Not of Men · · · · · · · · · · · · · · · 126
    The Disease of Crime · 132
    Militarization of the Police · 135
    Gun Control · 137
    Peers For Peace · 142
    The Exclusionary Rule · 143
    Voluntary Confessions and Eyewitness Identifications · · · · · · 144
    The Death Penalty · 147
    The War on Drugs · 150
    Criminalization in a Punitive Society · · · · · · · · · · · · · · · · · 155
    Prison Reform · 157
    Juvenile Justice · 164
    Life or Death · 165
    Rehabilitating Corrections · 166
    Civil Commitment of Sex Offenders · · · · · · · · · · · · · · · · 170
    Private Prisons · 173
    Martial Law and Concentration Camps · · · · · · · · · · · · · · 176
    Big Brother is Watching · 181
    What Can Be Done? · 186
The Most Valuable Rights · 189
    Freedom of Speech · 192
    Freedom of Religion · 194
    Freedom of the Press · 202
    The Illiberal Media · 203
    Freedom of Information · 205
    State Secrets Privilege · 207

    Political Censorship · 207
    Advertising Inherently Harmful Products and Services · · · · · 209
    Internet Neutrality · 211
Hope for Change · 213
Money Matters · 218
    What is Money? · 221
    A Brief History of American Finance · · · · · · · · · · · · · · · · · · 222
    The Great Depression · 226
    Banking Reform and Regulation · 227
    Deregulation · 231
    Aftermath of Deregulation · 233
    The Economic Casino · 235
    The First Failures · 238
    Black September 2008 · 240
    Recovery · 244
    State Banks · 248
    A National Bank · 249
    Student Loans · 252
    Reasonable Regulation and Transparency · · · · · · · · · · · · · · · 253
Free Enterprise · 254
    Capitalism · 258
    Corporate Power · 259
    Industrialization and Labor · 262
    The Dangers of Globalization · 267
A Smart and Simple Tax · 271
    Historical Background · 271
    Replacing the Income Tax · 274
    Should Taxation Be Used to Redistribute Income? · · · · · · · · · 279
    Tax Fraud and Cheating · 281
    Paying Our Dues · 283
A Political Evolution · 285
    A National Policy Referendum · 288

  Electing the President by Write-In Ballot · · · · · · · · · · · · · · · · · 291
  Voterism· 298
  A Peaceful Political Evolution· 299
Managing the Presidency · 302
Publication and Transition · 311
Health Care · 316
Energy and Transportation· 323
  Transportation · 324
  Energy · 327
Education· 330
Social Security and Retirement· 336
  Social Security · 337
  A National Retirement System · 340
The Election of 2012 · 345
The Power of Voting · 352
The Passage · 359
Epilogue· 367
Author's Note · 369
The United States Voters' Rights Amendment (USVRA) · · · · · · · 375

Sam
is an entirely fact-based political philosophy
narrated by fictional and real-life characters.

Dedication

For Joe and David,
who shared the dream,
but lived not to see the dawn.

Names

My father was Samuel Hubert Cox,
Who taught me to read;
His grandfather was Samuel Hampton Cox,
Who rode with Terry's Texas Rangers in the Civil War;
His grandfather was Samuel Cox III,
Whose father was Samuel Cox II,
Who, though of the Quaker faith,
fought in the Revolutionary War; and
Whose father, Samuel Cox I, disowned him for doing so.
The prophet Samuel, whose Hebrew name means "Name of God,"
Was dedicated by his mother at birth as a Nazirite, and
Whose deeds, as the last of the Old Testament judges,
are also recorded in the Noble Qur'an.

Sam's Ordeal

I can't recall the first time I met Sam. I'd seen him around the *Times* building for the past ten years or so, and from time to time when he would see me on the street, he'd tell me one of my columns "was a good one." Sam was homeless, but I had never seen him holding a sign or asking for handouts. His hair and beard might have gotten a little long and his clothes were well-worn, but he was always clean.

Sam frequented the *Times* loading dock and helped the crew throw the metropolitan edition on the trucks as the bundles came down the chute from the pressroom in the early morning. Afterwards, he usually used the dock restroom to clean up and to wash out a change of clothes, which he hung to dry in a back storeroom. Everyone liked Sam, including the dock boss, for unlike most street people he seemed to be without anger. There was, however, pain in his eyes and a limp when he walked.

He carried a backpack and often had a book in his hands as he shuffled along. A visit to the central library was a part of his daily routine, and he had his favorite overstuffed chair on the glass bridge high above the escalators. Sam read and dozed most mornings, as he watched the people come and go. In the afternoon, he could often be found surfing the Internet at the public computers on the second level.

Sam got his main meal each evening at the Rescue Mission and though thin, he wasn't malnourished. He looked to be around 40 years old, and except for his impaired leg and trembling hands, seemed to be in good health.

I had little cause to think much about Sam until one day in the summer of 2007 when he left a phone message for me one morning at work. When I called him back on his disposable cell phone, he told me he wanted to discuss a story with me.

Curious, I agreed, and he gave me the name and room number of a cheap hotel on the next block. I wasn't on deadline—I didn't have an idea for the next column, and he had piqued my interest.

Sam had rented a small hotel room with a bathroom on the third floor for a month. The room was clean. A hot plate and mini refrigerator were in the corner, and a chair was by the window overlooking the street, with a small table and stack of library books next to it.

I had brought along a couple of cold sodas, which we shared as Sam told me his story and related his plan. As a veteran of the first Gulf War he was gravely concerned for the troops fighting in Iraq, and he was determined to help bring them home. I found Sam to be a thoughtful, well-read, and articulate man as he explained why he had called.

Sam had graduated with top honors from high school in 1987, and his teachers had encouraged him to continue his education. College seemed beyond reach, however, since he was an adopted child of elderly working-class parents. An army recruiter sold Sam on enlisting for four years, so he would be able to help his parents and receive educational benefits when he got out.

After boot camp, the army sent him to Germany where he was trained as a tank driver. Sam liked his job; he didn't have to march, and he got to operate a 60-ton, 1,500-horsepower Abrams main battle tank.

The young man liked the German people, enjoyed the food, and used his time off to backpack around Western Europe touring the libraries and museums. He was saving money for college and looking forward to getting a degree, becoming a teacher, and traveling the world during summer vacations. Having been raised alone, Sam wanted to find the right girl, get married, and have a large family. He was counting the days until his discharge.

At first, Sam said, he hadn't paid much attention when Saddam Hussein invaded Kuwait in August 1990, but then his division was ordered to Saudi Arabia to participate in Operation Desert Storm.

His unit led the invasion on the western flank on February 24, 1991, and quickly penetrated the defense line. Wheeling about, his brigade executed a maneuver they had been practicing. Their tanks had been equipped with large bulldozer blades, and they were ordered to flank each side of the primitive trench system dug by the Iraqis in the sand and to plow it under. Sam told the emotional story.

The Iraqi reserves, mostly old men and boys, had been ordered into their positions at gunpoint and were expected to quickly run away. They had only light weapons, and there was nothing to stop us. We never gave them a chance to surrender. I just drove along at about 15 miles an hour as we buried thousands of them alive. Armored combat earth movers came along behind us and smoothed away any evidence of what we had done. Altogether, we covered up about 70 miles of trenches.

Later, I read that Dick Cheney, who was Secretary of Defense at the time, said there was a gap in the law of war that had allowed us to deny quarter. I don't know about that, but I have never been able to get that horrible image out of my mind. In my dreams, I keep running my tank on top of those trenches. Night after night, I can hear old men and young boys cry out to Allah and scream for their wives and mothers, as tons of sand poured down on top of them, crushing the air from their lungs and suffocating them to death.

Maybe it was karma, or just plain bad luck, but a couple of weeks later we were parked near a captured ammunition dump in Southern Iraq when the engineers blew up a large stock of rockets. We were downwind, and afterwards we all came down with what seemed like the flu. Later, we heard rumors that the rockets had contained sarin nerve gas, although our officers denied it. I was discharged a few months later, but my right leg had stopped working right and my hands had started to shake. The army and the VA told me it had nothing to do with our exposure, but I sometimes wonder: Is this my punishment?

Sam had become obsessed with the current Iraq War. Although the American body count was more than 4,000 and tens of thousands more had been grievously wounded, he agonized most over the 30 percent of returning soldiers who suffer from mental illness. Sam imagined them having the same kind of nightmares that had kept him awake over the years. He had been thinking about what he could do to stop the war and to bring the troops home.

Sam had considered fasting, but decided no one would notice. He briefly thought about dousing himself with gasoline and self-immolating in Pershing Square, but he concluded, that while such a drastic act might be noticed, few would care. Sam had an plan, but he swore me to secrecy before he revealed it.

He had seen a photograph on an Internet site of an eight-year-old Iraqi boy named Ali, whose fingers had all been blown off when he picked up one of the brightly colored unexploded canisters, that litter the Iraqi landscape. These canisters are the remains of cluster bombs used by the U.S. in the war—even though they have been outlawed by most nations.

Sam wondered how it would be to go through life without fingers, to be unable to pick up anything or to write. As he thought about the boy and the pain he must have felt, Sam conceived what he could do to oppose the war.

Sam proposed to fast for two weeks, except he was going to chew off one of his fingers each morning for five days, take the weekend off, and continue the next week for five more days until all of his fingers were gone. He would stop if President Bush agreed to immediately bring home the troops.

Sam's Ordeal

Accepting that concession was unlikely, all Sam asked of me was to write a daily column about what he was doing and why, publish photographs to prove his progress, and help him keep his location secret from the authorities.

Sam feared being arrested as a mental case, as he was determined to finish once he started. I had seen and heard a lot during my years in journalism, but this topped the cake. While I was perhaps a little less cynical than most old-timers, I wasn't convinced Sam was sane enough for me to go along with his scheme. I pushed with some hard questions. Why bite off his fingers? Why not just chop them off with a butcher knife on a block of wood? Isn't it disgusting to actually swallow and digest his severed fingers?

"Disgust is the very reason I am doing it," Sam said, "disgust with the horrible violence of war we are being forced to accept and 'swallow' every day."

It's not like Vietnam, where we saw the ugly and bloody images on the nightly news until we, as a nation, became sufficiently revulsed by the violence and death to force the government to stop the fighting. Today, embedded journalists and graphics make it appear war is a fun video game we can all play and win without having to see, smell, and feel the indescribable horror of it.

People have had to cut off their hands or feet at times in the past to free themselves from cave-ins or collapsed buildings. It is instinctual for an animal to chew off its paw caught in a trap. Am I crazy if I believe this is the only thing I can do to make people think about the death and destruction they are allowing to take place?

People must realize the war they are paying for is brutal, ugly, and disgusting, and that they are causing great harm to others and our own young people who fight on our behalf.

How else can I make ordinary people imagine how it would feel to be blown apart? If I literally bite off my fingers, one by one, and actually swallow them, don't you think people will be more likely to think about the violence being done in their name?

Of course, I'm afraid. It is just like a soldier going out on combat patrol knowing there may be improvised explosive devices planted along the road. Sometimes, people simply have to do what is right, without thinking whether it is crazy or not. We have to find the resources to take action deep within ourselves, down in our gut, rather than in our brains.

With your power as a journalist, you can cause things to change through your writing. I'm a homeless and unemployed veteran. What can I do? Together, we may make a difference. Once we consider the possibilities, don't we have a duty to at least give it a try?

I have no other choice. With or without your coverage, once I start on Monday morning, I will not stop until I finish. That is my vow. All I ask is that you give words and meaning to my actions.

We talked all afternoon. Since I had a history with Sam, I had a presumption in favor of his sanity. But, his proposal was crazy, and I initially wanted no part of it. Even so, without any mention of religion, I sensed a deep spirituality about him and wondered if this was how it felt to be in the presence of a martyr.

Sam exhibited a great depth of intelligence and clearness of mind, but there was also a goodness in his manner and a gentleness in his soul. He was offering an enormous sacrifice on the altar of peace. Much as I resisted the idea of helping Sam maim himself, I feared he would be in even more danger if I didn't agree to monitor his plan. I finally accepted that he had a story worth sharing, and the least I could do was to bear witness.

My syndicated column usually runs in about 30 newspapers on Sundays and Thursdays. I convinced my editors to budget a special series of daily columns for the duration of Sam's ordeal and quest for peace. Sam walked over to the *Times* building, and a photographer took a series of photographs of Sam and his hands.

Sam said he had a lot to think about before Monday, and I had a column to write.

The First Day

The first piece came out on a Sunday and didn't particularly attract a lot of attention. I simply told Sam's story, and readers may not have believed it. Having invested some of my personal credibility in Sam, I went to the hotel on Monday morning, wondering if he had the courage and will to do what he had promised. Using the key he had given me, I found him sitting by the window, a blood-stained bandage on his left hand.

According to plan, Sam had started with his left little finger, which he considered the least useful, and had bitten off the first two bones at the joint. He was tempted to use a knife, but had decided that a part of his commitment involved actually chewing and swallowing the finger.

We had agreed I would not watch—only document and report his progress. To avoid infection, Sam had first brushed his teeth, rinsed his mouth with an antiseptic mouthwash, and scrubbed his hands with antibacterial soap. Afterward, he had stopped the bleeding, applied an antibiotic ointment, and wrapped the stump and hand in a sterile dressing. I photographed his hand and recorded what he had to say.

Some say that war's a part of our nature, but not if we believe that humans are somehow special. How can we believe in a gentle and forgiving God who kills? If we're created in God's image, then shouldn't we be striving to end all war? I don't think we'll ever be able to travel to any significant place in the universe or into other dimensions until we overcome deception, hatred, and the violence of war.

World War II may have been America's last justifiable war, but even then, how can we defend the firebombing of civilians in Dresden and

Tokyo, or unnecessarily experimenting with the plutonium bomb on the people of Nagasaki?

I don't think war has been honorable since we stopped being able to personally look into the eyes of those we killed by our own hands. Certainly we can never justify intentionally killing noncombatants, and for the slaughter of children there can be no excuse, forgiveness, or redemption.

The Second Day

Tuesday's special column ran with the photograph of Sam's hand showing the mutilated finger. By the next morning, a few early emailed letters to the editor had come in and one of the anti-war blogs had picked up the column and begun to circulate it. Mostly, Sam was being treated as just another kook from LaLa Land.

I walked from the *Times* to Sam's hotel and found him with both hands bandaged. He said he hadn't been able to sleep—not because of nightmares from the war—but from dread of what he had committed himself to do at dawn.

The pain was so great in his left hand he had considered taking the ring finger on the same hand to save his right hand from pain, but he stuck with his plan and chewed off his right little finger as sunlight began to shine in his window.

Sam said the continual pain was more than he had expected, but he refused to take any medication. He had to experience the pain felt by those soldiers who had avoided death, but who were maimed for life, and by those whose mental pain seemed beyond all endurance. But mostly he needed to feel the pain of the children who suffer and die from the cowardly acts of those who glorify war.

Before we crossed the border in February 1991, the Air Force extensively bombed Iraq, but the strikes were not limited to military targets. To "overcome the will of the Iraqi people" to resist our invasion, we destroyed their power grid, water treatment plants, and sanitation systems.

Sam's Ordeal

After Saddam surrendered—and Bush Senior stupidly failed to order him out of the country—we imposed economic sanctions that prevented the Iraqis from rebuilding their infrastructure and denied them access to adequate food supplies and essential medicines. As many as a million Iraqis, half of whom were children, died as a direct result of the sanctions. How can we ever justify the deaths of those hundreds of thousands of children? Can their families ever forgive us? Will God?

The Third Day

Wednesday's special column ran with another photograph showing Sam's hands with both severed little fingers. Most of my subscribing newspapers had picked up the special column, and it ran across the country.

Telephone calls and emails to the *Times* were increasing; a couple of letters were published on the editorial page, and I was called for interviews by several radio stations. They were less interested in what I had to say than how to find and interview Sam. It was becoming increasingly clear to the public that Sam was determined to do what he had planned, and people were fascinated by the prospect.

As I took a circuitous route to Sam's hotel to make sure I wasn't followed, I was apprehensive about what I might find. I kept wondering how anyone, without being absolutely crazy, a religious fanatic, or under the influence of drugs, could chew off and swallow his own finger, much less do it day after day.

I found Sam passed out on his bed. The trash can contained a pile of bloody bandages, and there was a foul odor in the room. Sam aroused and told me his left ring finger wouldn't stop bleeding.

He had been wrapping a rubber band around each finger above the joint before he severed it, and afterwards he used direct pressure to stop the bleeding. That morning an artery wouldn't close off. Sam had finally cauterized the bleeding stump on the red-hot ring of the hot plate.

Sam: A Political Philosophy

I wrapped Sam in a blanket and opened the window, as he sat in the chair to talk and to sip some water. I asked him how, physically, he was able to bite off his fingers. Sam said he had researched the strength of the human jaw—it is actually as powerful as the jaws of many dogs. He knew, if he could just ignore that it was his own finger and quickly bite down as hard as possible directly at the joint, he could tear the finger away and sever any tendons or strips of flesh with his teeth.

I asked Sam what he thought about as he bit down on his fingers, and he said he concentrated on the image of the young boy, Ali, looking up into the camera and holding his small mutilated hands out in supplication.

Sam believed our political leaders had come to see themselves as military commanders, rather than statesmen, and that war, rather than peace, had become the primary objective of our government. He talked about the seeming enthrallment with war by a new generation of politicians who had never seen combat.

Nixon predicted that Clinton would win in 1992 because Bush Senior wasn't smart enough to keep the Gulf War going through the election, as Nixon had done with Vietnam in 1972. However, the '90s produced an adult reality version of the video war games that were becoming popular with teenagers.

A new breed of conservatives, the neocons, decided the American people would be better off without their European allies, whom they believed had lost their will to fight and their faith in traditional values.

These idiots had already forgotten that millions from other nations had died in World War II, along with our troops, to establish international organizations and effective laws to avoid war.

Most of these neocons were "chicken hawks," who had never served in the military. They had actually come to believe in an American Empire that should send its cavalry around the world and establish permanent military bases throughout the Middle Eastern frontier.

Much like spoiled boys who quickly tire of their latest toy, the neocons fantasized about deploying new space-based weapons to rain destruction down upon their enemies and even more exotic nuclear weapons, such as "bunker busters."

Funded by a group of equally deranged millionaires, the neocons gained influence over the corporate news media in preparation for the "New American Century" and set about to elect a president who shared their passion for violent games of war.

The Fourth Day

By Wednesday evening, several of the local television stations had picked up Sam's story, and the Associated Press put its first story about him on its wire service.

My regular syndicated column ran on Thursday and the *Times* dedicated a full op-ed page to letters. Even though the mail was running 50 to one in support of Sam, the paper balanced the page with equal numbers of pro and con letters.

The primary criticism was that Sam was obviously insane and the *Times* was facilitating a potential suicide. One ghoul offered to provide a barbeque so Sam could cook both hands at once. Those who supported Sam praised him for his sacrifice and for giving voice to their fears.

That morning, I found Sam in what appeared to be an altered mental state. When I photographed his hands with both missing ring fingers, he joked he would never be married because he no longer had a finger on which to wear a wedding ring.

Sam said his pain had become so terrible and unrelenting he could no longer acknowledge it in his mind; both hands were throbbing unbearably, and incessant pain was shooting up through his arms and into his chest, back, and neck. He was in a state of emotional, if not physical, shock.

Sam no longer slept—from time to time he just passed out for a few minutes. He was constantly thirsty and had drunk a lot of water. I helped Sam into the tub, bathed him, washed his hair, and helped him dress in clean clothes.

We sat by the window, and Sam told me what he thought about the President.

It's possible Bush Junior is smarter than Bush Senior. The son hired and promoted Karl Rove to help him lie and leak, while the father kept firing Rove for deception and deceit. But neither Bush will ever take a prize for commonsense or empathy. Stupidity may be genetic, but greed is learned, and the Bush family has a long history of selling out to the highest bidder—including the Nazis.

The neocons had stacked the Supreme Court with enough members of the Federalist Society to give the 2000 election to a simpleton, who was born with a silver spoon in his mouth and who had never learned to form a coherent sentence, much less think for himself.

Bought and paid for by the big corporations, it's no wonder that Bush Junior's first and most immediate priority was the removal of Saddam, who controlled the third largest pool of oil in the world. Clinton tried to warn him about terrorism, but Junior believed he could make a deal with Osama, since the bin Laden family had financially bailed Junior out of his failed businesses in the past.

The economy went down the drain as soon as Bush was elected; however, he felt the pain of the disadvantaged all the way to the bank, as he busily went about delivering tax breaks to his wealthy and corporate sponsors and destroying the public school system to keep the poor in their place.

Bush ignored every warning that bin Laden was planning to strike American targets using hijacked airplanes. He took a long vacation on his Texas ranch in the summer of 2001 and watched his dog, Barney, chase armadillos—as al Qaeda finalized its plans to attack America.

Bush's administration was on notice of the threat of imminent attacks, and they could have been prevented, but Bush was either too busy relaxing to be concerned or else he needed an excuse to play reality war games.

Where were you when the planes hit the World Trade Center? Our intellectually challenged president was striving to read a book about a goat to an elementary school class, and he was too stupid and uncaring to stop and attend to his people.

The Fifth Day

The picture in Friday's special column showed that Sam only had his thumbs and the fore and middle fingers on each hand, which we normally use in opposition for delicate tasks. If Sam stopped, he might be able to lead a somewhat normal life. But, there was no chance President Bush would end the war, and Sam had gone too far to quit.

With the AP story, Sam became national news. The President's press secretary was asked about Sam on Thursday for the first time, and he telegraphed the Rove party-line message. The President was saddened by those who are mentally ill and by those who choose to live on the street. Homelessness is a problem, and the President's program to stimulate the economy will provide jobs for everyone who wants to work. The press secretary deplored that the liberal *Times* was exploiting a sick veteran to sell newspapers.

It was an obvious effort to "swiftboat" Sam, but the corporate media couldn't find anything to exploit. Other than being homeless, Sam had little or no history. He had been a good student who had gone off to war, did his duty, and was honorably discharged. His parents had died, and he was the beneficiary of a small life insurance policy—which he had put in the bank.

Sam lived on the street, but he was respected by everyone who had contact with him. He washed dishes each night after his supper at the Rescue Mission. He had never been arrested, and he unfailingly treated others with dignity.

On the fifth day of his ordeal, I found Sam in a very weakened condition, with his left middle finger missing. He was in bed, and the usual trembling in his hands had given way to uncontrolled shaking. It was difficult for him to hold anything. Sam was worried about infection.

Despite his best efforts to scrub his hands and to treat his wounds with peroxide and topical antibiotic ointment, his hands were feeling hot. He knew he would have to go to the hospital if blood poisoning set in.

Sleep deprivation was also catching up with Sam. He had spent the night thinking about what he would say when I visited.

If the invasion of Afghanistan to capture bin Laden and to destroy al Qaeda was justified after 9/11, why didn't Bush finish the job? Why did he invade Iraq instead? Why is bin Laden still running around making videos threatening the United States? Oil's the simple answer. Afghanistan doesn't have any, and Bush and the neocons were determined to send the cavalry into Iraq and establish permanent forts to control the Middle Eastern oil supply.

The only problem was international law, which prohibited Bush from simply invading another country to take what he wanted, and the American people, who require something more than greed to go to war. To get his war Bush had to market it and create a demand for death.

This isn't the first time an excuse was cooked up to start a war. The Japanese attacked their own railroad in Manchuria in 1931, and Germany attacked its own radio station next to Poland in 1939. The Big Lie created by Bush, Cheney, Rumsfeld, and the rest of the War Gang was that Saddam had weapons of mass destruction—which he was going to give to al Qaeda.

It didn't matter that all such weapons had already been destroyed or that Saddam and bin Laden couldn't stand each other. Learning well from the Nazis, the Gang peddled its Big Lie to the American people, over and over, relentlessly, and the corporate media was its willing agent.

The Weekend

Sam survived the first week, and he had the weekend to recuperate. A medical doctor had secretly offered, off the record (because he didn't want to have to report his patient as being a danger to himself), to prescribe a strong antibiotic, without examining Sam. The doctor also suggested a regimen of vitamins and nutritional foods over the weekend to build up Sam's strength in preparation for the second week's ordeal.

Aileana MacDonald, a recently retired Navy nurse, had called me to volunteer her services. She agreed to stay in a room next door to Sam and administer the antibiotics, help treat his wounds, and be on call through a wireless monitor we installed between the rooms.

I asked Sam if there was anything special he would like to have with his supper? Although he did not normally drink alcohol, Sam said a small brandy would be nice. I went out and bought the most expensive bottle I could find, and Aileana and I joined him for a glass.

Sam rested and ate frequent light meals over the weekend. In spite of the continuing pain, he was able to get some sleep.

The *Times* provided him a laptop computer with satellite access to the Internet, so he could see the worldwide phenomenon he was creating, and I brought him the Sunday papers.

For the first time ever, the *Times* ran my regular column on the front page, above the fold. Sam's story was also reported by *The New York Times* and the *Washington Post*, and it was discussed on the Sunday morning political talk shows. CNN and MSNBC provided respectable coverage, but Fox News followed the party line and mocked the story.

The Sixth Day

On Monday morning, I found Sam sitting by the window. He said that starting all over was the hardest thing he had ever done. Sam had found a photograph on the Internet of a horribly burned baby in a Baghdad hospital, and he sat and seared the image into his mind, as he bit down on his right middle finger.

Sam was ready to continue talking about the war.

Bush and his lap dog, Tony Blair, did not wait for the United Nations to determine whether or not Saddam actually possessed weapons of mass destruction, or for Congress to act. They immediately started an intensive bombing campaign—without any legal authority—in hopes of provoking Saddam into a response that would provide a justification for the invasion they had been planning all along.

As a cover, Bush demanded that the United Nations take action, which it did. Inspectors went into Iraq and failed to locate any weapons of mass destruction. Bush ignored their findings and created more lies that Saddam was trying to purchase materials for nuclear weapons and that he had mobile chemical weapon laboratories.

His demand for a United Nations Security Council resolution authorizing an invasion of Iraq was properly opposed by three of our allies, but Bush and Blair decided they were above international law.

Bush went before Congress and flat-out lied about the presence of weapons of mass destruction and al Qaeda in Iraq. It's a felony crime to lie to Congress, but Bush did it without conscience and with criminal intent.

The "Downing Street Documents" have now proven what many suspected all along. Our invasion of Iraq was a part of a secret conspiracy at the very highest levels. It's a continuing crime against humanity.

The Seventh Day

I woke up Tuesday morning to find that "Sam's fingers" had become the most frequent search term used on Google—worldwide. *The Guardian* had published a magazine spread over the weekend, and *TIME* had obtained permission to use one of our photographs of Sam on its front cover.

When I visited Sam, he seemed to have gained a second wind. He was no longer worried about infection and appeared to have transcended any awareness of pain. When he showed me his left hand with the missing forefinger and its remaining thumb without an opposable digit, he determinedly gave me a "thumbs up" for the daily photograph.

Sam wanted to talk about the cost of the Iraq War.

Tens of thousands of Americans have had a family member killed or maimed by Bush's war games. He's spending five billion dollars on the war every month! He's already wasted 200 billion dollars, which could have been much better spent on schools, health care, and securing alternative sources of energy.

What have we purchased with the lives, limbs, and sanity of our brave young men and women, as well as our hard-earned tax dollars? Nothing but hatred, disgust, and ruin.

What about the Iraqi people? We didn't find any weapons of mass destruction when we invaded, but we will leave behind the residue of more than 3,000 tons of depleted uranium munitions when we leave. Every exploding shell or bomb scattered clouds of radioactive particles, which will remain chemically toxic for millions of years—causing deformed babies throughout the ages.

Now Bush is telling us our "noble cause" is to bring democracy to the Iraqi people and to "fight terrorism there before it comes here." He promises we will "stand down" when the Iraqi people are ready to "stand up." Unfortunately for our troops, the Iraqis are already standing up. They're resisting our illegal occupation of their country, and they'll continue to do so with all their might and with right on their side until we leave them alone.

Can we even conceive of the harm Bush's war has caused? At least 650,000 Iraqis have died! Percentage wise, how would we feel if we were invaded and two million Americans were slaughtered?

We have destroyed or allowed the theft of priceless cultural artifacts going back to the birth of human civilization. How would we feel if the Smithsonian was gutted, the Statute of Liberty was blown apart, the New York Public Library was burned, and our art museums across the country were looted?

We have created a civil war that is tearing apart the Iraqi nation. How would we feel if an invader allowed criminal gangs to rule our cities, if the West Coast withdrew from our country, and Alaska and Hawaii declared independence?

The Eighth Day

By Wednesday morning there was no longer any doubt that Sam had touched the hearts of millions of people around the world. Spontaneous demonstrations of support had begun to appear, and a candlelight vigil stretching across America was being planned for the evening.

The day before, Bush had responded to reporters about his vacation. He said he was just "hanging out." He had ridden 17 miles on his new bicycle, gone fishing, played a few hours of video games—just "keeping a balanced life."

When asked about Sam, the president said his "people" were looking into it and they were trying to get Sam some help through the Veterans Administration.

When I entered Sam's hotel room, I found him in a state of near shock. With his right forefinger now gone, he had only the two thumbs left. He couldn't hold a glass of water and had to sip through a straw. Aileana was attending him almost constantly during the day and most of the night, but he wouldn't allow her to be present in the early morning when he removed his finger. She spent the time talking and reading to him.

Sam said his hands felt like they were being constantly crushed under a red hot weight. I again asked him why he was so insistent on refusing any pain killers, even aspirin.

He said the Iraqi hospitals had been targeted by American forces to deny medical care to wounded rebels, and doctors did not have enough medications to treat their patients, including injured children, who suffered pain without relief. Sam was also growing increasingly worried about his ability to concentrate and focus on what he wanted to say.

How will history view Bush's war? What has it accomplished? The war has only lined the pockets of the big defense contractors and added billions to the national debt. Instead of a democracy, Bush has replaced a strongman dictatorship with a theocracy—one which will crush the rights of women and the freedom of religion.

Bush has destroyed the national integrity of Iraq. He has caused a civil war that will rage for decades. The country is now run by Kurdish militia in the north and by Shiite militia in the south, both of which have infiltrated the local police, and neither of which is controlled by the central government. The militias murder their opponents at will, without fear of prosecution. The system is every bit as repressive as that imposed by Saddam.

Sam paused...

Bush's idiocy has spawned thousands of terrorists, who will plague civilization for generations unless we do something, now, to convince the young people in the Middle East that we are not the modern crusaders.

We must prove we really do stand for the rule of law and that the American people are not imperialists, despite the insane ranting of those who claim to speak on our behalf.

The vast majority of humanity, almost 90 percent, believe the United States is the greatest threat to world peace: not Iraq, Iran, North Korea, or any other country.

America has become the instrument of evil in the world—it's almost as if the Antichrist had seized the levers of the greatest power on Earth.

It matters not the extent of our President's power or our private concerns. His sins will stain the souls of all those who remain silent while we still have the freedom to speak.

The Ninth Day

Hundreds of thousands of Americans had turned out for candlelight vigils the evening before in every major city in the country. Sam had touched the conscience of all who had one, and no one could fault his sincerity.

The truths spoken by Sam were becoming increasingly evident, and all frantic attempts by Karl Rove and his network of deception to divert attention from Sam's testimony had failed.

I had to drive through a mob of reporters and a mass of cameras when I arrived at the *Times* on Thursday morning. I had avoided granting any interviews or making any statements to the media. Not only was it Sam's story to tell, but the primary interest of other reporters was to locate and interview Sam—not to hear what I might have to say. *The National Inquirer* had offered $25,000 to anyone who would reveal his location.

By slipping in and out the back way and keeping a low profile, we had managed to keep the hotel management in the dark about what had been happening on the third floor, and Sam had never left his room. To avoid being followed, I no longer walked to my morning visits. Because of the media mob, I had hidden in the trunk of another reporter's car and was driven out of the *Times'* garage to the alley in back of the hotel.

Sam's left hand was now useless. He had bitten off the thumb at the joint, and there was only a stump remained to be photographed. He was very weak and remained in bed drifting in and out of consciousness. We discussed hospitalization, but Sam said he was too close to stop. There was only one more day.

Sam was fighting to remain coherent and avoid shock. He tended to ramble. Yet, he retained his amazing depth of understanding and wisdom. For the first time, however, I had to help him along with a few questions.

I asked him how long he thought the war would continue?

Bush Junior and his gang believe the war on terrorism they have started will go on indefinitely. They embrace a total war against a variety of enemies and avoid "clever diplomacy" or the need for allies. They want to extend the war to Iran and Syria, or into any other country that gets in their way.

Cheney says the war will continue at least as long as the Cold War... 50 years or more. Bush says he doesn't mind if he alienates the rest of the world, even if we're the only ones left... That's okay with him "because we are America."

The neocons in our government are constructing a string of forts along the Iranian border. They're building permanent military bases to house at least 50,000 U.S. troops in Iraq for decades into the future. It's a pipe dream to believe they will ever agree to willingly leave Iraq.

Bush refuses to set a time line for withdrawal or to commit himself to a complete evacuation, even if requested by the new Iraqi government. Most Democrats aren't any better. Some say we should be sending even more troops to Iraq, and the rest wring their hands about setting a deadline to bring them home.

All of these politicians, of both parties, are bought and paid for by the same corporations and special interest groups. They're all lying to us when they say we have a duty to stay until the Iraqis can defend themselves against terrorists. The only reason there are any terrorists in Iraq is because our troops are there.

We create three terrorist for every one we kill. The only sensible solution is for us to leave... Then they will stop coming.

I asked Sam what we should do to end the war?

We simply have to load up our soldiers and their equipment and bring them home. Immediately!

Of course we're responsible for Bush's war... for the disintegration of Iraq. We could save a few of the billions we're giving to Haliburton and use the money to pay for volunteer troops from neighboring Islamic nations to help keep the peace... temporarily... until the Iraqi people are able to govern themselves. That day will occur much quicker if we're gone... than if we remain. The cost to America will be far less.

He also had a few words for Congress and some advice for the soldiers fighting in Iraq.

The congressional resolution Bush obtained by his Big Lie only authorized him to use our military to defend the United States against the fraudulent threat posed by Iraq and to enforce nonexistent UN resolutions. Once it was established that Iraq possessed no weapons of mass destruction and was not affiliated with al Qaeda, any legal authorization to continue the occupation of Iraq expired.

Bush cannot... lawfully... on his own... change the mission in midstream. There is no longer any legal authority for our military to remain in Iraq. All soldiers of conscience should immediately refuse to obey any further orders of their Commander-in-Chief having anything to do with the illegal occupation of Iraq.

Bush's stupidity and greed have made war criminals out of all of us. Once we know the truth, we become accessories by our silence. Just like the good German burghers who lived next to the concentration camps, how long can we go on smelling the odor of burning flesh before we become equally as guilty in the eyes of the world as those who stoke the fires?

The Tenth Day

I didn't bother to go into the office on Friday morning. The street in front of the *Times* was almost completely closed off by television vans, and there was no way I could have gotten in through the mass of media and back out to meet with Sam.

A videographer accompanied me to Sam's room to record his final statement, and the *Times* planned to share the video with all other media outlets.

Before we could get to the hotel, I received an emergency call from Aileana. An artery in Sam's right thumb wouldn't stop bleeding, and she had clamped it with a hemostat. She said Sam had agreed to go to the hospital, but he wanted to first complete his videotaped statement.

I found Sam in bed close to collapse. He insisted that Aileana unwrap both of his hands so they could be filmed. It was a gruesome sight. His hands were bruised and swollen, and the finger stumps were scabbed over. A hemostat was attached to the stub of his right thumb.

Sam's voice was weak and hesitant, but his mind remained strong and he continued to believe he was making a difference.

I've had my say... More words would just be repeating... I pray enough people will join me in speaking out to force our government to listen to us and to stop committing crimes in our name.

We, the ordinary people in this great country, must take back our government from the wealthy... the corporations... and the special interests that have subverted it.

We must demand to vote in a national policy referendum every four years when we elect our president. We have the right to make our own policy... about the most important issues facing our country for the next term... and to hold accountable those we elect to carry out those policies.

The 2000 presidential election was stolen from the American people... The 2004 election results were largely based on computerized voting machines... operated by the very same corporations that profit most from their secret manipulations. The computerized vote in Ohio was clearly manipulated—which once again allowed Bush Junior to steal an election.

There is only one way for us to ensure that our vote counts... Each of us must take a moment to carefully write in the names of the persons we want to elect as our president and vice president... whether or not their name is on the ballot.

If all of us did this... and if it took days to count the ballots, we would show the world the true worth of our country and the American people.

All of humanity... all races... all creeds... could be proud of their contribution to the marvelous genetic pool known as Americans, rather than ashamed... We could transform our government into one deserving of respect... one worthy of emulation.

If we do these two simple things: Establish our own policy... and truly elect our own leaders... we can rest easy that we will never again commit crimes against humanity or threaten our neighbors. We can live at peace... with ourselves... and with the rest of the world.

We just have to get rid of these idiotic zealots... who have hijacked our government... and who use it to commit unspeakable crimes in our name.

I asked Sam what he was going to do next?

It might be nice to spend some time on campuses talking to students. Our generation has had its chance... we have to look to our young people... not just here in America... but in every country... and in every society... to think of others... rather than themselves... and to make the commitment to end war... forever.

We called an ambulance, and Sam was transported to the hospital where he underwent emergency surgery to stop the bleeding and to cleanse and trim the ragged edges of his wounds. He would require a series of operations to reconnect tendons and skin grafts to cover the stumps.

The future remained unsettled for Sam. With his notoriety and disability, he could no longer live on the street. A number of substantial offers had come in for him to sell his television, movie, and book rights. He's a survivor; I was sure he would figure it out.

Sam is a true hero. He has forever changed all of us and how we look at war. I have never known a braver person, and I was honored to accompany him on his mission.

Recovery

Sam's final comments at the end of his ordeal were televised and shown around the world, and collections of my columns about him were translated and republished in all the major languages. Although the Iraq War did not come to an end and the President did not immediately order the troops to come home, Sam's mission did contribute to a substantial increase in opposition to the war and a corresponding reduction in satisfaction with the President's job performance.

Combined with revelations about how the White House Iraq Group had criminally manipulated facts and public opinion leading to the war, the conviction of the vice president's chief of staff for lying to federal investigators, and the resignations of his major political advisor and Attorney General, it became apparent that an end to America's illegal occupation of Iraq was inevitable.

I visited Sam almost every day in the hospital during his recovery as we discussed his future. Since he could not return to the street, we had to make plans for his housing and living arrangement. I took him to my home when he was finally discharged.

Sam and I became more than friends. Neither of us had siblings and, in many ways, we became brothers. Sam had never married and he found comfort in my small family. My wife, Xiomara, thought he was a loving and caring genius, and Heather, my teenage daughter, believed him to be a very brave and gentle warrior.

Sam's Mental Health

As a journalist, I respected Sam's opinions and his ability to express himself. It was only natural that we considered writing a book about his political philosophy. As a nationally syndicated columnist, I was represented by a reputable agency, and Sam and I agreed the agency should shop the book. My agent, Naomi Washington, believed she could sell it to a major publisher.

The deal was not long in forthcoming, and the six-figure advance was more than sufficient for Sam to get by. Before I signed the contract; however, I wanted to make certain it was the best thing to do.

One night as we relaxed after dinner, I expressed my concerns. "Sam, the only worry I have is how this book deal is going to affect you. There's more to it than just writing a book. Are you ready to go out in public and defend your ideas? How are you going to feel when some pundit makes fun of you? Do you think you're healthy enough to deal with the pressure? Are you ready to rejoin society?"

Sam replied, "Going through what I did, with your help, I've finally dealt with what happened during the Gulf War. I may never be able to forget the screams as we buried those poor people, but at least I now feel I have done something to speak on their behalf. I've never talked to a shrink, but perhaps we should get a professional opinion."

I told Sam about a medical doctor I'd relied on for background information over the years, "Bill Vicary is not only a nationally renowned forensic psychiatrist, but he also serves on the board of directors of the Hollywood Free Clinic. He has volunteered his medical services there one night a week for years, and I'm sure he understands the problems of homeless vets."

Dr. Vicary agreed to see Sam. He scheduled a series of psychological tests, reviewed Sam's medical records, and interviewed Sam for several hours. Sam agreed the doctor could share his conclusions with Aileana and me.

Recovery

We went in for the results, and Dr. Vicary discussed the things that had most troubled him. The first was the revulsion factor. Thousands of years of human survival have given rise to emotional and physical feelings of extreme revulsion about certain things. We are nauseated at the sight and smell of filth and rotten things. We don't eat repulsive things, thereby avoiding getting sick and dying. The fact that Sam didn't simply cut off his fingers, but actually chewed them off and swallowed and digested them, causes most people to be repulsed by his acts.

Dr. Vicary said he carefully questioned Sam about his choice and was satisfied with his answers. Sam had deliberately chosen this most repulsive form of self-mutilation to graphically demonstrate against the horror of war. War is not clean—the bodies of little children are horribly torn apart, and their intestines are blown out of their little bodies. They are burned—they rot, they are covered with flies and squirming maggots, and they stink. Dr. Vicary acknowledged that cutting off his fingers using a scalpel and surgical techniques might be shocking, but the act would not have been as repulsive, nor would it have garnered as much attention to Sam's cause.

Sam was also questioned about self-destructiveness, especially his earlier thoughts about burning himself to death in a public place. Harming oneself can take many forms, and the degree of sanity can be gauged by the actual risk of death. What Sam ended up doing was dangerous, but was not necessarily life threatening. It was painful in the extreme and required more courage than that demonstrated by most soldiers, but it was not suicidal. Moreover, the way Sam carried out his plan suggested a cool, rational mind.

"Sam, the bottom line—in layman's terms—is that you're not crazy. While you've suffered some of the symptoms of Post Traumatic Stress Disorder, such as nightmares and withdrawal from social interaction, you do not have the levels of depression and despair required to satisfy the diagnostic criteria for clinical PTSD as defined by the American Psychiatric Association Diagnostic and Statistical Manual."

Dr. Vicary went on to say, "Your self-mutilation was not the result of a mental illness; in my opinion, it was a deliberate exposure to serious injury for a socially-desirable purpose—similar to the bravery displayed by soldiers during war, who have to repeatedly go into life or death situations."

"It appears to me, Sam, that your homelessness was a result of depression. It was not entirely unproductive. You managed to keep yourself clean, nourished, clothed, and well-informed through your own efforts. In my opinion, working on a book would be the very best thing for your health and emotional well being."

We signed the book contract, and we collected and banked the advance.

A New Home

Sam had expressed a desire to live at the beach, and we began to look for a place which was also convenient to my home and the newspaper office. Aileana began to drive him along the Los Angeles County coastline looking at the different neighborhoods.

Most homes were far too expensive; however, Aileana searched the Internet and found a large vacant house in Hermosa Beach near Five Corners, which was involved in a long-term probate. The parents had both passed away, and none of the grown children wanted to stay in the house while the complicated probate wound its way through the courts.

The two-story house was one of the first built in the area and sat on an unusually large double lot on the Strand—the concrete sidewalk that runs the length of the beach in front of the houses. The wood-shingled house had large picture windows in all of the rooms that faced the ocean and a brick-paved patio in front. A walk street runs along the south side of the house, where there is another patio garden shaded by a beautiful hand-crafted pergola covered with a purple flowering wisteria vine and climbing roses.

Recovery

The home had been built for a large family and, with six bedrooms, there was more than enough room for each of us to each have a study with a fireplace and ocean view. The estate executor had read about Sam's ordeal and, with the agreement of the heirs, signed a generous lease, with an option to buy.

Sam and Aileana had become friends during his recovery and rehabilitation. They were both quiet personalities who only spoke when they had something to say. She would quietly knit or surf the Internet while he sat reading or looking out the window, thinking about what he had done and what the future held.

Aileana is a redheaded, green-eyed Scot in her early 40s—a few years older than Sam. While she may have been plain in her youth, she's one of those women who age with grace and become more attractive with each passing year. Aileana had excelled in track and field in high school and college, and she still ran several miles almost every day.

She had never bothered to marry during her 20-year military career saying, "If the Navy had wanted me to have a husband, it would have issued me one during officer training." She had served around the world and was a Commander when she retired. Her last duty station was at the San Diego Navy Hospital, where she was in command of all nurses and corpsmen.

Aileana leaned to the right side of the political spectrum: "Even though as a military officer I always registered as an independent, I come from a long line of conservative Republican women."

Aileana joined Sam and me in our political discussions and often challenged our opinions with well-considered viewpoints. As we discussed the book and began to organize the subject matter, we found Aileana's contribution often provided a valuable balance. Moreover, her graduate degree in English, with a minor in computer science, and her facility with Internet research offered a resource that could only improve the book.

Taking advantage of the opportunity, Sam and I worked out a contractual arrangement with Aileana that included a monthly salary and a percentage of the royalties. In addition to caring for Sam, her duties included research, questioning, and editing as appropriate.

We had a number of discussions about how the book was to be organized. We settled on a method of presentation in which I would research and write generalized narratives on the various subjects to provide the reader with necessary facts and background. Sam would present his take on the issues and offer his creative ideas and philosophical thoughts.

In my columns, I had italicized Sam's verbatim statements, without quotation marks. This method seemed to have worked well, so we decided to continue my narration and Sam's italicized commentary. Aileana's specialized research and occasional observations, challenges, and comments would be set forth in an italicized Avenir font.

We contracted with a secretarial service to transcribe Sam's tape-recorded observations and commenced what turned out to take longer than we initially expected.

Sam's Philosophy

Sam and Aileana quickly settled into a routine at the beach house. Although she had never had children of her own, Aileana was raised in a large family, and nurturing came natural to her. She established a regimen of nutrition, exercise, and intellectual stimulation to complete Sam's rehabilitation—as they planned their meals, shopped, and worked together to prepare at least two sit-down meals a day.

Because Sam had left the first bone on each finger and his thumbs, with physical therapy, he was able to oppose the stumps of his thumbs with the stumps of all but his little fingers. As he regained strength in his arms and hands, he assisted Aileana in the kitchen and garden.

Aileana coaxed Sam to jog with her on the beach each morning, weather permitting, to either the Manhattan Pier to the north or the Hermosa Pier to the south.

Oftentimes they would stroll along the Strand or the surf line at sunset talking about their progress and their writing plans for the next day. Frequently, they debated the various issues that Sam was interested in, as he developed his ideas and sharpened his presentation. With her sharp and probing questions and alternative points of view, Sam said she should have been a trial attorney instead of a nurse.

The outline we agreed upon called for Sam to start with a metaphysical overview of the human condition and the planet we occupy in order to provide a foundation for his political philosophy.

We all agreed that the human society we live in is at a precarious place and what we each do or don't do can make a difference. The essential question is whether we, as a species, will survive or become extinct.

The genius of Albert Einstein was demonstrated by his ability to step aside in his mind and view the universe and its physical laws from a place where the rest of us had never ventured. Likewise, Sam said he wanted to "step out of the box and imagine we are regularly visited by unseen benevolent time travelers from another dimension whose sole mission is to identify and document the truth about Earth and its inhabitants."

He asked: "What conclusions would these truth seekers draw about who we are, what we are doing to ourselves, and why? Freed from political lies and religious distortions, what would their report say?"

Humans are quite simply the most marvelous species that has ever evolved on Earth. Increasingly they have adapted Earth's environment to their needs and have multiplied to fill every habitable niche of its surface.

They have created a magnificent and cooperative worldwide culture based on their ability to work together in solving complicated problems. In doing so, they mostly communicate the truth and usually demonstrate respect and civility in their interactions.

In our travels to every country, every city, and every village, and in our visits to every home, every apartment, and every hut where humans live, we mostly find parents who love and educate their children and who wish for them a better and safer existence.

Everywhere, we find people who help others in need and who communicate their discoveries, inventions, and creations in making life easier for all. The essence of humanity is that they usually tell each other the truth, and the truth they mostly tell is that they care for one another.

Humans are, however, infected with a disease—the viruses of deception, hatred, and violence. Diseased individuals commit crimes against others and the public peace, and in some societies they are severely punished for their illnesses and incarcerated or put to death, without any attempt to cure them.

Worst of all, societies that come to be governed by diseased individuals can be led into committing massive acts of violence against their own people and to making war against other societies.

Several generations ago, such a war involved most of the societies on Earth. It led to the slaughter of millions and ended with the use of atomic weapons. From the ashes of destruction, however, arose a worldwide organization of all nations united in their pledge to avoid belligerency and war in the future, to obey international laws, and to respect the human rights of all individuals.

Humans practice a variety of faith-based religions, all of which claim to represent the ultimate word of their "God," to the exclusion of all other beliefs. Governments vary in their responses to religion. The most enlightened governments allow individuals to practice their religion of choice and refuse to support or endorse any particular religion. Other, more repressive governments represent a particular religion, rather than individuals, and prohibit all other expressions of faith.

Although most religions provide a basis for ethical decisions by their adherents, they are also relied on by some practitioners to validate and justify the most violent and uncharitable acts against those who disagree with them.

Just over 200 solar orbits ago, immigrants to a sparsely populated continent with abundant natural resources united their various states into a new form of government. They declared that individuals have the right to life, liberty, and the pursuit of happiness, and they established constitutional law that preserved basic freedoms including the freedoms of expression, assembly, and religion.

Although the society was initially destructive of the indigenous people and tolerated human slavery, it learned from its mistakes and came to provide the greatest freedom and opportunity available on earth.

Sam: A Political Philosophy

The best, the bravest, and the brightest found their way from all over the world to this new society where they were accepted and protected. The genetic pool became robust, and the level of intellectual knowledge and accomplishment came to exceed all others.

Indeed, it was this society that provided the balance in the last worldwide conflict between freedom and totalitarianism and which led all other nations to unite against war. While it was the only society that used atomic weapons, it was also the only one whose members came to walk on the moon.

Sad to say, all of this is at great risk. The government of this great nation was illegally seized by a cabal of diseased zealots who continue to dominate it through their mastery of lies and deception, their control of information, and the force of arms.

Claiming to believe in the principles of a small, but powerful, minority of religious fundamentalists and to act in the name of their God, these sick men and women secretly worship at the dark altar of corporate greed and world domination.

Since gaining office, these zealots have eliminated taxes and regulatory restraint on their wealthy and corporate sponsors; sought to destroy public education; reduced health care for working people and poor children; eliminated constitutional protections; incarcerated dissenters and criminals at rates exceeding all other nations; curtailed the freedom of expression; attempted to impose their narrow religious beliefs on others; and expanded the intrusion of government into the private lives and decisions of its citizens.

Although existence of the entire human civilization is threatened by global warming, air pollution, and shrinking supplies of fresh water, these zealots, who are suffering from an epidemic of ignorance and avarice, have refused to ratify an international agreement to reduce industrial emissions, overturned and reversed years of beneficial environmental regulations, and authorized the destruction of forests and the pollution of fresh water sources, all to the benefit of their corporate bosses.

Sam's Philosophy

In order to militarize space and to divert tax money into corporate accounts, the zealots withdrew their nation from an effective antiballistic missile treaty and abrogated agreements against space-based weapons. They refuse to sign an international agreement against the use of cluster bombs, which indiscriminately and disproportionately kill children, and they continue to deploy weapons containing depleted uranium. To protect themselves from prosecution for war crimes, the zealots have withdrawn their nation from the International Criminal Court Treaty.

Pretending to act against international terrorists and weapons of mass destruction, while secretly seeking control of a vast pool of petroleum for his corporate benefactors, the morally and intellectually deficient head of the illegal cabal ignored the wishes of the international peace organization and ordered the military invasion of a weak society—which in truth posed no risk of harm to his nation. As a result, perhaps as many as a million innocent civilians have been killed and maimed, including thousands of babies and little children.

Although the illegal war is opposed by the vast majority of all other societies on earth and no evidence of justification has ever been found, prisoners continue to be tortured and detained indefinitely without trial, and there is no end in sight.

The plague must be contained before it wipes out the efforts of all those who have labored to improve the lives of their children.

While the disease thrives on the power of deception and acts to destroy the common means of communication, humans have again demonstrated their amazing resilience and ability to adapt to changing conditions. They are seeking a cure through personal interaction using electronic computers and the cooperative media they refer to as the Internet. This then may be their salvation.

Someday a computer, such as the one used to communicate this report, may grace the altars of freedom around this planet and throughout the distant worlds that her children, the truth seekers of tomorrow, will discover—if they survive!

Aileana said, "Samuel, I don't know if I completely share your belief in the inherent goodness of humankind, but there is authority for believing we are visited from outer space."

Did you know that ancient Iraq was known as the "Land of the Watchers?" Fragments of the Book of Jubilees found in Israel among the Dead Sea Scrolls tells the story of Jared, the father of Enoch, and includes this amazing statement: "For in his days, the angels of the LORD descended upon Earth—those who are named The Watchers—that they should instruct the children of men, that they should do judgment and uprightness upon Earth."

Public opinion polls consistently report that most people believe there is intelligent life beyond earth and that we are regularly visited from outer space. The French Office for the Study of Unidentified Aerospace Phenomena recently posted more than 10,000 documents about UFOs on the Internet; however, in most countries, including the United States, such files remain Top Secret.

The issue presented by Sam's observations is not whether we are in fact watched, but rather what an unbiased and disinterested observer would actually discover about humans. The watcher could conclude that we are better than we, ourselves, think we are. All in all, we agreed it is far better to commence a political philosophy from a viewpoint of health and inspiration, rather than one of self-hatred and despair. Otherwise, why start?

A Nurturing Society

One of the reasons Sam had enlisted in the Army was to see the world; however, his youthful dreams of travel were replaced by adult nightmares of his wartime experiences. Rather than getting married and happily vacationing with a wife and children, Sam came to wander the streets of Los Angeles carrying a heavy load of guilt and physically suffering from the Gulf War Syndrome.

As Sam recovered from his ordeal with Aileana's care and support, he began to think about all the places he had never been. He shared these dreams with Aileana, who had enjoyed her travel in the Navy and, with her encouragement, they began to make plans for a working vacation across America.

We often talked about the society that might result from a peaceful political evolution in America. We could see around us the decline of the working, middle, and small-business classes as a consequence of President Bush's war on terror and his policies; however, it was less clear what ordinary voters really wanted and needed from their government.

Sam and Aileana proposed a research tour of major cities where Sam would appear in a series of town hall meetings sponsored by the local Chamber of Commerce, the League of Women Voters, the local Federation of Labor, and the student body of a local university.

The primary question for discussion at each gathering would be what the participants want and expect from their government. Sam and Aileana would drive a rental car to another major city for another round of discussions, randomly stopping to ask the same question of ordinary people they encountered along the way. They would then fly to another city and repeat the same process over a two-week period.

Learning the entire trip could be written off their taxes, Aileana applied her superb organizational skills to the project. She arranged a schedule that combined a series of leisurely drives through some interesting countryside, with a concentrated research program at each end.

My daughter, Heather, who was attending UCLA, was recruited to accompany them during an extended spring break. She was to act as a liaison to students and serve as the recorder.

After the research crew flew out of LAX on their quest to identify the goals of our society, I took some vacation days and went down to the beach house to start constructing a word picture of the reality show we actually live in. It's not an easy story to tell because it requires a lot of statistics to draw an accurate image, but I was determined to keep it simple as possible.

Xiomara, my school-teacher wife, joined me for our own working vacation at the beach house. The daughter of immigrant parents from Mexico, raised in the tough neighborhood of West Long Beach and trained as a teacher at Cal State Long Beach, she taught ESL (English as a second language) to children of poverty in the public schools of South Central Los Angeles. Her commute from the beach house was about the same as it was from our home on the Westside, and we looked forward to our time together. Too exhausted at the end of each day to do much more than share a meal, she reviewed the drafts of my work each weekend, as I tried to describe the society we actually live in, rather than the one we wish for.

What Happened to the American Dream?
Americans survived World War I, the 1929 stock market crash, the Great Depression, and World War II. Coming out of the last great war,

A Nurturing Society

American's demand for the good life was based on a healthy self confidence, supported by the New Deal programs, and was fueled by accumulated personal savings, consumer demand, the GI Bill of Rights, and a vigorous labor movement.

For almost eight years between 1945 and 1953, President Harry Truman presided over the postwar economic boom in which many, if not most, American families came to enjoy a comfortable life style primarily paid for by the husband's single income. This was the "American Dream."

We bought new homes in the suburbs, our mothers stayed at home to manage the household, we attended newly constructed neighborhood schools, and we walked home to play on safe streets. We enjoyed the latest gadgets, especially television, and our society was orderly. The era was epitomized by *The Life of Riley*, a radio and television sitcom, that starred William Bendix as an assembly-line worker in a Southern California aircraft plant.

Today, the ever-rising cost of housing, health care, child care, fuel, and higher education, combined with the loss of union protection for most workers and the shifting burden of taxation to all workers from their employers, has rudely awakened us from the American Dream. If Riley were to wake up from his nap in the backyard hammock today and look around, we might hear his famous line, "What a revoltin' development this is."

There are still some who live the good life, primarily the upper-middle class and the wealthy, and there are many who still live in poverty. Just because there are millions of us in between, does not mean we are still enjoying the bounty of the middle class.

We in the middle are vulnerable, as we are being pushed down to the bottom by the socially and economically privileged. The poorest and most disadvantaged among us are growing in number and declining in strength.

Although America is the richest country in the world, the government sets our annual minimum wage at just $12,168 per year, and 37 million of us—one out of every eight—earns less than the almost $20 thousand a year established as the official poverty line for a family of four. Over the past six years, the number of officially poor people has grown by five million, and now includes 12 million children.

These findings by the Census Bureau in 2005 only begin to tell us the story about the poor of America. The Bureau relied upon 12 alternative measures of poverty, and all but one are higher than the official poverty line. One of the alternatives is similar to that used by the National Academy of Sciences, which identified 41.3 million Americans living in poverty.

Among all developed nations, the United States has the highest level of poverty. Of the millions who live in poverty, 744,000 are homeless. About 41 percent of these poor people are in families, and as many as 200,000 of them are children. Families with children constitute the fastest growing group among the homeless.

On any given day, only half of America's homeless can find space in a shelter; the other half are forced to live on the street. Many of these poor people work; however, their earnings are insufficient to pay for shelter, food, clothing, and transportation.

Low-wage jobs began to pay more during the 1990s; however, starting in 2001 and adjusted for inflation, they have fallen back almost to the level of 1979. Half of the 4.3 million retail sales clerks earn less than $9.20 per hour, and almost one-third of all Americans, more than 90 million, are barely making it on an income of less than $11 an hour.

Working in fast food and takeout joints, cleaning houses, mowing lawns, trimming trees, fixing tires, changing hospital beds, and earning little more than the minimum wage, millions of Americans are going without health insurance, receive no vacations or sick leave, have no savings, live from paycheck to paycheck, and are teetering on the brink of poverty.

Barely above these bottom-tier earners are the millions of young people who have graduated from two- and four-year colleges—who have discovered that their degrees qualify them only for dead-end jobs behind rental car counters, or as "assistant managers" and "independent contractors," without benefits or overtime.

For many of these disillusioned workers, who once expected to live the American Dream upon graduation from college, there is the burden of unpaid student loans and the humiliation of moving back in with their parents.

The inequality of income between those at the bottom and those at the top continues to grow. Using the last available figures, we find that in 2005 the top one percent of Americans received the largest share of the national income since 1928. Their income rose by an average of more than $1.1 million each, or 14 percent; however, the average income of the bottom 90 percent fell by 0.6 percent.

Collectively, the 300,000 Americans at the top earned almost as much as the 150,000,000 at the bottom—double the gap of 1980.

The disparity of income in 2005 was the greatest since the previous peak in 1928. The top 10 percent earned almost half of all reported income, and the top one percent garnered almost a quarter.

Between 1997 and 2005, the average income for all but the top 10 percent of earners fell by 11 percent, when adjusted for inflation. During the same period, the income of the top .01 percent skyrocketed by 250 percent.

The inequality of income is compounded by the inequities of taxation. Because of inaccuracies in reporting—or successful concealment—the Internal Revenue Service can locate and tax only 70 percent of business and investment income; however, because of mandatory payroll deductions, the IRS easily taxes 99 percent of wages paid to workers. At the same time, federal tax revenues from corporations has declined by two-thirds since 1962.

Unsurprisingly, the concentration of wealth is found where the income flows. Between 1983 and 1997, 85 percent of Americans lost real net worth as the nation's wealth was shifted to the top 10 percent.

These top 10 percent individuals enjoy almost 71 percent of the collective wealth and of those, the top one percent hoards nearly 39 percent of America's treasure—which is just about equal to what the bottom 95 percent of Americans are left to share.

Strangely enough, when asked in a poll several years ago, nearly 90 percent of Americans still believed they were in the middle class.

Most Americans know they are not in the upper class, and they don't want to think they are in the lower class. So, just where are they? First, most really, really do want to believe in the American Dream, but individually, they really, really earned only a median wage of less than $25,000 per year in 2006. They may feel better if we use the average wage of $37,000; however, that is skewed upward by the exorbitant incomes of our modern moguls.

In addition to these almost-poverty-level wages, most American workers have lost their union protection; they no longer have health or life insurance provided by their employer; they may or may not receive any vacation or sick days off, and they probably receive pay only for mandatory legal holidays. So, how are people getting by?

One answer is productivity—also known as plain old hard work. Between 1947 and 1973, the average married couple's income grew by 115 percent and was mostly produced by a single paycheck. Since 1973, the average couple's income has grown only by 33 percent; however these couples are now working an *additional* 533 hours, or 13.3 weeks a year to produce their income.

Another answer is the term "household income" now being used by economists and the corporate media instead of individual income when measuring the salaries of ordinary workers. This assessment adds up the income of everyone over the age of 14 in a family who is working. In 2006, the median household income was $48,201; however, it took two or more earners to earn that income at every level above the very bottom.

A Nurturing Society

In 2003, only seven percent of U.S. households with children were headed by husbands who worked and wives who stayed at home. By 2005, 35.5 million families were headed by two breadwinners, and today approximately 26 million mothers work outside the home or in home-based businesses.

Department of Labor statistics reveal that almost three quarters of all American mothers with minor children were in the workforce in 2004. Of these, 62 percent had preschool children, almost 12 million of whom were in daycare.

Depending on where the family lives, the cost of childcare can amount to 10 percent of the household income produced by two-income families. In California, the average annual cost of childcare, $4,022, exceeds the cost of full-time tuition in state universities by almost a thousand dollars.

The middle class, to the extent that it means anything like the good life enjoyed by Chester A. Riley, has been squeezed out of existence. A single wage-earning, median income American worker now earns slightly more than the poverty level. Without another source of funds, he or she can no longer buy a home, maintain health insurance, allow his or her spouse to remain at home to care for the children, build a secure retirement, or provide a college education for children. He or she cannot even afford to live in a modest apartment without having a roommate to share expenses.

Today, the middle class lifestyle can be enjoyed only by the upper-middle class and the wealthy. This does not mean the American Dream is no longer possible; it's just that it is increasingly becoming more of a dream and less of a reality.

While Sam, Aileana, and Heather were out taking the pulse of the nation, I was enjoying my time off from writing the column, as Xiomara and I house-sat the Hermosa Beach home. I continued to research and write about the economic state of the United States.

Mine was by far the easiest task, as I was up early each morning and usually completed my daily writing objectives by the time the sun came up. I made coffee and fixed breakfast for Xiomara, saw her off to work, and welcomed her home in the evening. On the weekends, we had leisurely breakfasts at a small café on the Strand, napped in the afternoon, and often sat on the patio with a glass of wine and watched the sunset.

Heather or Aileana usually called us each evening, and we talked about their progress and experiences.

It was becoming clear that appearances in multiple cities was more than Sam could physically handle. He remained in good spirits and was energized by his reception and interaction with the discussion groups, particularly at the colleges; however, there were also requests for interviews by the local media and other unscheduled demands upon his time. Sam was not complaining, but Aileana was concerned about his loss of stamina.

During a conference call from a small bed and breakfast they were staying, Sam agreed to cancel the remaining town hall meetings. He wanted to continue the driving portion of the journey, however, saying it was restful, and in many ways the informal contact with people along the way had proven more productive than the structured meetings. They decided to slow down. Heather was usually the designated driver, as they leisurely enjoyed the remaining sights and the wonderful people they encountered and visited with along the way.

Xiomara and I met the research crew in the baggage claim area at LAX upon their return, and we were distressed by Sam's appearance. He was only 40 years old, but he looked older and more than tired. The trembling of his hands seemed to have increased, and his limp was worse.

We dropped Sam and Aileana off at the beach house, and I urged him to take some time to rest before we continued with the book. Aileana immediately got him in to see a doctor, and she enforced a strict regimen of rest and nutrition.

A Nurturing Society

I went back to work at the newspaper and started banging out my columns. Fortunately, the governmental circus in Washington DC produces no shortage of waste and other political manure, and I was able to settle back into the routine without too much effort. I was, however, eager to hear what Sam had to say about his trip. We talked on the phone—he said he'd read what I had written about the destruction of the middle class, and he believed it supported what they had learned. Sam said he'd be ready to start after a few more days of rest and contemplation.

I drove down to Hermosa Beach on a Saturday morning, and Aileana and I listened to Sam as he talked about America's promise: "The American Dream is not dead. It's sick and tired; it's sore and wounded, but it struggles on. It's threatened as never before; however, I believe it will survive. We just have to reestablish the principles upon which our society was founded and defend it against those whose greed knows no limits and whose allegiance is without boundaries."

America and the Dream are inseparable and interdependent. The Nation's founders abandoned the rigid class systems of Europe and substituted a principle that one's place in our new democratic society was based on individual talent and effort, rather than the class into which one was born.

With hard work and thrift, workers could provide their children with a better education and increased opportunities, easing the way for their upward mobility. More than the ability to just accumulate possessions, the Dream allowed every American to fulfill his or her capabilities and to enjoy the respect of others for their efforts.

The Declaration of Independence established the Pursuit of Happiness as one of our inalienable rights, and Benjamin Franklin counseled new Americans to work hard and pay their debts.

Abraham Lincoln defined the elements of a just, generous, and prosperous free labor system: "The prudent, penniless beginner in the world, labors for wages awhile, saves a surplus with which to buy tools or land for himself; then labors on his own account another while, and at length hires another new beginner to help him." The Protestant work ethic taught us that God's grace was revealed by the rewards of hard labor and thrift.

Industrialization, machines, and assembly-line production shifted the dynamic of the Dream; however, it was recharged by advances of the labor movement, the availability of consumer goods to reduce drudgery, and higher wages to purchase them.

Following World War II, a fairly well balanced free enterprise system and supportive government programs came together to better ensure the good life to all who were prepared to work for it.

Inequalities based on race and gender continued to make it more difficult for some to achieve the Dream; however, civil rights legislation, court decisions, and government regulations began to reduce overt discrimination. At the same time Americans were making choices about what we wanted our government to do for us and what we would do for ourselves.

We chose to provide our own health care, often as a fringe benefit of employment, and to accept a reduced safety net of unemployment and welfare benefits in exchange for an improved chance to get ahead through hard work and savings. Somewhere along the way to the good life, however, the deal got changed for most of us.

The numbers of workers engaged in creative endeavors continued to grow as new products and services were created. At the same time, the numbers of American workers actually producing the new goods and services fell sharply, as production and support jobs were shifted to other countries.

The value of long-term employment, with benefits, continued to depreciate as employers substituted temporary employees and independent contractors, without benefits. Sadly, the ability of the labor movement to protect the good jobs was diminished by the failure and withdrawal of government support and regulation.

As more and more American families became dependent on two incomes to survive, the secure middle class was replaced by a new

A Nurturing Society

working-middle-class, whose children are increasingly stuck on the plateau where they are born.

Only the upper-middle-class children have the good health, education, financial resources, and connections to get the best jobs. For all the rest, irrespective of merit, the Dream has increasingly become a nightmare of frustrated desire and thwarted opportunity.

As Sam paused for a moment, Aileana offered a challenge: "Isn't it possible the failure of the American Dream may also be the result of some basic changes in our society resulting from the 'me generation'?"

These children of the Baby Boomers were indoctrinated with a belief from birth that they can be "anything they want to be," irrespective of their effort or ability. Many of these children grew up with an enhanced sense of entitlement which fails, in many cases, to account for reality.

Once they graduated from college and didn't find their dream job waiting for them, a large number of these "me firsters" simply laid back and waited to strike it rich. They refused to concede the possibility of failure, and thus never realized that overcoming failure is one of the basic paths to success.

As time passed and success wasn't quickly served up, many young people became depressed and blamed others for their lack of immediate reward.

I also think that members of this generation failed to connect the benefits of hard work and delayed gratification with achievement of their goals. The new easy way versus the old-fashioned hard way is the same attitude that drives lottery sales and encourages a belief that success is as much a matter of luck and good fortune as thrift and hard work.

We may have also failed to adequately instill a sense of duty to community in the "me" generation, the members of whom appear to be excessively focused upon themselves and who overlook the interests of others. The book, "Bowling Alone" extensively *documents the breakdown of civil society, as we have become more disconnected from our families, neighbors, communities, and nation.*

Heather came in while Aileana was talking and had something to say about the subject. Heather had been the primary liaison with college students on the research trip and shared her observations: "Volunteer activities by young people have actually been on the increase, by more than 12 percent over the last decade. In just three years, between 2002 and 2005, volunteer activism by college students increased 20 percent. Each year, America's 60 million young people volunteer 2.4 billion hours of public service, which is worth $34.3 billion to our society."

> These efforts demonstrate the evolution of a post "me" generation more willing to recognize and act upon a duty to society. Eighty million young people were born into the successor 'Y' generation, or 'Gen Y,' between 1978 and 1996.
> Recent surveys confirm that 81 percent of young people have volunteered just during the past year, and that 61 percent of teens through 25-year-olds feel a personal responsibility for making a difference in their world. Two out of three college freshmen believe it's essential or highly important to help others in difficulty.

Heather found a difference, however, between those who go to college and those who don't, between children from the upper-middle-class and the working class, both in volunteerism and in political commitment. "It appears that those who are receiving the least from our society are the least willing (or able) to give anything back, and those who feel the least powerful are less likely to try to do anything about it."

One survey of 18 to 30-year-olds found 80 percent registered to vote; however, another survey of the overall population of young adults, found only 60 percent were registered to vote. Only 22 percent of young people regularly vote, compared to 42 percent of older voters and 35 percent of 30 to 49-year-olds.

Gen Y children are the most diverse American generation ever, with almost 40 percent minorities. They gave their vote to Kerry in 2004, and they voted for Democrats over Republicans by 22 percent in the 2006 congressional elections. By their actions and by their votes, they have the power to transform our culture, our society, our nation, and our government.

I had just read an interesting book on the subject which seemed to confirm what Heather was saying. *Millennial Makeover* focuses on the generation born between 1982 and 2003. Diverse and positive in attitude, Millennials have been raised with access to the Internet, Facebook, YouTube, cell phones, Twitter, and texting.

Millennials are in constant communication with their friends and are the most socially tolerant generation ever. They "are much more likely to feel empathy for others in their group and to seek to understand each person's perspective."

"All this offers both a hope and a challenge," Sam said. "We have to do a better job of showing our young people how they individually benefit from service to the greater good and by participating in the political process."

Most importantly, to the extent that today's young people are being deprived of the Dream, we have to restore the Promise.

The American way of life cannot survive the permanent division of our society into an overseer class of opportunity and a working class without dreams or the hope of advancement."

We continued to talk about what people had to say during their trip. After lunch, Aileana insisted that Sam take a nap, and we agreed to continue the next day—if Sam was up to it.

Xiomara and Heather went to church the next morning, and I drove down to the beach. Sam had rested and was ready to talk about what he believes Americans want and expect from their government.

I mentioned a Pew poll in which a majority of Americans thought "seeing that one's children are better off than oneself is the essence of living the American Dream." The poll also found, however, that, "Earnings of men in their 30s have remained surprisingly flat over the past four decades." and that, "Family incomes have improved during that time largely because of the wholesale entrance of women into the work force."

Sam had done his homework and responded, "The Dream is still alive, but less so in America than in other countries. Here there is more than a 40 percent chance that the child of someone in the bottom fifth of earnings will end up at the same place. In every other industrialized nation, there is a substantially greater chance that children will do better in life than their parents. Americans want their government to help them prepare their children to improve their lives, rather than to impose obstacles in their path."

He was ready to talk about what he learned from the American people.

To effectively support the dreams and ambitions of ordinary people, Americans want their government to make decisions based on what is best for them, not upon what may be best for major political contributors and their lobbyists.

They want their government to be an ethical model for society, not riddled with corruption and scandals. Voters of both parties expressed a strong desire to see a reduction of partisan fighting in government.

Security and safety are obvious concerns; however, most people want their government to place its emphasis on serving—rather than on protecting them. Americans fear excessive protection and are prepared to take personal risks to preserve their freedoms.

A Nurturing Society

Americans want a government that nurtures and cares for the society that elects it. Indeed, this is their overriding demand. All other objectives, needs, and expectations are subordinate to this duty of our elected government.

As individuals, we are first members of our families, then our cultures, our communities, our states, and our national society. These are our primary affiliations, and our governments, at every level, must be oriented to our individual needs and the needs of our collective societies.

Our societal relationships and identities will survive and will continue to shape our futures long after the usefulness of any particular government has expired.

A government that does not nurture the society that elects it is not representative; it is ineffective at best and repressive at its worst. Every member of society has a duty to resist and to change any government that does not serve the collective good. We have consented to be governed, and one of the few powers we retain is the withdrawal of our consent.

Mothers, primarily, expressed a feeling of being abandoned by their government in regard to their families. They are outraged by the fact that America is the only industrialized nation in the world that does not require any paid maternity leave.

Aileana said that it was even worse than a simple failure to provide paid maternity leave.

America ranks at the very bottom of all nations, 170 of which provide paid benefits and 98 of which require at least 14 weeks with pay. Although lower- and middle-income parents can claim a $1,000 tax deduction for each child in day care, the actual benefit to the parent is the reduced amount of taxes saved, rather than a dollar-for-dollar offset credit against taxes.

For the poorest of earners, there is no benefit at all. Moreover, since child care costs an average of 10 percent of household earnings, even if the deduction were a credit, it does not come close to compensating for the cost of child care required to allow parents to work.

Why should parents have to pay taxes on money they have to spend to earn the income that is to be taxed?

Nodding his head in agreement, Sam continued.

American workers are the most productive in the world, as we have been forced to work harder and longer hours for less and less pay. Americans work longer hours and take fewer vacations and holidays than the workers in other industrial countries.

Not only do we want an appropriate reward for our work—we also want to have more time to enjoy the life earned by our effort.

Our families, communities, and society are primarily important to us, and we expect our elected government to at least equally support our side of the labor equation versus the demands of our employers.

We are the citizens of America, not the corporations!

Everywhere we traveled, Americans told us that they want jobs that pay well enough for them to support their families and provide their children with the ability to succeed in life.

Americans want our government to force employers to keep their promises to workers and to enforce legal obligations. Workers want their government to recognize there is a difference between the interests of individual workers and businesses and there are inherent inequities in their bargaining power. Government's primary duty of protection should be to workers rather than their employers.

Workers want the security of knowing their income and savings will not be exhausted by medical emergencies. Whether provided by their employer as a benefit or supplied by their government as an entitlement, American workers want, indeed they demand, the same quality of health care enjoyed by their bosses and by their elected officials.

There is no good reason why working parents should be forced to watch the suffering of a child because of the unavailability of health care—for whatever reason. Their pain is more than a shame. It is a national disgrace.

A Nurturing Society

Every family in America has the right to demand that its children be protected by the very best health care system in the world. It is the duty of every elected representative to satisfy that demand, not to seek ways to avoid it, or to line the purses of their corporate sponsors.

One of the most common concerns we heard across the country was the need to correct the inequality of the tax system. Americans do not object to paying their fair share of taxes; they do demand, however, that everyone, including the wealthy and their corporations, also pay their fair share according to the extent they benefit from our government.

Workers are not stupid, and every payday they can readily see the exact burden of taxes they bear. They have no choice except to pay the withholding tax, but they expect that their burden will be fairly shared.

Individuals are increasingly concerned about the inordinate power of big business, especially multinational corporations that owe no particular allegiance to America. These companies earn billions in profits each year, and their managers and officers earn salaries that dwarf those paid to all of our elected representatives, including the President.

Corporations have no loyalty to their employees and no reservations about eliminating well-paying jobs for Americans and shipping the jobs overseas to increase their profits. At the very least, government should discourage the outsourcing of jobs by eliminating any corporate tax incentives for doing so.

Our government has a duty to ensure that individuals are protected against corporate greed at every level. Corporations are not entitled to vote, and they should not be allowed to subvert our elected government by buying off those we elect to protect us against their enormous power.

Workers also told us they were afraid that employers will not adequately fund and protect their retirement obligations. Most Americans believe their government should force employers to keep their promises to provide adequately-funded retirement plans.

Many workers are also worried that their elected representatives will fail to take necessary steps to ensure the long-term solvency of Social Security, or that they will give in to pressure from financial institutions to convert Social Security to a voluntary plan managed by financial corporations.

Quality and enjoyment of life is vital for personal happiness, and our elected government should nurture our creative instincts and interests. Educational authorities must ensure that music, art, dance, and theater receive at least as much support as sports.

Encouragement of innovation and creativity is essential if America is to continue developing new products, services, and technologies to successfully drive our economy into the future.

I had heard similar concerns about public education expressed many times by Xiomara, my aptly named educational warrior-wife. She often talks about the impossible burden of having to constantly test the poor children she battles for, while depriving them of the joy of creative endeavors. She believes schools have to be something more than education factories engineered to supply the labor needs of Corporate America.

In President Roosevelt's last State of the Union address in January 1944 shortly before he died, he said: "We have come to a clear realization of the fact that true individual freedom cannot exist without economic security and independence." He called for a "second Bill of Rights under which a new basis of security and prosperity can be established for all regardless of station, race, or creed." These included:

> The right to a useful and remunerative job in the industries or shops or farms or mines of the nation.
> The right to earn enough to provide adequate food and clothing and recreation.
> The right of every farmer to raise and sell his products at a return which will give him and his family a decent living.
> The right of every businessman, large and small, to trade in an atmosphere of freedom from unfair competition and domination by monopolies at home or abroad.

A Nurturing Society

The right of every family to a decent home.
The right to adequate medical care and the opportunity to achieve and enjoy good health.
The right to adequate protection from the economic fears of old age, sickness, accident and unemployment.
The right to a good education.

Sam agreed that Roosevelt's call for a second Bill of Rights could form the basis of a nurturing society, but thought an earlier president said it even better. "President Lincoln concluded his Gettysburg Address with, 'we here highly resolve that these dead shall not have died in vain—that this nation, under God, shall have a new birth of freedom—and that government of the people, by the people, for the people, shall not perish from the earth.'"

Sam said, "Our government must be for the People, otherwise it has no rightful place in our lives."

Aileana, a thrifty Scot, was concerned about the cost.

How can a government that is permanently obligated to care for and nurture the members of its society survive financially? In 2006, the national debt exceeded $9 trillion, interest payments on the debt exceeded $406 billion. When "entitlements" such as Social Security and Medicare are added to interest payments, discretionary spending is reduced to one-third of the budget, down from two-thirds in the early 1960s.

How can a future government respond to changing situations if discretion in allocating tax resources is eliminated?

Sam said, "Back in 1936, the economist John Maynard Keynes recommended that governments 'prime the pump' by reducing taxes on lower income workers and by spending taxes on job programs. The economy booms when we invest our money in the lives of ordinary people, and it contracts when we give our money away to the wealthy and waste it through unnecessary defense spending."

Sam: A Political Philosophy

Bush Junior cut taxes by a trillion dollars in 2001 and by $350 billion in 2003 in an effort to stimulate the economy, but unfortunately for the rest of us, these cuts primarily benefitted his wealthy constituents and did little economically except to increase the deficit.

The tax savings of Reaganomics do not trickle down to the rest of us—if the wealthy sock away their savings in trusts and investment accounts.

Democrats are more likely to focus government spending on social programs, and Republicans are more likely to spend money on the military. The consequences of these spending decisions reverberate through the society.

Aileana was surprised when she looked at the actual data: "Contrary to what a lot of people have thought—including myself—by every measure, Democratic presidential administrations appear to have been much better for the economy than Republicans."

Looking at the S&P 500 Index over the last century, we can see that Democratic administrations have produced returns of 12.3 percent, while Republicans have produced only eight percent. Democratic control over Congress produced stock returns of 10.7 percent, while Republican control produced only 8.7 percent.

Democratic presidencies produced price gains of 13.4 percent on Dow Jones stocks, while Republican ones only produced increases of 8.1 percent. Since 1930, the Gross National Product has grown 5.4 percent during Democratic administrations and only 1.6 percent during Republican presidencies.

There were 33.6 million jobs created during the 12 years of the Carter and Clinton administrations, while only 24 million were created during the 19 years of the Reagan, Bush I, and Bush II administrations.

At the same time, the growth in debt held by the public went up only $0.6 trillion during the Carter and Clinton years, while it skyrocketed $4.3 trillion during the Reagan and Bush years.

Sam had the last word: "if."

A Nurturing Society

If we do everything in our power to reduce wasteful spending on stupid wars and concentrate our wealth on ensuring that our government nurtures our society; if we help working parents to feed, house, and educate their children; if we ensure that every person has the very best health care in the world; if we unite together to ensure a free enterprise system that respects and rewards hard work; if we ensure an equitable system of taxation; and if we respect the unique contribution of every individual, we will create a society unequaled in history—one that will carry us together into an unimaginably happy, creative, and productive future.

This is what is meant by the pursuit of happiness—this is our destiny.

The Way of Women

Sam's slow recovery from the rigors of the research trip was attributed by his doctor to the chronic effects of his exposure to unknown chemical and nerve agents during his Gulf War service. The tremors in his hands increasingly interfered with even the limited use he retained, and he was having difficulty jogging on the beach with Aileana as far as the nearby piers.

Perhaps even more than the physical limitations, Sam missed the freedom of running on the beach, and he became increasingly despondent and depressed. Aileana insisted that Sam become more active and encouraged him to help her with the gardening. After researching which trees would do best at the beach, she purchased three mature dwarf citrus trees in large wooden planters for the front patio. Sam helped supervise the installation of the orange, lemon, and lime trees and setting up the watering system.

Heather was sitting with Sam in the patio one day after school as a teenager on a skateboard came by being pulled along the Strand by a large dog running full tilt. She said, "Sam, you ought to get a dog." Heather had loved dogs from a very early age and had taken on the responsibility of raising and caring for several, including our current terrier, Buster. She told Sam, "Come on. It can't hurt to take a look."

Heather and Aileana began to drag Sam out of the house to the local animal shelters to look at dogs that were up for adoption. At first he was reluctant, but one day at the ASPCA, he saw a young mixed-breed

German Shepherd and Golden Retriever female looking longingly out of her cage, with her head cocked sideways, an inquiring look on her face. She had one ear of each breed, one ear up, one down, and a beautiful red rust coat with gold highlights.

Sam asked Heather, "Can we get her out of the cage for a visit?" Heather made the arrangements, and they took the dog to a large fenced grassy area. The dog began to race around in circles, and when Sam called to her, she ran directly into him, knocking him on his backside. She was jumping around playing with him, and Sam began to laugh, saying "She's trying to kill me!" He was hooked. It was mutual love at first sight.

After going through the adoption procedures, the day came for the dog to be brought home. As a stray, she had never been named, and Sam, recalling their first romp, said "She looks like a killer dog to me." So, the "killer dog" became "K.D." and from that point on, Sam's protector and companion. We bought a crate for her to sleep in and placed it in Sam's bedroom, but K.D. quickly decided she preferred to share Sam's bed.

Heather did a little research and informed Sam, "You're legally entitled to have a service dog accompany you, not only for company, but also to help with things you find physically difficult. If you're interested, I'll help you to train K.D. to assist you, and *maybe* to stay off the bed." Sam readily agreed. K.D. was registered in the program and issued a coat designating her as being "in training." She began to accompany Sam everywhere he went—the proverbial man's best friend.

K.D. was naturally clever and easy to train. She quickly learned to bring in the newspaper, turn on and off the light switch, and fetch Aileana whenever Sam needed assistance. Equally important, K.D. began to accompany Sam as he walked on the beach each day. Sam continued to experience a loss of function in the use of his hands and legs, but his attitude improved tremendously—he exercised more, and his depression evaporated.

Sam: A Political Philosophy

As the chapter on a nurturing society was being completed, we discussed how to bring about changes to the government that would best result in more caring programs. Aileana expressed her reservations.

In all my travels and in everything that I've ever read, it seems that the most socially responsible countries with the most effective health and child care programs also have the highest percentage of women in elected positions. At the same time, there is no question but that the United States is at or near the bottom in most categories of representation by women. We should devote a special chapter to the role of women in government and the ways in which they can make a superior contribution to a more nurturing society.

As a result of his reading of history and as a part of his personal philosophy, Sam had some unique thoughts about the role of women in the development of human civilization.

The received wisdom today is that women in ancient civilizations were little more than the property of their husbands and that, little by little, things have been getting better for them. But, this belief may be because men have written the history. The truth of the matter seems to be something entirely different.

As they dig down through layers of settlement and back in time through thousands of years at sites all over the world, archeologists often find that the oldest civilizations were more advanced than many that came later. And, as they dig down, as far back as 30,000 BCE, they deduce from the carved stones and fired clay figures that these earliest civilizations honored women and lived in peace, rather than worshipping male gods and engaging in war.

During the Neolithic Period, starting around 10,000 BCE, the development of farming and the maintenance of livestock led to permanent settlements. Neolithic life, as we are now learning from the digs, was not necessarily idyllic, for earning a living is hard, children are always hungry and, if we live long enough, we all grow old.

The Way of Women

Perhaps it was the human need for comfort from the physical demands of life and from the emotional pain of death that caused us to seek answers through concentrated prayer to an unseen creator who was the Mother of all life on Earth. Throughout the Neolithic Golden Age, the Mother Goddess was honored for her gift of life, and she provided comfort against the harshness of existence.

The growth and expansion of agricultural societies in the Neolithic provides physical evidence of a widespread worship of goddesses. One source is Catal Hayuk, a settlement in western Turkey that dates from the Sixth and Seventh Millennia BCE, where archaeologists have uncovered evidence of many shrines, or cult rooms, in which representations of a goddess (or goddesses) figure prominently.

Excavations yielded a terra cotta statue of a woman seated on a throne and flanked by two lions. This statue may be the earliest evidence of the cult of Cybele, which originated in Asia Minor. During the later Greco-Roman period, Cybele continued to be represented as a goddess sitting on a throne, holding a tympanum, and associated with lions—either two lions flanking the throne or a single lion across her lap.

While there always may have been tribal conflict in the past, all life had been sacred and metal was too valuable to waste on weapons. Restricted to even the most ingenious flints, bows, arrows and spears used for hunting, there had been little threat of large-scale organized combat, or species extinction.

Then war was born!

With a language and writing, but more devastatingly, with horses, wagon chariots, and bronze weapons, male warriors introduced the government of kings and shifted worship from the Mother Goddess to her son.

These kings sat on their thrones and depicted themselves as having tamed the lions! When their armies swept into the river valleys of China, India, and Iraq and around the Mediterranean Sea and across Europe, the peaceful people had to use their precious metal for blades instead of tools, and all that remains today are the deeply buried memories of our Mother Goddess.

For thousands of years discrimination against women has been institutionalized, not only by governments, but also by religions. God tells women in the Old Testament that for the disobedience of Eve, he will multiply their pain in childbirth and that their husbands shall rule over them. In the New Testament, Paul taught that man, not woman, is the image and glory of God, and that women were created for the sake of men. And the Qur'an tells us that men are the managers of women and that Allah gave wives to men so they might live in joy.

We can only wonder how far human civilization would have advanced by now without the destruction of wars and the subjugation of our life givers.

The immediate question we have to answer is how we can overcome and reverse thousands of years of discrimination against women and use their qualities of compromise, collaboration, and compassion to establish governments that are oriented to and nurture the societies that create them.

Aileana was more than happy to research and comment on the role of women in government, and, in her usual manner, she had no reluctance to say her piece.

The founders of the United States were all men. Indeed, the Declaration of Independence says all men are created equal. There is no mention of women. As these equal men labored over a constitution for the people of the United States, Abigail Adams wrote her husband urging him to "remember the ladies and do not put such unlimited power into the hands of their husbands." John Adams responded, "I cannot but laugh. Depend upon it, we know better than to repeal our masculine systems." These "equal" men prevailed; however, and women were left out of the Constitution.

Following the Civil War, the Constitution was amended to guarantee the equal protection of the law to all "persons;" however, *the Fourteenth Amendment counted only "male citizens" in determining representation in Congress, and the Fifteenth Amendment extended voting rights to all men. There was no mention of women, even though women had been in the forefront of the political battle to secure equal rights for former slaves.*

My great-great-grandmother was very active in the Suffragist Movement to secure the right of women to vote, which got started back in 1848. However, the Nineteenth Amendment, which guaranteed that right to my grandmother, was not ratified until 1920. Three years later, the Equal Rights Amendment (ERA) was first introduced into Congress to rectify the exclusion of women from the Fourteenth Amendment. Simply put, the Amendment states, 'Equality of rights under the law shall not be denied or abridged by the United States or by any state on account of sex.' It took almost another 50 years to get the Amendment out of Congress and to a vote of the States; however, the time limit for ratification expired in 1982, with only three states left to go.

"To this day, any rights I have as a woman exist only because of statutes, not because they are guaranteed by the Constitution," Aileana exclaimed.

One of the main arguments contributing to the failure of ratification of the ERA was a concern that women would be subjected to the draft and could be sent into combat. Thirty years later and after six years of the war on terrorism, that argument is no longer valid, as women are now serving in almost every element of the military, not just in nursing and support operations.

Women sailors were killed during the terrorist attack on the U.S.S. Cole, and military women died during the 9-11 attack on the Pentagon. Women are now flying combat aircraft and are deployed on the front lines in Iraq. Because of this exposure they are being horribly wounded and killed in numbers far greater than in previous conflicts.

Although more than 58,000 troops were killed in the Vietnam War, only eight of them were women. In just the last four years, however, more than 100 military women have died in the Iraq War, of a total of more than 4,000 troops killed. Hundreds more women have been severely wounded and thousands more have been sexually assaulted by their officers and the soldiers who serve with them.

Sam had a suggestion.

For all of its dithering about what to do about the Iraq War, there is one thing Congress could do on a bipartisan basis to honor the women who have been injured, mentally and physically, and who have so courageously given their lives in the War on Terror. Congress should once again pass the Equal Rights Amendment, this time without a deadline, and should submit the Amendment to the States for ratification.

Aileana agreed the ERA should have a better chance for ratification by the states today, but she had concerns about the chances of getting it passed by Congress and about women legislators in general.

The ERA has been reintroduced into Congress every year since its defeat in 1982, including the current session. Now renamed the Women's Equality Amendment to the Constitution, the Amendment has a record 209 cosponsors in the House of Representatives and 17 in the Senate, who have promised to bring it to a vote before the session ends.

The Amendment has been introduced into at least five state legislatures; however, conservative opposition is already forming. Among other things, state lawmakers are being falsely warned that passage would allow same-sex marriages and would deny Social Security benefits for housewives and widows.

Perhaps women would not need a constitutional amendment to protect them if they were adequately represented in government; however, the truth is they are not. More than half of all Americans are women; however, Congress has fewer than 20 percent women senators and representatives, and the state legislatures have only 23.5 percent women lawmakers.

Although female representation nationally has increased from 12 percent in 1981, the number elected by each of the two major parties has changed dramatically. In 1981, the parties were about equal; however in 2007 there were 1,187 Democratic women legislators and only 534 Republican women.

Worldwide, the United States ranks 67th of 134 countries in women legislative representatives. This lack of representation may account for the additional fact that the United States ranks at the bottom of the wealthiest countries in all indices of child welfare.

Studies have shown that women legislators have different policy priorities than men. One Rutgers University survey found that women are more likely to give priority to women's rights as they relate to the family and society and are more liberal on major policy issues. They are more likely to operate in public view than in secret and are more responsive to other groups which have been denied full access to the policymaking process.

The countries with the greatest percentage of women representatives include Denmark, Norway, and Sweden. There are no constitutional provisions or laws that require a high level of women representation in these Scandinavian countries; however, their political parties have adopted nomination methods on their own to ensure that 40 to 50 percent of their candidate lists are women. It is no surprise that issues which are important to women are also important to the governments in these countries.

Worldwide, more than 40 countries have included positive measures for the election of women in their constitutions, and there are about 50 countries in which the political parties have voluntarily introduced quotas into their nominating rules. The question is what can we do to increase female representation here in the United States where each party nominates a single candidate for each elected office?

Sam: A Political Philosophy

Sam was listening and thinking about ways to improve women representation. "First," he said, "women must vote!"

In safe districts, where one party or the other holds a significant majority that pretty much ensures the election of their proposed candidates, parties should adopt a policy to nominate qualified women for these offices.

In every legislature, women representatives should recognize and organize the strength of their numbers, even if in the minority, and should insist that every piece of legislation takes into account the concerns of more than half of the population served—women.

Finally, women voters should demand that their elected representatives, men or women, Republican, Democrat, Green, Libertarian, or Independent, address the unique needs of women in every aspect of the legislative process.

Aileana expressed a fear, "Although the United States holds itself out as a leader in the women's rights movement and seeks to display our system as a showcase for freedom, it's clear that past gains are being eroded by the evangelical and neoconservative movements."

Why is it that there are so many fewer Republican women representatives than Democrats? The Republican Party was once a leader in women's rights and was the first party to include ratification of the Equal Rights Amendment in its platform. It was also the first to remove it—in 1980, when Ronald Reagan was its presidential nominee.

The Republican Party I was proud to be raised in has entered into a shameful marriage of convenience with the Christian evangelical movement and the vows were pronounced by the high priests of neoconservatism. Neither of these movements holds the rights of women in high regard, and the political strength they have gained has been at the expense of women.

There is enough shame to go around. The United States is the only democracy that has failed to ratify The Convention on the Elimination of All Forms of Discrimination Against Women that was adopted in 1979 by the United Nations General Assembly, signed by President Carter, and has since been ratified by 90 percent of the UN members. The Convention not only defines discrimination, it also requires signatories to undertake specific measures to end discrimination against women in all forms.

Discrimination against women in the United States takes many forms and the consequences are a matter of life and death. Women die and their children suffer because the U.S. fails to provide adequate health care for pregnant women and childbirth.

How can it be justified that the United States ranks 41st in an analysis of maternal mortality rates in 171 countries, even behind developing nations such as South Korea? One in 4,800 women in the United States carries a lifetime risk of dying during pregnancy, while only one in 16,400 in the 10 top-ranked industrialized countries will die.

With the rising cost of health care, fewer women are able to obtain the care they need to remain healthy for their families and those they care for. A high percentage of women, particularly those without insurance, delay or go without the care they need and fail to fill prescriptions for prescribed medication.

Not only are women failing to receive health care generally, but they are also failing to receive preventative care for their unique risks. For example, the number of women receiving mammograms and pap smear testing is decreasing, as more and more women find themselves without health insurance and unable to pay for these preventive medical procedures.

It was once unusual to find women and children in homeless shelters; however, the number of homeless families has increased by 35 percent since 1989, and it is estimated that between 70 and 90 percent of homeless families are headed by women and many of the children are preschoolers. If the current trends hold, most of homelessness in America in the future will be single mothers with children.

Sam: A Political Philosophy

Many of these homeless women are victims of spousal and sexual abuse and suffer from a variety of mental illnesses, including post traumatic stress disorder. With the increasing number of women serving in the military, many of these homeless women are veterans of the War on Terrorism.

All forms of violence against women continue to increase. In just the last two years, there has been a 25 percent increase in domestic violence and a 25 percent increase in rape and sexual assault.

Because women still earn only 77 cents for every dollar earned by men and because so many of them are the sole support of their households, they are discriminated against in preparing for retirement, With an income that barely covers current expenses, many women are unable to save for retirement, and because they often have to take time off from work to care for their children or parents, their Social Security benefits suffer. Today, three-quarters of the elderly who live in poverty are women.

A recent book by Witter and Chen offers some hope, however. Because women are working, they are delaying marriage, they are becoming better educated, and they are living longer. They are increasingly making the purchasing decisions of their households, and they are controlling more of the nation's wealth. Women-owned businesses are also on the increase, especially by women of color.

The most encouraging finding is that women care about the future, as evidenced by the fact that they are contributing to the causes they believe in and they are volunteering their time.

There was one remaining area of women's rights that Aileana wanted to discuss specifically as being central to the unique health care needs of women and that she believed must be addressed by the political process. It's a highly personal subject that she wrestled with for some time before she decided to talk publicly about it.

The only options available to me after I graduated from high school were to attend the local community college part-time and go to work as a receptionist in a doctor's office. I continued to live at home with my parents and date my high school sweetheart. The arrangement quickly became complicated when I found myself pregnant as a result of our prom night fling. Although we had talked about marriage, neither of us wanted it immediately.

Looking back, I realize how smart we were to trust our instincts. Had we married then, especially under those circumstances, it would have resulted in a painful divorce within a year or two. On top of that, I felt so inadequate to parent a child. Even if I had dropped out of school, I was still living at home, and I was too immature and needy myself. How could I possibly take on the responsibility of another life when my own was so unsettled?

I knew right away I was pregnant and decided to terminate the pregnancy immediately, before the embryo was more than a few cells. My boyfriend left the decision up to me. Since we were both adults, however immature, it was our decision to make.

I didn't discuss it with my parents, because I was sure at that time they would not understand. I found out many years later this would not have been the case, but I had no way of knowing it back then.

The doctor did not press me when I stated my decision in my usual emphatic manner. I rather wish he had. The procedure was totally legal, and safe, and quite common, but it was still painful and felt somehow cold. Perhaps if I had received a few hours of counseling before having the abortion, I would have been clearer in my own mind about my own ambiguities.

As I matured, I experienced a deep emptiness. I did not understand this emptiness until I realized I still grieved for the unborn child, the child I did not allow myself to have because I felt so personally inadequate.

With this knowledge, would I advocate to other women not to have abortions? Certainly not. I still believe that this is a highly personal decision and each woman has the right to decide for herself, based on her circumstances and needs. I go so far as to say the man should have little, or no, say in the matter.

How many men would tolerate laws that deprive them of their personal choices? For example, how many would approve of a law to limit population growth through forced vasectomies? Hah! And don't get me started on new laws in some states that try to prohibit abortion even when the mother's life is at risk.

It is simply outrageous that women's lives are being sacrificed for the opinions of a few, primarily male, religious extremists. This is no better than a witch hunt!

You know, I have had a rewarding career. I got my nursing degree, thanks to a scholarship from the state university. I volunteered for the Navy Nursing Corps after graduation and was commissioned an officer. I traveled the world on interesting assignments and advanced through the ranks.

Even so, I have often wondered how different my life would have been if I had been forced to give birth to a child when I was unprepared. I still feel sad about it, both for the child and for myself, but I know I would have been a poor mother at that age.

Either way, it was my life and my body and my decision! I agree with that bumper sticker that says, "Keep your laws off my body." Those men who make laws regulating my choices about my body violate something very deep within me. Since it's illegal for men to rape women literally, it feels as though they are figuring out how to rape women figuratively, through laws that have no respect for women.

With President Bush's judicial appointment of men with intolerant views of women and their rights, there is a great risk that Roe v. Wade will be reversed and the states will be allowed to legislate away the right of women's choice. In its last abortion decision, the Supreme Court overruled its own precedent and allowed an anti-abortion law to stand that included no provision to protect the health of the woman.

Abortion bans have been introduced in 14 states, and four states have already enacted "abortion bans-in-waiting" laws that will become active if the Supreme Court rules against women's choice. And you know who will suffer the most? Poor women. They will not be able to fly to another country or pay for expensive procedures from real doctors working under the cloak of darkness, which you can be sure wealthy women will do.

Poor women will be forced to pay for unsafe and unsanitary abortions, or turn to the solutions of my grandmother's day. They will insert coat hangers in their uteruses, and expose infants to extreme cold or neglect, hoping the baby will die of pneumonia.

The craziest part is that a vast majority of Americans support a right of women's choice. As many as two-thirds of registered voters fear that Roe is at risk, 42 percent believe the matter is too important to leave to the states, and 70 percent do not want the government to interfere when abortions are medically necessary.

Since as many as one in four pregnancies in America is terminated by abortion, it is likely that the real support for women's choice is much higher than indicated by polls.

One thing is certain. Legal abortions are very safe and non-threatening to a pregnant woman's health, but women suffer horribly wherever it is illegal. And, if the right to a legal abortion is taken away, women will be forced to resort to illegal and unsafe means.

A global analysis of the incidence of abortion worldwide has shown that the abortion rate has nothing to do with whether it is illegal or not; it has most to do with the availability of safe means of contraception.

Do you know what really prevents abortions? Safe and affordable contraceptives! Which brings up another disturbing trend in *the anti-abortion movement—the concurrent campaign against all contraception.*

The very same groups that oppose universal health care and government support for child care also oppose contraception and freedom of choice, and this opposition is making itself felt in government programs.

Government funding of contraception has been cut by as much as 60 percent since 1980, and in some cases Medicaid eligibility rules deny contraception benefits to many poor women who otherwise qualify for pregnancy care.

The government has been shifting contraception funds to abstinence programs which have little effect on teenage pregnancies. While these programs may delay initial sexual experiences for a few months for some girls, these young women are much less likely to use contraception when they do decide to engage in sex.

Rather than a success, these abstinence programs are a national scandal. Teen pregnancy in the U.S. is the highest in the industrialized world. Then, with legal abortions less available, 50 percent of these vulnerable teenage girls are forced to leave school to care for their children.

What kind of future do most of them have? How about their children? Are the "pro-lifers," who are so aggressively depriving them of choices, going to help these poor mothers, or their poor children?

This abstinence mentality has also resulted in opposition to vaccinating girls against the human papilloma virus—which is responsible for 4,000 deaths from cervical cancer in the United States each year.

This same deaf, dumb, and blind mentality results in opposition to providing the "morning after" emergency contraception pill to rape victims and may lead, ultimately, to a prohibition against birth control pills altogether.

The Way of Women

Most threatening is the recent promotion of state constitutional amendments that define life as beginning at conception. Such amendments would effectively outlaw all abortions, even those performed to save a mother's life, and would prohibit any contraceptive method that prevents the implantation of fertilized eggs in the uterus. The definition would also stop the in vitro fertilization of multiple eggs unless all were introduced into the mother's uterus, irrespective of viability or deformity.

I can't believe there are so many people who have so little concern for women! These same people who want to force women to raise children they are unable to care for are the first to deny mothers the financial and health care assistance they need to raise their children. They certainly don't want responsibility for thousands upon thousands of children at risk! It's as though they just want to punish women because they are women.

The truth of the matter is that there is broad support for proactive public policies regarding contraception and reproductive health care. Seventy-six percent of voters want to see comprehensive sex education in the public schools, and almost 73 percent want to make it easier for women of all income levels to obtain contraceptives. People understand best the risks and human temptations of their own lives.

Our common sense tells us that it's far better to prevent pregnancies and sexually transmitted diseases than to force people, primarily women, to live with the consequences of the stupidity of those with the power to force and enforce their religious dogma on others. Whatever happened to the separation between church and state?

This whole subject makes me so angry it is hard to speak about it in neutral terms!

Sam shared Aileana's concern about the dark tunnel women are moving through on their path to equal rights, but he had another take on the issue.

Sam: A Political Philosophy

Those who want to use the law to deprive women of their freedom of choice must keep in mind that, under different circumstances, laws can be passed to limit the number of children and to require women to undergo forced abortions. Once we give the government power over our bodies and our personal choices, laws can change with shifting policy initiatives.

We have seen such laws enacted and enforced in China, and we could very easily be confronted with them in the United States. Population control is an issue, worldwide, and is far more likely to result in birth restrictive control laws instead of fetus rights' laws.

The pragmatic optimist, Sam glimpsed light at the end of the tunnel.

Once upon a time American women were more likely to identify themselves as Republicans rather than Democrats. The Republican Party was first to support the Equal Rights Amendment, and more women voted for Richard Nixon than John Kennedy. Starting with Ronald Reagan and his abandonment of support for the ERA, however, American women have increasingly supported Democrats, while men have increasingly supported Republicans.

All women, irrespective of party, are concerned about equality under the law, equal pay for equal work, prevention of violence against themselves and their children, increasing their political leadership, and preserving their freedom of choice.

Since women of all ages are more likely to vote than men, these shared concerns should unify them to ensure that all candidates of all parties address their concerns and provide solutions. If all women voted, our government would never again be the same—it would be immeasurably better for all.

Aileana concurred, "Of course, you're right and the facts prove it."

Al Gore won the women's vote by 11 percent in the 1980 election, and 51 percent of women voters chose John Kerry, while 55 percent of men voted for George Bush. Interestingly, an even higher percentage of women of color (75 percent), unmarried women (62 percent), and young women (56 percent) voted for Kerry.

The Way of Women

Unmarried women of voting age, those who have never been married, or who are divorced or widowed, make up 42 percent of all registered women voters. However, 21 million of these unmarried women voters did not vote in the last election. Shame on them! If they had voted, and in the same proportions as married women voters, Kerry would have received millions more votes than he did, certainly enough to have made a difference in the close election.

These women who did not vote tend to earn less money and to be less educated than the average, and they are most vulnerable. As a demographic, the group is increasing rapidly as the percentage of married couple households has continued to decrease to less than 50 percent.

Unmarried women can and will make a difference in their lives and for all of us—if they vote. All women must join arms and march united to the polls. Irrespective of whom they vote for, women can help focus the political process on matters that are most important to them and elect representatives who will listen to them and act on their needs.

As usual, Sam had the last word.

Although the rights of women have improved in our society, their special needs and their potential contribution requires that their participation and representation be effectively mobilized at every level of government and in regard to every issue.

Questions such as family health care, abortion, infant mortality, and child care cannot be fairly answered without the experience or empathetic and collaborative influence of women.

The use of force by law enforcement and the military will never be effectively controlled without the negotiating and conflict resolution skills of women.

Girls need to be encouraged to speak out on every issue and to participate in every element of our society, and women must actively seek every elective and appointive office.

Let us place ourselves in the caring hands of the women of our society. May it please all we consider holy for them, not only to care for our children, but also to cast their votes with love and wisdom to ensure the future well-being of all of us.

Outlaw War

With Heather's assistance, Sam was able to train K.D., and we all attended her graduation at the Service Dog Academy. She was issued a dashing gold coat identifying her as an "ADA Service Dog," within the meaning of the Americans with Disabilities Act.

Now qualified, Sam and K.D. were legally guaranteed equal access to all places where the general public is allowed, including restaurants and airplanes.

One evening after work, I drove down to the beach house to talk with Sam in more depth about the futility of war. I found a note from Aileana saying she and Sam had taken K.D. down to the beach to watch the sunset.

Aileana had told Sam about the elusive "green flash" popularized by Jules Verne: "If there is a green in Paradise, it cannot be but of this shade, which most surely is the true green of Hope." The flash occurs, but rarely, due to the refraction of scattering light waves at the instant the sun disappears over the ocean horizon, and Sam and Aileana had started going out to the surf line each evening with K.D. to watch for it.

I heard the front door open, and K.D. came bounding into my study shoving her face into my lap looking for a scratch—which she got. She was joined by Aileana and Sam, who excitedly told me about the sunset, "The atmospherics were perfect. Just as the final tip of the red sun disappeared behind the ocean, there was a split-second flash of a brilliant emerald color. At the same moment, the dog catcher drove up to write us a ticket for having K.D. on the beach."

Aileana said, "Samuel must have dropped her leash and K.D. was merrily chasing some sandpipers down the surf line. The animal control officer told us that dogs were prohibited from the beach. I told him that K.D. was a certified service dog, and he said that was great, but she had to be on a leash to be of service. We all laughed, and he let us go with a warning."

Then we turned to the subject I had come down to discuss. Although the Iraq War was the original catalyst for our relationship, Sam and I had decided to reserve the subject until after we thought about what kind of government would have the capability to confront and resolve the horrors of war. Even so, an abhorrence of war remained central to Sam's political philosophy.

In preparation for writing the chapter, Sam, Aileana, and I each researched and prepared papers on issues of interest, and we were working out the organization. A cool ocean breeze was blowing, and Aileana had started a wood fire in the fireplace. K.D. was curled up on a hooked rug in front of it. It was a real L.L. Bean moment.

We had each taken a different approach to the problem. Even with the end of the Cold War, Aileana had grave concerns about the continuing threat of nuclear weapons, and I was agitated by President Bush's illegal preemptive Iraq War and his never ending war on terrorism. As usual, Sam offered a holistic view that encompassed the entire subject from the origins of war to an out-of-the-box alternative. The beginning was easy: We started with the stupidity of war and the idiots who glorify it.

The Stupidity of War

In 1795, James Madison observed: "Of all the enemies to public liberty war is, perhaps, the most to be dreaded because it comprises and develops the germ of every other. War is the parent of armies; from these proceed debts and taxes . . . known instruments for bringing the many under the domination of the few. . . . No nation could preserve its freedom in the midst of continual warfare."

While most of us are probably in agreement with Madison, it is unlikely that America's defense contractors will ever concur. Things were not looking too good for them at the end of the 1990s as the Cold War ended and the United States was cutting defense budgets. Since 9-11, however, the profits of our top weapons manufacturers have soared: Lockheed Martin - 22 percent; Northrop Grumman - 62 percent; General Dynamics - 22 percent; and Boeing - 61 percent.

Globally, we humans are now spending more on our militaries and their armaments than on anything else—more than a trillion dollars each year. Of this, the U.S. military budget is almost as much as the rest of the world's combined spending, and the Pentagon currently accounts for more than half of the federal budget's discretionary spending.

The 2005 U.S. military budget was more than seven times larger than the Chinese budget, the second largest. It was almost 30 times as large as the combined military budgets of the eight countries usually identified as rogue states—Iran, Iraq, Syria, Sudan, Libya, North Korea, Sudan, and Cuba.

Sam said, "It's not just the cost of war and the diversion of precious resources from more beneficial goals, nor is it just the loss of lives and the maiming of our youth; war is simply stupid in the extreme. Violence may not be inconsistent with basic animal nature, although that itself is debatable; however, war is contrary to human culture and everything spiritual that connects us to a greater reality."

What caused the Germans to voluntarily surrender their freedoms, tolerate a police state, accept detentions without trial, ignore mass murder, and accede to starting a war in which millions died? The same question can be asked today about Americans who are acting in much the same way.

Sam: A Political Philosophy

If war is contrary to our personal and religious beliefs, why do we willingly allow our elected leaders to subvert our freedoms and commit mass murder in our name? The answer may lie in our ability to psychologically ignore the consequences of governmental violence in exchange for the security we are told it brings. In our ignorance, we deny the inherently moral character of humanity and imagine our victims to be less than human.

Before World War II, the United States continued our forefathers' mistrust of standing armies and tailored the size of our military to fit the perceived threats of changing times. Following the war, however, the United States engaged in a massively expensive Cold War to contain the spread of communism from the Soviet Union, our former ally. In doing so, we ultimately established more than a thousand military bases in at least 100 countries around the world.

The United States has come to view itself as the indispensable nation required to maintain its global supremacy so as to isolate and destroy evil wherever it is found.

The theory of containment is usually attributed to a memo written by George Kennan, who served as the State Department's policy planning chief in 1947. Those who subsequently adopted the policy of containment, however, failed to heed Kennan's argument that we did not need to defeat the Soviet Union, in which were planted the "seeds of its own decay." He suggested that we patiently avoid confrontation and histrionics and adopt a political, rather than military, response.

In another letter at the same time, Kennan said, "Let us find health and vigor and hope, and the diseased portion of the earth will fall behind of its own doing. For that we need no aggressive strategic plans, no provocation of military hostilities, no showdowns."

For the past 60 years, the United States has ignored Kennan's wise advice and has blindly followed a flawed and delusional policy of military confrontation and political disengagement, and humanity has paid the price.

Outlaw War

Kennan lived for 101 years, long enough to warn us, just before Bush Junior illegally invaded Iraq, that the United States cannot "confront all the painful and dangerous situations that exist in this world . . . That's beyond our capabilities."

Associated with all of the stupid things our government has done to preserve our security has been the concurrent concealment of its idiocy. James Madison once observed that the right that controls all other rights is the right to get information. In other words, if you don't know what's going on, you only think you have rights.

We have been kept in the dark about so many very serious things for so long that we don't know what to believe or disbelieve. Everything is secret—even our mistakes—especially our mistakes.

Did you know that between 1944 and 1970, we secretly dumped 64 million pounds of nerve and mustard gas agents, 400,000 chemical bombs, mines and rockets, and more than 500 tons of radioactive waste into the ocean just off our coastlines?

Are you aware that the United States has severely contaminated hundreds of thousands of acres of land around the world at its current and former military bases? Can you believe that our own domestic drinking water supply has been contaminated by leaked rocket fuel and industrial solvents from military sites, and that these substances will cause cancers in our descendants for hundreds of years?

Sam was especially concerned about what the violence of war does to the psyche of the young men and women sent to fight, and how the resulting changes in their personalities affect all of us, particularly the way we view ourselves and how we deal with problems.

Among the secrets of the Vietnam war is a study conducted as a result of the My Lai massacre that confirmed at least 320 other atrocities by U.S. forces. Unwarranted attacks were frequently made against families in their homes and against innocent farmers and fishermen, and a violent minority of soldiers murdered, raped, and tortured without fear of punishment. Although the records were declassified in 1994, they have since been removed from public view by the Bush II administration, which has failed to learn from past experience.

The War in Iraq
Today, we are committing the same crazy violence in Iraq, where as many as a million Iraqi civilians have died as a result of our invasion. Innocent people are regularly gunned down by military convoys because they get in the way—they don't slow down fast enough, or simply because the troops are angry, bored or frustrated. A young girl is raped, her family is murdered, and they are all burned to conceal the crime.

Prisoners are abused and tortured—all in furtherance of the war on terrorism. Although we saw a few photographs of the horrors of Abu Ghraib, hundreds of photos and videos remain classified to avoid public outrage. Reportedly, these include images of American soldiers beating a prisoner almost to death, raping a female prisoner, and acting inappropriately with a dead body, as well as tapes of Iraqi guards raping young boys.

Contrary to the laws of war, we drove nearly 200,000 people from their homes in Fallujah and occupied their hospitals to deny medical care to the casualties of our aggression. Those who remained or tried to escape were targeted by military weapons, including cluster bombs and white phosphorus—that causes horrible burns. Tens of thousands of homes were destroyed, entire neighborhoods were flattened, and the city became a wasteland. We destroyed the city to save it from those who rebelled against our occupation.

The United States justifies its use of white phosphorus, and it has refused to sign the Convention on Certain Convention Weapons that includes specific restrictions on the use of incendiary weapons. When used as it was in Fallujah, however, white phosphorus is considered a chemical weapon and is forbidden by the Chemical Weapons Convention.

The U.S. has also refused to sign the Ottawa Agreement that bans conventional cluster bombs and artillery shells, and it has used tens of thousands of these weapons in Iraq, including almost 60,000 pounds since major hostilities ended in April 2003.

Each bomb has hundreds of bomblets, about the size of a soda can, that contain tiny shards of razor sharp steel. About 5 to 15 percent of the bomblets fail to explode on impact and appear to be colorful toys for curious children to pick up and play with. More than 1,000 Iraqi civilians have been killed by these cluster bombs in Iraq. It was the image of a young boy who had lost all of his fingers that originally drove Sam to undergo his ordeal.

Most people don't know just how extensively the United States relies on air power in Iraq with the consequence that tens of thousands of civilians have suffered "collateral" injury and death. We routinely drop 500, 1,000, and 2,000 pound bombs, and we fire rockets and cannons from aircraft at buildings without knowing if civilians, including children, are inside. It is estimated that 13 percent of all violent deaths, as many as 78,133 and as much as 50 percent of all children's deaths, have been caused by coalition air strikes in Iraq.

Referring to civilian casualties as collateral damage misstates the very nature of modern war that has come to specifically target civilians, who now account for 90 percent of all war deaths. With the invention of airplanes and missiles, warfare has come to focus as much on degrading the will of the populace as the defeat of armies.

During both the Gulf War and the current Iraq War, we destroyed the entire infrastructure of society required for the survival of the Iraqi people, of whom we have killed as many as a million non-combatant men, women, and children.

The United States has imprisoned thousands of individuals without trial or due process of law since the invasions of Afghanistan and Iraq, and our military is presently detaining more than 24,500 prisoners in Iraq, including 800 juveniles, and thousands more in Afghanistan.

At least 26 prisoners have died under circumstances defined as criminal homicide, including beatings, suffocation, freezing, and other forms of torture, and this number does not include all the killings ruled to be justifiable homicide. Other than for a few slaps on the wrist by commanding officers, there has been no accountability.

During our own war for independence, General Washington ordered that all prisoners be treated with the humanity for which we were fighting. As a result, prisoners were trusted to march from one location to another without guards and, at the end of the war, one in four Hessian prisoners chose to remain and become American citizens.

Is it any wonder we are so hated—not for our freedoms as Bush Junior says—but for our denial of freedom and humanity to others? Is it any wonder that our poor troops, men and women, come home from war filled with self-hatred for what they have been forced to do and doubts about whether anyone can still love and respect them—whether anyone will ever be able to understand what they have endured?

Aileana had something to say about President Bush bragging that "the advance of freedom in the Middle East has given new rights and new hopes for women . . . the systematic use of rape by Saddam's former regime to dishonor families has ended."

The truth is that the war in Iraq and Afghanistan has not only killed thousands of innocent women and children, but it has also resulted in a devaluation of their quality of life and elimination of human rights within their societies.

Under Saddam's government, Iraqi women were the most liberated women in the Middle East. The 1970 Iraqi Constitution formally guaranteed equal rights to women, and they could attend school, own property, vote, and run for public office.

Women were allowed and encouraged to hold advanced positions in government, education, and commerce. All of that has changed. Iraqi women now fear to leave their homes and are subjected to rape by armed gunmen (including both militia and U.S. soldiers).

Outlaw War

The 1970 Constitution has been replaced by one incorporating Islamic law which suppresses women, who are required to be veiled in many areas and to be accompanied by male relatives. No longer are women free to gain higher education or to work in their professions.

The status of women in Afghanistan is little improved from the Taliban era, as most areas outside Kabul remain under the control of tribal warlords, who impose Islamic law.

Sam was shaken by what Aileana said.

Have we no self-awareness of the effect such violence has on all of us? Where's our common sense? Do we think the yellow ribbons on the back of our SUVs absolve us of guilt? We need to show some feelings. We Americans have done great harm to others—and to our own.

More than 38,000 troops have been injured in Iraq, not including thousands who have suffered undiagnosed brain damage, and tens of thousands more who have suffered lifelong emotional injuries, such as anger, isolation, sleeplessness, anxiety, and antisocial behavior.

When these young men and women return home, unable to continue fighting, our government demands they return their enlistment bonuses, denies them adequate medical and psychiatric care, and refuses medical and psychiatric disability payments. The backlog of veteran disability claims exceeds 391,000, and it's taking an average of almost two years to process their appeals.

Thousands of these tormented young people have come back to the United States forever traumatized by their experiences. More than 121 veterans of Iraq and Afghanistan have killed another person after their return to the United States in a cycle of destruction and self-destruction. In addition to forced drowning, choking, stabbing, and physical assaults, more than half of these veterans used a gun. Their victims were service associates, relatives, spouses, significant others, and their own children, including one two-year-old.

Four hundred thousand veterans are now homeless in America. More than 4,256 veterans committed suicide in just one year, and their suicide rate is twice that of nonveterans. The highest suicide rates are suffered by those who have just been fighting the War on Terrorism.

Aileana said one of the reasons she retired early was her feelings of hopelessness and failure at not being able to better care for the young military personnel who ended up in her hospital.

The San Diego Naval Hospital where I served is one of the premier military hospitals. Even so, I found that, while the administration and Congress were always able to borrow money to buy more weapons, they continually shortchanged those who had to use them.

Walter Reed Hospital in Maryland is one of the primary treatment centers for wounded troops from the Middle East wars. The hospital has long been known as the crown jewel of military medicine; however, the unremitting flow of the severely wounded has overwhelmed its capacity. A Washington Post investigation last year revealed it had become a "holding ground for physically and psychologically damaged outpatients . . ." who "suffer from brain injuries, severed arms and legs, organ and back damage, and various degrees of post-traumatic stress." Outpatients recovering from severe injuries outnumber hospital patients 17 to 1 and are housed in deplorable conditions.

Those suffering from post traumatic stress disorder receive short shrift. Patients are heavily medicated with a cocktail of antidepressants and left to find their own way until they are returned to duty, discharged, or kill themselves.

The Veterans Administration continues to cover up the number of veterans who have attempted suicide. While publicly putting the number at 800, an internal email revealed that more than 12,000 try to take their lives each year. Much of the time group therapy was the only help offered by the VA.

Those returned to duty are often heavily medicated to allow them to perform their duties. The military continues to dole out drugs, including potent dextro-amphetamines, to keep soldiers going. One of the most disturbing medications is propranolol, which has been given to troops to submerge any pangs of conscience they might suffer as a result of their violence acts against others.

Heavily medicated and repeatedly deployed, today's troops are becoming zombies, outfitted with Kevlar body armor and night-vision goggles, with little hope for a healthy and productive reintroduction to civilian life.

Since the military primarily draws its enlisted recruits from the working class, there is little hope for these young men and women once they return home from having done their duty.

Sam said, "Just talking about this makes me want to cry, but we have to stand up and speak out for these young men and women who have been placed in harm's way and then abandoned by their government."

Are we surprised that more than 4,698 Army soldiers deserted in 2007, an increase of more than 2,000 from 2006, or that hundreds of enlisted troops and officers are refusing to be deployed to Iraq?

The Uniform Code of Military Justice requires soldiers to obey lawful orders; however, it also provides a right and imposes a duty to disobey illegal orders. Although Congress passed a resolution authorizing President Bush to use the Armed Forces to defend the national security of the United States and to enforce relevant United Nations Security Council resolutions regarding Iraq, it never declared war on Iraq.

Bush Junior unilaterally ordered the invasion of Iraq, saying that Iraq "has uniformly defied Security Council resolutions demanding full disarmament;" that "the Iraq regime continues to possess and conceal some of the most lethal weapons ever devised;" and that Iraq "has aided, trained and harbored terrorists, including operatives of al Qaeda." Time has now revealed all of these justifications to be false and that Bush knew they were lies as he spoke them.

Neither members of Congress, nor the people of the United States have delegated power to Bush to conduct an illegal war. Every member of the military has the right and duty to disregard any and all orders to fight in illegal wars.

As Thomas Jefferson said, "Whensoever the general Government assumes undelegated powers, its acts are unauthoritative, void and of no force."

Sam stopped talking, and a heavy silence descended on the three of us, as we contemplated the enormity of the crimes we were confronting and the great harm that has been done in the name of peace. K.D. got up and shoved her face in Sam's lap. He idly patted her head as he looked out the window at the ocean, and tears rolled down his cheeks. Aileana stood behind him and began to massage his shoulders, "How about we take a break, review our papers and get some rest before going on?"

Preemptive War

I had been researching the concept of preemptive war, which has become the formal policy of the Bush administration, and I had prepared a brief summary.

In the past, the use of military force was considered to represent a failure of diplomacy; however, the Bush II administration officially relied upon the preemptive use of violent coercion as a "multiplier." Vice President Cheney claimed that force "makes your diplomacy more effective going forward, dealing with other problems." President Bush viewed the deployment of proactive military violence as a lesson learned from 9-11, that "this country must go on the offensive and stay on the offensive."

The United Nations was established by the people of the world to protect international peace and to avoid a repeat of World War II, which destroyed millions of lives. We all agreed to peacefully settle our international disputes, and we accepted a very limited right to wage war against another nation.

Outlaw War

When the United States ratified the Charter of the United Nations, it became the supreme law of the land, binding on all subsequent presidents, including George W. Bush.

At the beginning of the Cold War there were suggestions the United States should launch an attack on the Soviet Union before it became too strong. In 1953, after he reviewed plans to attack the USSR, President Eisenhower stated, "All of us have heard this term 'preventive war' since the earliest days of Hitler. I recall that is about the first time I heard it. In this day and time . . . I don't believe there is such a thing; and, frankly, I wouldn't even listen to anyone seriously that came in and talked about such a thing."

Shortly after 9-11, President Bush adopted an official policy of preventive war that is contrary to international law. The United Nations Charter provides, "All members shall settle their international disputes by peaceful means in such a manner that international peace and security, and justice are not endangered . . . . [and] shall refrain in their international relations from the threat or use of force against the territorial integrity or political independence of any state."

Bush's National Security Strategy sought to prevent enemies from even threatening us with weapons of mass destruction. He proposed to defend the U.S. "by identifying and destroying the threat before it reaches our borders. While the United States will constantly strive to enlist the support of the international community, we will not hesitate to act alone, if necessary, to exercise our right of self-defense by acting preemptively against such terrorists."

Previously, a preventive attack by a nation required the existence of "an imminent threat—most often a visible mobilization of . . . forces preparing to attack." President Bush, however, claimed the power to "adapt the concept of imminent threat to the capabilities and objectives of today's adversaries." He said, "The greater the threat, the greater is the risk of inaction—and the more compelling the case for taking anticipatory action to defend ourselves, even if uncertainty remains as to the time and place of the enemy's attack."

Sam read my paper and was prepared to talk about it several days later when we met to continue work on the book. He said, "In the very beginning, when the United States adopted regime change as an objective and when Bush Junior threatened he would use military force against Iraq unless Saddam and his two sons left the country, he committed a war crime."

When we failed to find any weapons of mass destruction in Iraq—when it was proven that Saddam had not been supporting al Qaeda, and when it was apparent that the majority of the United Nations Security Council had been right in not approving the invasion, Bush demonstrated the very reason why preemptive war is illegal.

What if we're wrong? What if our "intelligence" is faulty? We then stand with blood on our hands accused of murder for all the world to see. It matters not that we arrogantly ignore the verdict and have the power to avoid punishment.

America's finest young women and men are being maimed and killed every day in Iraq in an illegal war intentionally started by our president. More than 4,000 American soldiers have died, tens of thousands more have been grievously wounded, and the war is costing us more than a billion dollars a week.

In just the last two years, our government has spent almost six-and-a-half billion dollars on thousands of projects in Iraq by the Corps of Engineers, while slashing millions from its budget to protect New Orleans. Thousands of National Guard troops from Louisiana, Mississippi, and Florida were sent to fight the illegal war in Iraq, depriving those states of the emergency resources they needed to cope with hurricanes Katrina and Wilma.

What else has the war accomplished? American citizens have been imprisoned without trial or access to counsel; we are building concentration camps in America and operating secret prisons around the world where torture of prisoners is approved and condoned in violation of international law.

Outlaw War

Without question, Saddam Hussein was a brutal dictator who oppressed his own people, and without a doubt, few would have cried real tears at his demise. The people of Iraq, however, did not welcome us with candy and flowers as promised. Hundreds of thousands of them have died since our military invasion, two million have been displaced, and they continue to resist our occupation.

Although elections have been held and a constitution approved, a civil war between religious factions is shattering the national integrity of Iraq. The new central government is powerless, and its corrupt military and police have been infiltrated by local militias, who torture, murder, and imprison their opponents without fear of punishment.

This is not the first time we have engaged in a war that has proven to be a mistake, nor will it be the last, unless we find a better way to defend ourselves against real or contrived threats to our national security.

Since World War II and the Korean War, the United States has repeatedly deployed its military into other countries in a series of undeclared wars. These wars have resulted in the deaths of thousands of American soldiers, widespread destruction of the targeted nations' infrastructure, and extensive civilian casualties. None of these wars produced any lasting political advantage to the United States.

We have to recognize that it is war itself that is stupid, just like the idiots who glorify it and who cause the rest of us to aid and abet their criminality. Humanity does not have a choice. We will either treat and cure the disease of violence and war, or it will destroy us. We no longer fight with bows and arrows, swords, and spears. Our modern weapons destroy not only massive numbers of human lives, but the very environment we live in.

Nuclear Weapons

Aileana said, "I remember the apprehension I felt as I listened to Vice President Cheney, Condoleezza Rice, Donald Rumsfeld, and President Bush talk about Saddam's weapons of mass destruction and the deep-seated fear I felt as I imagined nuclear weapons in the hands of terrorists."

Coming from a solid middle-class Republican family, I was raised to respect our government, and as a military officer, I was trained and acculturated to obey orders. I believed my Commander-in-Chief when he said Saddam could launch a biological or chemical attack in as little as 45 minutes and that Iraq was rebuilding its nuclear weapon facilities, and I trusted Secretary Rice when she said "We don't want the smoking gun to be a mushroom cloud."

When I learned after the invasion that these were all lies and that the leaders I had trusted were liars, I had no honorable choice but to retire from the Navy and resign my commission in order to speak out. It is no longer the weapon programs of Iraq, or even of Iran, that I fear. I am concerned, of course, but I am terrified by our own weapons of mass destruction and the fact that those whose fingers are on the triggers are unworthy of our faith and trust and who act as though they are mentally unstable.

President Bush and his gang of neocons are the most dangerous people on earth because they do not appear to have any moral reluctance to destroy millions of lives to make their insane dreams come true.

Aileana had completed a comprehensive review of the current deployment of nuclear weapons by the United States, including the routine use of depleted uranium.

Depleted uranium (DU) is left over from the processing of fissile material for nuclear weapons and power plants. Uranium, being the heaviest naturally occurring metal, has the ability to cut through concrete and steel when machined into tank rounds and bullets.

The United States first used DU weapons by tanks and attack aircraft against Iraqi forces in the Gulf War. However, our military has vastly expanded its use in the Iraq War, including smaller bullets used in rifles and pistols. The earlier war was mainly fought in the desert, but DU weapons are now regularly targeted against Iraqi rebels in urban areas.

A DU shell disintegrates at high temperature when it strikes a hard surface giving off a cloud of microscopic uranium dust that remains radioactive and poisons the surrounding area for billions of years. DU dust can be inhaled into the lungs before migrating to other organs and bones where it causes cancers. DU is highly toxic and easily binds with DNA causing fetal mutations.

Tens of thousands of American troops have been exposed to DU, and the consequences of its use will be with us for generations—and with those in Iraq we supposedly went there to liberate.

Even more scary than the routine use of depleted uranium, our current policy regarding the use of true nuclear weapons is highly dangerous and destabilizing. The United States appears to have abandoned the goal of nuclear disarmament and is disregarding and discarding the treaties we have already signed. Our President is actually considering the use of tactical nuclear weapons against nonnuclear nations, such as Iran.

Commencing in 1968, the Nuclear Nonproliferation Treaty has now been signed by most countries. The Treaty was envisioned to eventually eliminate all nuclear weapons. Those states, including Iran, that did not possess nuclear weapons as of 1967 agreed to restrict their use of atomic energy to the generation of power and not to develop nuclear weapons.

Countries, including the United States, that did possess nuclear weapons, promised to divest themselves of the weapons over time. Several countries, including Israel, India, and Pakistan, never signed the Treaty, and North Korea subsequently withdrew its signature. Each has developed nuclear weapons.

Although the United States promised in 1968 to work towards the elimination of its nuclear arsenal, the Bush II administration not *only budgeted billions of dollars for more advanced nuclear weapons, delivery systems, and manufacturing facilities, it also adopted more aggressive guidelines for their use and deployment. In the past, it was the policy of the United States to consider nuclear bombs as a deterrent weapon of last resort against other nuclear powers, but no longer.*

As a part of President Bush's policy of preemptive war, he targeted nuclear weapons against the nations of Russia, China, North Korea, Iraq, Iran, and Libya, several of which possess no nuclear weapons. He threatened the use of nuclear weapons to deter a "large-scale conventional military force" and as a response to undefined "surprising developments." In addition, President Bush adopted guidelines allowing for preemptive nuclear strikes against "rogue enemies" accused of possessing or developing weapons of mass destruction.

In 2003, President Bush defined a "full-spectrum" global strike as the capability to deliver nuclear and conventional weapons in support of both national and theater objectives. In support of that directive, Secretary Rumsfeld approved a top secret "Interim Global Strike Alert Order" in 2004 ordering the military to assume and maintain readiness to preemptively attack hostile countries, specifically Iran and North Korea, that were suspected of developing weapons of mass destruction.

The global strike plan specifically allows for the use of thermonuclear weapons to destroy hardened targets. Any ambiguity regarding the use of these weapons was eliminated by the Pentagon's 2005 Doctrine for Joint Nuclear Operations, which provides that "Integrating conventional and nuclear attacks will ensure the most efficient use of force and provide U.S. leaders with a broader range of strike options to address immediate contingencies."

Sam said, "These changes in U.S. policy are dangerous for several reasons, not the least of which is a resumption of the nuclear arms race between the U.S. and Russia, but also because they anticipate the casual use of tactical nuclear weapons in conventional warfare. This can only encourage other nations, such as Saudi Arabia, Syria, Egypt, Taiwan, and Japan to go nuclear."

One does not even have to be sympathetic towards Iran to understand why it might consider obtaining nuclear weapons, surrounded as it is by nations with nuclear weapons and repeatedly threatened with nuclear attack by a super-powerful nation. This is especially true when Iran sees the deference paid to other nations, even weak ones like North Korea, once they obtain nuclear capability.

We must reverse direction regarding our threatened use of nuclear weapons before it is too late. Next, we must accurately identify the real nuclear threats and take steps to overcome them.

The United States must immediately affirm that we will respect all existing treaties and accords wherein we have made promises regarding nuclear weapons, and we must adopt effective polices to ensure our compliance. Specifically, the U.S. should ratify the Test Ban Treaty and take concerted steps with other nuclear nations to comply with and effectuate the Nuclear Nonproliferation Treaty.

It is disturbing there are those who believe that, in a world free of nuclear weapons, we could be held hostage by any nation that suddenly developed nuclear capacity. Contrary to the delusions of the Bush administration, one of the most effective elements of the Nuclear Nonproliferation Treaty has been its verification procedures administered by the International Atomic Energy Agency (IAEA). We must remember that the IAEA was effective and accurate about the absence of weapons of mass destruction in Iraq and that it was our President who was lying to us.

In a joint article, former political leaders George P. Shultz, William J. Perry, Henry A. Kissinger, and Sam Nunn recently wrote: "Nuclear weapons today present tremendous dangers, but also an historic opportunity. U.S. leadership will be required to take the world to the next state—to a solid consensus for reversing reliance on nuclear weapons globally as a vital contribution to preventing their proliferation into potentially dangerous hands, and ultimately ending them as a threat to the world."

Currently, there are four nations, North Korea, Israel, Pakistan, and India, that possess nuclear weapons and who are not subject to the Nuclear Nonproliferation Treaty. Of these, North Korea appears to have only a very limited capacity. The three remaining nations are all considered to be friendly to American interests. Why then are we not taking aggressive steps to bring them into the fold?

Even though the United Nations Security Council directed Israel in 1981 to place its nuclear facilities under IAEA safeguards, the resolution has been steadfastly ignored by both Israel and the United States. Instead, Bush Junior recently gave a hundred harpoon missiles to Israel to be armed with nuclear warheads and deployed on Israeli submarines in a further destabilization of the region.

Rather than attacking Iran for seeking nuclear capability, the U.S. has a golden opportunity to reaffirm the benefits of the Nonproliferation Treaty and bring all nations into compliance with international law. The United States will never have the moral standing to influence these hold-out nations until we ourselves comply with the Treaty.

As a first step, the U.S. should withhold all foreign aid, military or otherwise, from any country that is not a signatory to and in compliance with the Nonproliferation Treaty.

Aileana asked, "Even if we are able to achieve nuclear arms control and bring all other countries into compliance with the Nonproliferation Treaty, what are we ever going to do with all of the leftover fissile material and nuclear waste? The United States and Russia each have tons and tons of weapons-grade uranium and plutonium in their stockpiles."

American stockpiles of nuclear weapons and materials are thought to be generally secure. However, Russia has retrieved all nuclear weapons previously deployed in other states in the former U.S.S.R., and there are more than 20,000 warheads and enough uranium and plutonium to make another 40,000 warheads spread across Russia. Much of this material is stored in poorly defended facilities protected by underpaid guards and faulty physical security.

Russia has engaged in a program to reprocess highly enriched uranium down to a degraded level that can't be used in nuclear weapons; however, huge quantities of uranium are stored at approximately 130 nuclear generating facilities around the world.

These vast quantities of nuclear materials truly represent the greatest terrorist threat in the world—far more than that posed by Iraq formerly, or Iran potentially. It is not hard to imagine a few pounds of fissile material finding its way into the hands of any terrorist prepared to pay the price and the means to construct a bomb.

Or, just imagine the hundreds of ready-made, so-called "suitcase nukes," developed by both Russia and the United States to be used by their special forces. These one-kiloton weapons weigh less than 100 pounds and can be easily concealed and detonated at locations in urban areas to cause widespread damage and loss of life. Even if these weapons have degraded, the weapons-grade plutonium could still be used in dirty bombs.

"I have been reading about former U.S. senator Sam Nunn," Sam said "who once thought that nuclear weapons guaranteed the safety of America; however, he has come to believe the United States would be far safer in a world without nuclear weapons. According to Nunn, 'We are at a tipping point, and we are headed in the wrong direction.'"

The United States has spent more than $10 billion helping Russia dismantle surplus Soviet nuclear weapons, upgrading security at its sites, and assisting unemployed nuclear scientists to find jobs; however, there are areas beyond the reach of the program. Nunn established the privately-funded Nuclear Threat Initiative to assist in the disposal of nuclear stockpiles in dangerous situations not covered by the U.S. law he sponsored in the Senate.

Nunn also envisions the creation of an international nuclear fuel bank to process and store nuclear materials for use by nations wishing to engage in the production of nuclear power. The bank would avoid the construction of nuclear refineries that are incredibly expensive and technologically challenging and, once constructed, can be used to increase the concentration of uranium from that required to generate power to weapons grade.

A number of nations have expressed an interest in civilian nuclear power, and Nunn believes a nuclear fuel bank would provide a reliable fuel supply for these nations and would prevent others from cheating in the enrichment of nuclear materials. If such a fuel bank were in operation, there would be no practical need for North Korea, Iran, or any other nation to engage in domestic nuclear enrichment programs.

Finally, Nunn wants to see an international treaty that prohibits the creation of all new fissile material.

I have gained a great deal of respect for Nunn and his thoughtful recommendations, and have heard of no better solution to resolve this greatest nuclear threat to our security and safety. The United States does not have a choice. We must quickly act to secure these vast quantities of fissile materials.

As a final step toward eliminating nuclear weapons entirely and the risk of nuclear waste generally, the United States should sponsor an international agreement that places all nuclear materials in the hands of the United Nations, creates a nuclear fuel bank for all existing enriched nuclear material, and eliminates the enrichment of new fissile material for the conceivable future.

Military Industrial Complex

Although I agreed with Sam in principle, I told him I had great doubts whether our defense industry—that depends on the war machine for survival—would allow one of the primary justifications for its existence to be eliminated. For example, the nation's three nuclear warhead laboratories have now been privatized and want to replace current warheads with improved and even more destructive models. These new systems could cost more than a trillion dollars and would further destabilize relations with Russia.

"It's true that it may not matter what the people want," Sam said, "if the politicians continue to listen to those who pay for their campaigns, rather than those who elect them. Even so, we should take a closer look at this powerful industry that has become an integral part of our military." I volunteered to brief the issue.

In his final address to the nation in 1961, President Eisenhower talked about the creation of a "permanent armaments industry of vast proportions" in association with an "immense military establishment." While recognizing the need, he warned that, "we must not fail to comprehend its grave implications. In the councils of government, we must guard against the acquisition of unwarranted influence, . . . by the military industrial complex. The potential for the disastrous rise of misplaced power exists and will persist."

Eisenhower continued, "We must never let the weight of this combination endanger our liberties or democratic processes. We should take nothing for granted. Only an alert and knowledgeable citizenry can compel the proper meshing of the huge industrial and military machinery of defense with our peaceful methods and goals, so that security and liberty may prosper together."

Looking to the future, Eisenhower said:

> Down the long lane of the history yet to be written America knows that this world of ours, ever growing smaller, must avoid becoming a community of dreadful fear and hate, and be instead, a proud confederation of mutual trust and respect. Such a confederation must be one of equals. The weakest must come to the conference table with the same confidence as do we, protected as we are by our moral, economic, and military strength. That table, though scarred by many past frustrations, cannot be abandoned for the certain agony of the battlefield.

Disarmament, with mutual honor and confidence, is a continuing imperative. Together we must learn how to compose differences, not with arms, but with intellect and decent purpose.

Aileana said, "It shouldn't surprise you to know that an autographed photograph of President Eisenhower occupied a place of honor on the living room wall of my parent's home. More so than any subsequent Republican president, he best represented the ideals and promises of the party established by Abraham Lincoln."

In 2006, world governments misappropriated more than $1.2 trillion from their citizens, better spent for other things, and wasted it on the purchase of weapons of war, a 37 percent increase in just ten years. The number increased to $1.5 trillion in 2007.

The United States remains at the top of the expenditure chart, accounting for more than half of total sales, followed by Russia, Britain, Israel, and France.

Thirteen of the top 20 defense manufacturers are located in the United States. These businesses are subsidized not only by the spending by the U.S. on armaments, but also by the generosity of our government in providing billions in foreign aid to other countries that is earmarked to purchase U.S. arms, rather than to assist their citizens to live a better life.

Such aid can be both destabilizing and counterproductive. For example, the United States offered to sell 36 F-16 fighters to Pakistan for its use in the ongoing armed conflict with India, and then turned around and offered India the opportunity to purchase 126 of the same fighters.

Israel has been the top recipient of foreign aid from the United States for years, averaging close to $3 billion annually, allegedly to keep the nation safe from its threatening neighbors. However, the U.S. signed a deal with Saudi Arabia, which remains in a formal state of war with Israel, to provide that nation with $6 billion in arms.

In 2007, the U.S. Defense Department notified Congress of the "possibility of military sales" to other countries more than 52 times. Between September 2005 and September 2006, the Bush administration approved the sale of $21 billion in weapons to foreign governments. This is more than double the amount for the previous year.

The U.S. government directly negotiates these arms agreements, in effect acting as a salesman for the manufacturers. America leads in the sales of missiles and military ships, as well as military training. In 2008, the militaries of 138 nations will be taught how to use these weapons by U.S. military trainers.

Many U.S. arms customers are undemocratic regimes in the developing world with poor records of human rights. By propping up these unstable governments, the weapon sales undermine global security and, in many cases, the best interests of the United States. The Bush administration increasingly used new "military assistance accounts" to allow the Pentagon to bypass legal restrictions on training and arming human rights abusers.

The United States not only sells exotic high-tech military equipment, but the business of its small-arms industry is also booming. The U.S. remains one of the principal suppliers of new rifles, pistols, machine guns, and grenade launchers to the world.

In addition, according to the Federation of American Scientists, "the Pentagon gives away or sells at deep discounts the vast oversupply of small/light weapons that it has in its post cold war inventory." The ease by which these small weapons can be passed around contributes to ethnic, religious, and sectarian conflicts throughout the developing world that have killed more than five million people since 1990.

Military prowess is often a just matter of one-upmanship, with victory usually going to the boy with the biggest toy. In effect, we say, "This year we'll sell to you and next year to your enemy. That way, you will have to come back year after next with more cash in hand."

Sam laid aside my weapon industry paper and picked up the *Los Angeles Times* from the table. Pointing to the front page, he said, "It's not difficult to figure out why the national debt is increasing by $1.4 billion a day, or nearly $1 million a minute, or why it will have almost doubled during Bush Junior's tenure to more than $10 trillion by the time he leaves office. Every one of us already owes almost $30,000 for the cost of his dirty little war and the killing machine he's driving."

What we need is greater control over the international sale of weapons. In fact, the United States should sponsor an international treaty to prohibit the sale of arms by any one country to another.

Although it might not be possible to completely eliminate all military weapons as a matter of international law, everything possible should be done to discourage the production of arms, even for a nation's own use.

In the meantime, and to the extent it remains necessary, the entire United States defense industry should be nationalized. Our government acts as its sales force around the world, and these are essentially public companies acting for the profit and benefit of private owners.

We might as well own them outright and eliminate their excessive profits. The Seattle Journal for Social Justice published an article suggesting that defense corporations should become federally chartered, publicly-controlled companies. This sounds like an excellent idea!

Among the primary benefits of a publicly-owned defense industry would be the reduction or elimination of their aggressive lobbying and campaign contributions, neither of which is in the nation's best interests. In the current conflict, these industries have not only failed to deliver essential military supplies in a timely manner, but they have also failed to take advantage of the benefits of new information technology.

The lack of competition between just a couple of large bidders and interlocking relationships between contractors and the Pentagon elevates the guarantee of profits above a commitment to performance.

Military Mercenaries

One of the most invidious consequences of the commercialization of war has been the growing use of private military contractors by the U.S. military and their threat to freedom. According to Pulitzer Prize-winning historian David M. Kennedy, "Since the time of the ancient Greeks through the American Revolutionary War and well into the 20th Century, the obligation to bear arms and the privilege of citizenship have been intimately linked. It was for the sake of that link between service and a full place in society that the founders were so invested in militias and so worried about standing armies." Not only is today's all-volunteer military no longer representative of all ranks of society, "without respect to background or privilege or education," it is increasingly being augmented by hired contractors to perform many of the duties previously performed by citizen soldiers.

Civilian camp followers have always tagged along with armies to perform auxiliary tasks such as food, laundry, and supply services. Under the laws of war, these supply contractors are entitled to be treated as prisoners of war if captured; however, contractors or mercenaries who engage in combat are defined as unlawful combatants and are not entitled to the protection of the Geneva Conventions.

In its attempt to privatize every government function that can be performed by their corporate sponsors, the Bush administration hired more than 100,000 civilian contractors in Iraq, and almost half are illegally working as private soldiers.

Although they are performing combat duties, these mercenaries operate with little or no oversight by the U.S. military or other legal constraints. All such contractors were granted immunity from Iraqi prosecution by Bush's civilian administrator before the election of an Iraqi government. Moreover, the vast majority are engaged in tasks for the State Department and other agencies, and they are not subject to any form of military discipline.

Sam: A Political Philosophy

In Iraq, our ambassador's security is provided by paramilitary operatives employed by Blackwater International, which has received government contracts valued at more than one billion dollars. Blackwater operates the largest private military base in the world, where it trains mercenaries. It has a fleet of 20 aircraft and deploys 20,000 troops.

Most of Blackwater's private soldiers received their initial and advanced training at the expense of the U.S. military; however, most left the service for the far greater pay offered by the private contractors for doing the same job.

Blackwater pays as much as $1,000 a day for the services of former special-operations personnel compared to about $150 day which a Green Beret with 20 years of service receives. Individual supervisors and managers are paid as much as $350,000 a year for tasks ordinarily performed by active duty officers who receive far less, and their salary does not include as much as $850,000 in overhead, insurance, and profit costs. Keep in mind that the President, as Commander-in-Chief of the military, only earns $400,000 a year.

The U.S. government deployed Blackwater mercenaries to New Orleans following Hurricane Katrina, and Blackwater is presently constructing an 800 acre training facility along the Mexican border. The Blackwater president told Congress in 2005 that Blackwater could "respond to the Customs' and Border Patrol's emerging and compelling training needs."

Blackwater was hired by the CIA in 2002 for classified missions and recently formed a new company, Total Intelligence, to provide intelligence services to commercial clients. According to the company, it will operate a "24/7 intelligence fusion and warning center" that will monitor civil unrest, terrorism, economic stability, environmental and health concerns, and information technology security around the world.

Sam said that in his 2007 State of the Union Address, Bush proposed the formation of a Civilian Reserve Corps to "function much like our military Reserve. It would ease the burden on the armed forces by allowing us to hire civilians with critical skills to serve on missions abroad when America needs them."

The Reserve Corps would legitimize America's illegal deployment of mercenaries and would allow them to engage in all traditional military roles.

This entire movement toward contracting for military and law enforcement services is a very dangerous thing.

There are laws to protect us from the involvement of the military in law enforcement operations and that define the role of the military in our government. All of these laws are thrown out the window, however, when our government hires mercenaries to do things that are most threatening to our personal security and freedoms.

We have seen the death and destruction caused by unregulated mercenaries in Iraq, and we have to imagine the result if civilian contractors are hired to enforce the laws or to provide internal security in America.

The United States must immediately discontinue the deployment of all civilian contractors in traditional military and law enforcement roles. No other policy will serve to protect us here at home and those abroad to whom we have a duty to protect under international law.

Outlaw War

Our work on the war chapter was more extensive and was taking longer than we had expected, and I told Sam and Aileana that I had to spend a couple of weeks attending to newspaper business. My assignment editor had requested my participation in the interviews of the 2008 presidential candidates for editorial endorsements and wanted me to dedicate a series of columns to the election.

John McCain had sewn up the Republican nomination earlier in the primary process, and Barack Obama had finally secured the Democratic nomination over Hillary Clinton. It was an exciting opportunity for me to interview the next president of the United States, no matter which candidate won the election.

Aileana said, "Sam, maybe it's a good time for you and me to take a real vacation. The research trip was interesting, but it certainly wasn't relaxing. Since you've never been to San Diego, how about if we go down and I'll show you the town?"

Sam enthusiastically agreed, and Aileana began to make the plans. She found a hotel in Ocean Beach that welcomed guests with dogs. It was located adjacent to the dedicated dog beach along the channel leading from Mission Bay to the ocean.

They loaded K.D. into Aileana's car and set off down the freeway to San Diego, while I got to ask a couple of "wanna-be presidents" what they thought about war and nuclear weapons—among other things.

Sam and Aileana spent two weeks in San Diego visiting Balboa Park, the Gaslamp Quarter, Sea World, the Point Loma Lighthouse, La Jolla, Old Town, and other sights. As a service dog, K.D. accompanied them everywhere they went, including a personally guided tour of the Naval Medical Center, where Aileana formerly commanded the nursing and hospital corps.

Xiomara, Heather, and I drove down to the beach house the weekend they returned. There were presents for all of us, and as we sat on the patio looking at photographs and talking about their trip, Sam said he might want to settle in San Diego after we finished the book.

I told them about my interviews with the presidential candidates and what they had to say—and what they wouldn't talk about. We agreed to get started on the remainder of the chapter.

I had asked each of the candidates what we could have, or should have, done differently about Iraq. I asked Sam the same question. Sam had obviously given the subject much thought, probably more than the actual candidates. He responded with a quoted question.

Thomas Jefferson once asked, "Will nations never devise a more rational umpire of differences than force? Are there no means of coercing

Outlaw War

injustice more gratifying to our nature than a waste of the blood of thousands and of the labor of millions of our fellow creatures?"

Drawing on our collective wisdom, we may finally be in a position to positively answer Jefferson's question. If we are honest with ourselves, the only logical conclusion is that waging military wars against other nations and their innocent people is not only immoral in some cases, but also downright foolish in most.

America's dispute is often with some petty despot who poses a far greater risk of harm to his own citizens and neighbors than to us. Why then should we throw away the lives of our young soldiers and waste billions of our dollars slaughtering and immolating thousands of the dictator's innocent victims, while earning the hatred of the people for generations to come?

Why not adopt a national policy of avoiding war against other nations and their innocent people as a matter of principle? We should outlaw war unless our country is actually attacked—as at Pearl Harbor.

Instead, to confront the danger posed by foreign dictators who threaten to physically injure our citizens or to seriously harm our national interests, we should adopt an alternative policy based upon a law enforcement model in which Congress declares the dictator, personally, to be an "outlaw," instead of declaring war against the nation.

The word outlaw has a very special meaning—different from common usage. It's an Old Norse word for someone who was outlawed or banished as a punishment. An outlaw was outside the protection of the law; his property was seized by the crown; and he could be killed without recrimination.

By treating these dangerous dictators like the criminals they are, we can use existing legal means to deprive them of support and separate them from power.

Aileana said, "interestingly enough the United States, along with most other nations, signed a treaty in 1928 that renounced war as an instrument of national policy.

The Kellogg-Briand Pact simply says, "The . . . Parties solemnly declare in the names of their respective peoples that they condemn recourse to war for the solution of international controversies, and renounce it, as an instrument of national policy in their relations with one another."

The parties agreed "that the settlement or solution of all disputes or conflicts of whatever nature or of whatever origin they may be, which may arise among them, shall never be sought except by pacific means."

The treaty failed to prevent World War II, which erupted ten years later, but it is still in effect and binding on the United States. All a president has to do to establish a policy outlawing war would be to announce she or he was going to obey the law of the land. Of course, there are real-life situations that would test the policy.

I asked Sam what could be done differently to deal with dictators such as Saddam Hussein in Iraq. What should a president do?

Based upon deceptive evidence, and although more than half of us had serious misgivings about it, Congress empowered President Bush to wage all-out war against the Iraqi people on behalf of all of us. At a time when we were enduring an economic recession, he gained the power to waste billions and billions of our hard-earned tax dollars, better spent in other ways, to bomb Iraq and punish Saddam's victims.

What if, instead, we had been blessed with an enlightened president who had wisely presented the case against Saddam to Congress and (assuming there was a true threat) was able to establish that Saddam actually represented a serious danger to our national interests? If convinced by the evidence, Congress could have passed a joint resolution declaring Saddam to be an outlaw.

Congress could have directed the President to file a lawsuit against the government of Iraq in the World Court of Justice in The Hague. The President could have been authorized to use reasonable force and other legitimate means to secure the personal appearance of the outlaw at the World Court to defend his government against the charges.

Outlaw War

In essence, Congress could have issued an authorization or "warrant" for the President to take Saddam into custody and to "arrest" him and his dangerous behavior.

What then? Would we have expected the President to run over and personally kick in Saddam's door, toss him against the wall and frisk him? Certainly not the cowardly President we are currently cursed with. No, one of the things professional police officers have learned the hard way is that it's bad tactics to immediately rush an armed and barricaded suspect.

A lot of brave cops and innocent people died unnecessarily before law enforcement professionals learned to take as much time as necessary to secure the premises, bring in the SWAT team, turn off the utilities, clear the neighborhood, engage in negotiations, and obtain the release of hostages.

Only when all else fails and only when delay increases the risk of harm to the hostages, do professional police officers fire in the tear gas, toss the flash-bang grenades, and storm the premises. Innocent people and brave officers may still die, but at least decisions to use deadly force are made in a reasoned and deliberate manner pursuant to established policy and only after all other alternatives fail.

Would an outlaw war model work? Would it be a smarter policy? We will never know unless we try it.

Shouldn't we have taken the time to make a better case for invasion to ourselves, our allies, the United Nations and, most importantly, to the poor people of Iraq and to others in the Middle East?

We had the technological ability to bomb the Iraqi people with audio and video tapes, take over their airwaves, and spam their computers with emails, not to spread false propaganda, but to prove to them they had more to fear from Saddam than from us.

We should have demonstrated our respect for the antiquity of the Iraqi culture, recognized their individual desire to protect their families, and sought to reassure them that we wanted to avoid harm to them, their institutions, and their cultural heritage.

Sam: A Political Philosophy

We should have shown the Iraqi people we were not interested in their oil wealth, only to ensure it was used for their welfare, not for building palaces for Saddam and his family.

Relying on international and Islamic law and by appealing to their common sense, we should have asked the people of Iraq to move away from the outlaw who had seized power over them and to let us help them to free themselves from his domination.

Wouldn't it have been money well spent to offer a substantial individual reward, generous financial aid, and the elimination of economic sanctions to the surviving Iraqi government that deposed the tyrant? Wouldn't it have been a far better investment than the billions we have already wasted and the billions more to come? By not targeting the people, the resulting government would more likely be representative, rather than repressive. It would certainly have been more stable and democratic that the one the Iraqi people ended up with.

Should push come to shove, the armed elements of our Defense Department continue to be the mightiest military force in history and the most effective in the world today. Surely, the brilliant military planners in the Pentagon could have conceived and created myriad plans and actions to keep Saddam on the ropes, personally, until such time as he gave up, his own henchmen sold him out, or when a few brave volunteers had to go in and "arrest" him—and what he was doing—by taking the outlaw into custody, dead or alive.

Building upon a smart instead of a dumb war policy, wouldn't we (and the United Nations) be in a better position in the future to cope with violent dictators and unstable nations?

Shouldn't we at least consider the alternative?

I asked, "If you were the Commander-in-Chief, Sam, what would he do about the military?" He laughed and said, "Well, assuming that I were miraculously elected president against my wishes, I would have to first accept that there would be some things within my power and there are other matters that would require the cooperation of Congress to achieve.

Outlaw War

I would immediately do what I could on my own, and I would work with others in government to bring about fundamental change. Mainly, I would adjust the focus of the military's mission and do some reorganizing, but I would not seek to eliminate the military.

We live and shall continue to live, at least for the foreseeable future, in an imperfect world, one in which it is foolish to fail to recognize that there are dangers lurking in the shadows along our path for which we must be prepared. If we are smart and if we successfully confront these dangers, however, in a way that prevents them from reoccurring or mutating in the future, we can look forward to the time when peace prevails and violence is a distant memory.

In the meantime, we must venerate those who dedicate their lives to the attainment of peace, as we must honor those who fight for us by defining their task so as to minimize the risk of harm to them and to best achieve mission objectives.

Existing U.S. policy is to offensively project our military power around the world to protect the interests of the United States and to defend what has only recently been nationalistically characterized as the "Homeland." At the same time, we are increasingly deploying military assets within our country against our own citizens in order to protect the Homeland security.

The first thing I would do is to clearly define the primary mission of our military as the defense of the American people against external threats. The Department of Defense is and should be for our defense, not policing.

I would reaffirm the Posse Comitatus Act and order that the military, including its contractors, play no role in the internal enforcement of laws within the United States.

The United States presently operates more than 750 military bases around the world at a cost of approximately $365 billion per year. With the existing inventory of intercontinental ballistic missiles, stealth bombers, carrier fleets, and cruise missiles, the U.S. has the ready ability to project its might anywhere in the world without the necessity of most of these military bases.

Sam: A Political Philosophy

If I were Commander-in-Chief, I would order most of our troops to come home, and I would work with Congress and other nations to close down the vast majority of these bases and seek to reduce the military budget by up to 75 percent.

The remaining military budget of $115 billion a year would still be almost double that spent by the next two nations, China at $62.5 billion and Russia at $62 billion

Wisely spent, those billions should purchase sufficient security for the people of the United States against any realistic and foreseeable external threats in a manner that encourages respect and which does not engender hatred from the rest of the world.

The saved $365 billion would go far in providing health care for all Americans, properly educating our children, preserving our Social Security retirement system, and adequately funding space and science programs that would forever make us stronger than any potential enemies.

One of my first orders would be that every member of the military, irrespective of rank or assignment, be first educated as a medical corpsman, well beyond basic first aid training.

Before we teach our young women and men to take lives, we have to ensure they understand the sanctity of life and that they respect the essential humanity of everyone, including our enemies.

We must also do everything in our power to save the lives of those who are placed in harm's way on our behalf and who are injured. Hopefully, with time and the reduction of combat, the medical training would become more important and valuable than the military training.

With this mission and training, we will also be able to rely on our military to respond to disasters, natural or otherwise, within our country and around the world, and to render effective aid and assistance to those most in need.

Throughout most of our history, the United States used its army for much more than combat, and they performed a wide variety of socially-beneficial tasks. Colonel (and later president) Zachary Taylor said, "The ax, pick, saw, and trowel has become more the implement of the American soldier than the cannon, musket, or sword."

Just as they performed as "nation builders," the military can once again be used to help the people of the world, rather than to kill their children in senseless wars.

The respect gained from such activities will far more effectively protect the security of the people of the United States than any arrogant display of naked military power.

Aileana said that she couldn't agree more with universal medical training for all personnel, but having experienced the reality of war firsthand, she wondered what could be done to ensure victory once our military had to be committed.

Sam replied, "I too have seen the horrors of war and have given much thought to successfully fighting necessary battles. We must recognize that we will never again fight war with massive armies such as was done in World War II, and hopefully, we will never again undertake to occupy a nation such as Viet Nam, Afghanistan, and Iraq.

"Given the availability of technologically advanced weapons and the nature of modern warfare, we should be able to reduce the size of our military services to a level that allows us to effectively defend Americans *and* to protect our overseas interests"

In-depth military training could field a coherent, mobile, well-equipped, highly-trained, and tactically facile force of fighters capable of kicking ass in multiple languages, each one poised to respond worldwide to any disaster, natural or military, that excites our common concern, and each one individually committed to bringing home all who share the risk of danger and death.

Advanced justice training would enable those most capable of more refined individual discretion to work more independently in exercising authority of force outside the United States in actions not requiring group weapons and tactics.

In other words, should the need arise, we have to be able to surgically remove or neutralize individuals, anywhere—regarding whom Congress has, upon evidence of imminent danger, issued an "arrest" warrant—without harming their innocent victims.

The military's airlift capacity should be available during peacetime to shuttle patients and their relatives to advanced medical treatment centers around the country, and during a military emergency, we should be able to quickly transport troops to any trouble spot in the world.

Combined with the technological spin-off generated by a free and exploring society, the actual use of military force would likely become increasingly rare, but would forever remain rapid in its deployment tactics and decisive in its strategic effects.

Americans excel in their ability to creatively discover technological solutions to difficult problems. We have to balance the essential need to spend money on scientific research and to do so wisely in precisely operating on the conflicts of the future, rather than to waste resources on material used to fight the wars of the past.

Conflicts in the future that cannot be solved by compromise and negotiation may be resolved by using sensors, robots, drones, and unmanned vehicles operated by technically-sophisticated and dedicated young women and men.

Rather than being the stupid, overweight, and cowardly bully on the block, we should shape our military to be more like the confident and brave young person with a black belt in karate, who quietly avoids conflict, but who is prepared to defend herself and her friends and to defeat the bully, if forced to do so.

Aileana said, "The people of other nations now consider the United States to be the world's bully, and we are perceived by many to be the greatest threat to world peace; however, if we are ever going to overcome this perception we must acknowledge that our offensive military policies have a bipartisan origin.

Outlaw War

It was President Carter who enticed the USSR to invade Afghanistan and who declared that the United States would use military force if necessary to defend its national interests in the Persian Gulf region. And it was President Clinton who launched an air attack on Serbia based on questionable justification—without the backing of the United Nations Security Council—and who attacked Bagdad to deflect attention from his impeachment proceedings. Clinton also erroneously bombed a pharmaceutical factory in Sudan and was the first president to approve "extraordinary renditions."

It has been estimated that the long-term cost of the wars in Afghanistan and Iraq could exceed $3.5 trillion. Beyond the monetary costs, we must consider that the result of continued war in a technological age may extinguish the future of collective humanity.

As President Eisenhower once wisely observed: "Every gun that is made, every warship launched, every rocket fired, signifies in the final sense a theft from those who hunger and are not fed, those who are cold and are not clothed." We exist only for the future well-being of our children, and their health and happiness is most threatened by unceasing war.

Sam agreed, "Each war sows the seeds of hatred from which the next is grown, and wars will continue so long as we kill and injure human beings by choice in our efforts to impose our political will upon others."

We must break the cycle of hatred if we are ever to win the war against terrorism. We are a nation whose citizens have the potential freedom and institutions to control its military and which has the power to remove dangerous foreign outlaws without causing the deaths of their innocent victims and the destruction of their victim's means of existence.

Irrespective of the motivations of those who purport to lead us, we the ordinary people of the United States abhor war and the slaughter of innocents. We are not war criminals, and we cannot abide the commission of crimes under the guise of self-defense.

We have an obligation to humanity to demonstrate our compassion, strength, and imagination, and we have a duty to our children to avoid wasting their lives and futures in senseless wars when we can better accomplish our political aims by other means.

Sam spoke during these last few minutes with great emotion, and he had never been so eloquent. He was pleading his case to an unseen audience, trying to convince its members that they had to surrender their familiar ways before they destroyed their families, their nation, and humanity. As he concluded, he sat quietly with his eyes closed, then he looked up and his eyes came to focus on a distant place.

Is war inevitable? Can't we overcome it—cure it like any other disease? I cannot believe that eternal peace is impossible. We must have hope for something better. I believe in a rational universe, one in which peace is the standard. There can be no other logical answer.

A Safe, Just, and Civil Society

The sun had broken through the "June gloom" that blankets coastal Southern California with overcast mornings in the late spring, and I was on my way to the beach house to spend a workday with Aileana and Sam. Heather was tagging along to visit with K.D., and she was chattering away about a conflict she was having with her "BFF" (best friend forever). I was half listening and thinking about where we were going with Sam's book.

Sam had initially focused his philosophy on questions of war; however, the war on terror was also interfering with the privacy and civil rights of Americans. The fallout had brought the entire issue of internal policing to the forefront of his thinking.

It appeared the subject of justice was going to be as difficult and extensive as our review of militarism, yet Sam felt it was a necessary extension of many of the same issues.

As I sensed that Heather was nearing the point of her story, I tuned in as she shared her differences with her lifelong girlfriend, who was now more interested in boys than youth politics. I gave my beautiful Mexican-American daughter my full attention and was pleased by what I saw.

Named for my mother, Heather had certainly inherited the best genes from both Xiomara and me—a living example of the "hybrid advantage." I cared for my young Hispanic princess in the way of fathers in all cultures, and the love she returned was something a woman can give to no other—neither mate nor child. She respected her old man and what he was doing and wanted to be a part of it. What more could a guy ask for?

As we opened the gate to enter the patio, we could hear K.D. barking inside, but she stopped when Heather called her name at the front door. We found Sam in his study and he wanted to show off his new watch dog. Sam had been praising K.D. when she barked whenever the patio gate opened, and her service training had advanced to a new level.

They had been walking on the Strand when a darkly dressed man had suddenly appeared behind them. K.D. wheeled about and began to bark, and Sam quietly encouraged her. He asked me to go outside the study and come back inside. Sam told K.D. to "watch 'im" as I returned, and she began to bark at me. Then, when Sam told her that it was "okay," she stopped, sat down, and offered her paw for a shake.

Heather sat down on the couch and spoke to K.D. in "dog talk." K.D.'s tail began to wag so fast that it appeared to be a propeller. She was so excited she couldn't understand why all of her 65 pounds shouldn't be in Heather's lap. After a little more dog talk, the two of them decided to go for a stroll—with the promise of a treat at the Strand Café.

Sam was grinning like a Cheshire Cat. When I asked him if was because of the way the political winds were blowing, he said he and Aileana had even better news. "Actually, we have good news and we have great news. The good news is that I'm going to be a father, and the great news is that the baby's mother has agreed to marry me."

I was beyond delight. It had been apparent to all of us that Sam and Aileana's relationship had been evolving over the months as they traveled and worked together. Their joy was infectious as they shared their wedding plans.

"Samuel and I would like for you, Xiomara, and Heather to stand with us," Aileana said. "You folks have truly become more than friends, and we can't think of anyone we'd rather share the experience with."

They wanted to get married on the beach at sunset, with just my family (and K.D.) as witnesses. The two of them were deeply spiritual and had written their own vows. They asked if I knew of anyone to officiate.

I told them I could probably get Judge Judi—not the television personality, but my friend, the real Judge Judi Jones, a retired Superior Court commissioner. After years of hearing juvenile matters, I was sure she could legally tie their knot. They said they would like to have the ceremony as soon as they could get their license, and I agreed to make the arrangements.

Aileana passed around a plate of hot, freshly-baked scones, and we settled down with our tea and coffee to map out where we were heading. She had prepared a subject outline on her laptop that she began to revise and expand as we talked about the justice system and its challenges.

We agreed to start with the domestic justice system before confronting issues such as the government's illegal monitoring of private communications, secret investigations, torture, preventive detention, establishment of privately-operated prisons and concentration camps, and the use of civilian mercenaries and the military in domestic law enforcement.

As a young man, Sam had once considered a career in law enforcement before he settled upon teaching, and he had often read about the subject as he sat in his comfortable chair in the Central Library. His interest continued, and he had called me a few weeks before to tell me he would like more background before taking on law enforcement policy and philosophy.

My trusty Rolodex once again saved the day, and after a few phone calls, Sam and I had appointments to visit with two retired Los Angeles Police Department administrators who were willing to share their experiences, knowledge, and professional connections.

Ed Davis had served for nine years as the chief of police and was known as the "father of community policing." Jim Fisk was perhaps the most intellectual command officer who ever served on the LAPD, having scored first on every promotional exam, including his last one for chief, when Davis was appointed instead.

Fisk was a scholarly, quiet, gentle man; however, the Police Commission had not believed he was tough enough to lead the Department. He retired and accepted a professorship at UCLA's Institute of Government and Urban Affairs.

Ed Davis had gone on to serve several terms in the California Senate and had recently retired to his home in Chatsworth. Sam and I found him sitting by his swimming pool on a warm afternoon.

Always gregarious, Senator Davis was more than happy to share his philosophy as we sipped ice tea.

> I worked in Planning and Research when I was a young police sergeant and helped develop the Department Manual; however, William Parker, who was chief at the time, would never let me write the first volume on policy. As a lawyer, he was afraid of lawsuits and always said he carried his policy in his hip pocket and every officer on the street knew exactly what it was.
>
> The day I got my chief's badge, my first order was that the Policy Manual be written. It took two years, a lot of hard work, and many arguments, but finally the command staff and the Police Commission agreed on what the principles and philosophy of policing should be in the City of Los Angeles. We published the manual, and we put it in every city library for everyone to read.
>
> It wasn't enough to say the motto of the Department was *To Protect and To Serve*. We had to define exactly what that means. I've been called a populist—and a lot of other things over the years including "Crazy Ed"—but most basically I believe the

role of the police in America is or should be that *the People and their Police are Peers for Peace.*

Although police officers work for the various state and local governments established by the people, there is a deeper, more profound relationship between individuals and *their* police—one that is key to the definition of a free society.

Law enforcement based upon fear, repression, and punishment cannot serve to preserve freedoms. To the contrary, such a system is destructive of freedom.

A free society requires a law enforcement that respects and appreciates the Constitution and its protections. One of the stupidest things I hear today is that we have to give up some of our freedoms to ensure our security.

We cannot post a police officer in every front yard or on every street corner, nor should we tolerate such an intrusion in a free society. The system can be effective only when the people and their police work together for a peaceful community.

Individuals have to have the courage and motivation to report crimes when they see them happening, to stand up as witnesses in prosecutions, and to discourage crime in their daily lives.

We have to encourage an inhibition in young people against becoming criminals, and we can best do this by setting a good example. This not only means that parents should not get drunk or do drugs in front of their children, but they also shouldn't shoplift, cheat on their tax returns, or resort to violence words or actions when they get upset.

Every situation is different, and what we want are officers who are capable of exercising discretion in making decisions to ensure that each case is handled judiciously; however, we also have to have written policy to make sure that people are treated equally and not discriminated against. It's a delicate balance.

Sam: A Political Philosophy

Davis spoke favorably about the policing approach implemented by New York Police Commissioner William Bratton in New York City in 1994. Emphasizing crime prevention over making arrests, Bratton believes that attention to minor crimes prevented larger crimes. "He has been successful in reducing the number of crimes by aggressive "stop and frisk" policies and targeting high crime areas, but law enforcement officers in New York City, Los Angeles, or any other jurisdiction cannot forget that they are representatives of the communities they police—not an occupying army."

Senator Davis spent the remainder of our visit providing additional background about the law enforcement function and the difficult political problems it presents. He was generous with his time and invited us to return if necessary.

On our way back from the Valley over the Sepulveda pass, we stopped off at UCLA to meet with Jim Fisk. He had retired from teaching full time, but maintained an office on campus as a professor emeritus.

We found Jim to be a soft spoken and professorial deep thinker. As a deputy chief, he had commanded the Department's community relations efforts and had provided the intellectual foundation for its philosophical policy. Once he had grown comfortable with our interest and intentions, Professor Fisk began to talk about the emotional and psychological aspects of law enforcement.

A tall and physically fit man with a gentle demeanor and intelligent eyes, he quietly smiled as he reached across and took one of Sam's wrists in his large hand and squeezed. "This is the essence of law enforcement. How we as a society arrest and take our own into custody defines, most basically, the essential nature of our society." An articulate teacher, who had presented the material many times in the classroom, the professor continued:

A Safe, Just, and Civil Society

If we must be deprived of our physical freedom, we want the arrest to be done by someone whose allegiance is to our local government and the people who elect its officials. Law enforcement in a free society must be performed, to the greatest extent possible, by city, county, and state officials, in that order. The current trend of federalizing crimes is one of the greatest threats to individual freedoms.

Law enforcement officers must not only be trained to use force in making arrests, even to kill another person who threatens the lives of others, but they must also be trained to do so in a manner that is consistent with Constitutional guarantees. They are authorized to use only the minimum amount of force required to accomplish the objective.

Police work is different from the military function, in which soldiers are simply trained to kill with the maximum available force. Officers have to be able to turn on the ability to fight—and to always win—but they have to be able to immediately turn it off. Coolness, rather than anger, is the mark of a professional officer.

Police officers are never allowed to lose or to retreat. They cannot just say "uncle" and let a dangerous felon walk away, but at the same time, they cannot allow their emotions or fears to control the situation or to punish a resistor. There are few jobs that are so stressful and dangerous, both physically and emotionally.

American law enforcement is truly a profession. Many of our new officers have college degrees, and they all undergo comprehensive training to comply with the Peace Officer Standards and Training requirements now established by every state.

The selection process is rigorous, including academic testing, physical agility, multiple interviews, psychological and polygraph testing, and comprehensive background investigations.

These are the good boys and girls, now grown up—those who mostly stayed out of trouble, did their homework, and played sports. They helped around the house and didn't give their parents too much grief.

We hire and train them, and then we put them out on the streets to do an almost impossible job. Every day they are confronted by disrespect, and they have to wade through blood and other consequences of violence. They have to resist bribes and greed in a society that is increasingly glorifying the pursuit of wealth.

They have to deal with the dark side of our society and the very worst of human behavior, but at the same time, they are not allowed to become insensitive to their experiences. Otherwise, they become incapable of doing the job in the manner we expect. Cynical and violent officers often become uncaring "robocops" who themselves act unconstitutionally and commit crimes.

Even officers who survive the first year or two with their basic humanity intact learn that only other police officers understand what they have to go through. They begin to lose touch with their old friends and increasingly find it difficult to talk about their experiences—even with their own family.

Many lose the ability to experience intimacy with their spouses and significant others, as they keep more and more secrets. They begin to hang out together, to drink together, and to reinforce their own negative attitudes and behaviors.

Professor Fisk paused for a moment and continued with tears in his eyes, "Police work takes these very fine young women and men, puts them through a meat grinder of deception, hatred, and violence, and after a couple of years, many of them suffer emotionally."

> We send these young, brave warriors for peace out day after day to deal with the tears, trash, and turmoil of our society. We expect so much of them, but we give them so little. More than a paycheck and the promise of a retirement, they need understanding, respect, and support. They stand between us and the abyss.
> I worry that we will increasingly militarize our law enforcement function—that a time will come when we will impose an immediate death penalty for crime by shooting down violators, mount machine guns on our police helicopters, and deploy armored cars in our local neighborhoods and drones above our cities. When these things occur, it is not only civil law enforcement that will be dead, it will also be the law itself and our free society that will have passed away.

He concluded by saying, "The thing I fear the most, right now, is that we are doing nothing about the swift erosion of our freedoms by the federal government. We have been so caught up in getting ahead in life and buying stuff that we have failed to notice, or to care that our own government has come to constitute one of the greatest threat to the well-being of Americans, perhaps more so in the long run than international terrorists or domestic criminals.

> We have acquiesced in searches without warrants, domestic wiretapping, preventive detention, draconian prison sentences, and private prisons. Much like boiling a frog alive by gradually raising the temperature of the water, I am terrified by our own inertia and inaction. The time to jump is now, for the times are perilous.

Professor Fisk referred us to various written materials and invited us to return and meet with other faculty members, should we have an interest in doing so.

We took him up on his offer, and over the next couple of weeks, Sam and I met with the dean of the law school and the heads of the political science and sociology departments. We learned that the history of the United States is closely tied to its system of justice.

A Government of Laws and Not of Men

From its beginning, America has been a nation of laws. Colonists brought English law with them, including the Magna Carta and the common law. Once here, they founded representative government, passed laws, and established courts. When the colonists resolved to declare their independence from England, they relied on the Magna Carta in citing numerous violations by King George III.

With a written Constitution—which supplanted the Magna Carta—and the Bill of Rights, Americans achieved a political and legal standoff between the vulnerability of individual rights and the overwhelming power of government. These rights depend on a delicate balance of power, or independence, among the legislative, the executive, and the judiciary, especially the courts.

The rule of law was not easily achieved, nor was its definition immediately clear. During the administration of John Adams, the Federalists controlled both Congress and the Presidency. They passed legislation to prevent seditious attacks on the Federalist government by newspapers and to deport people born in other countries who opposed them.

As they were being defeated by the Jeffersonian Democratic-Republicans, the Federalists attempted to assert lasting control over the judiciary by dramatically expanding the number of courts and by filling all vacancies through last-minute appointments.

The constitutionality of the Judiciary Act of 1801 became an issue when newly-inaugurated President Thomas Jefferson ordered his Secretary of State, James Madison, to withhold the undelivered judicial commissions. A lawsuit quickly ensued.

In deciding *Marbury vs. Madison*, the Supreme Court under Chief Justice John Marshall ruled that the Constitution provided the Court with the power to review statutes passed by Congress and signed by the President, including the Judiciary Act.

Marshall stated: "The government of the United States has been emphatically termed a government of laws and not of men. It will certainly cease to deserve this high appellation, if the laws furnish no remedy for the violation of a vested legal right."

Following the tradition of English common law, American society was founded upon the trust that aggrieved persons could always find an effective remedy at law—rather than resorting to violent self-help or vigilantism. Our civil society is based on shared community responsibilities and benefits—rather than tribal dependency.

The American justice system has not always been just, with some bad laws and twisted judicial decisions depriving people of their rights, rather than enforcing their rights. Low points include both the Fugitive Slave Act and the *Dred Scott* decision, in which the Supreme Court ruled in 1857 that Congress had no authority to prohibit slavery in federal territories. The Court ruled that people of African descent, whether or not slaves, could never be citizens. They could not sue in court—they were merely private property, which could not be taken from their owners without due process of law.

The Civil War was a failure of law, in which the Southern States believed they had the constitutional right to secede from the United States. Its result was the emancipation of the slaves and Constitutional amendments prohibiting slavery and guaranteeing the rights of former slaves to vote. Congressional statutes passed to enforce these rights, however, were consistently invalidated by the Supreme Court.

In 1883, the Court ruled Congress lacked the authority under the Fourteenth Amendment to outlaw racial discrimination by private organizations and individuals. Thirteen years later, in *Plessy vs. Ferguson*, the Supreme Court upheld the constitutionality of official racial segregation, even in public facilities.

The failure of the Supreme Court to uphold individual rights continued until Franklin Roosevelt and Harry Truman appointed more sympathetic judges between 1933 and 1953.

The trend continued under President Eisenhower, who based his judicial appointments primarily on character and ability, rather than politics. Following his appointment of Earl Warren as Chief Justice in 1953, the Supreme Court issued a series of opinions over the next two decades upholding the civil and criminal rights of individuals against the power of government.

In 1961, Justice Tom Clark, who had earlier served as President Truman's Attorney General, wrote the majority opinion in *Mapp vs. Ohio* that expanded the federal court's "exclusionary rule" to the states in refusing to allow evidence unlawfully seized in violation of the Fourth Amendment to be used in criminal trials.

Justice Clark reasoned that it is not the exclusionary rule that allows criminals to go free just because a police officer made a mistake; "it is the law that sets him [the criminal] free." He said, "Nothing can destroy a government more quickly than its failure to observe its own laws."

In 1966, Chief Justice Earl Warren, another former prosecutor, wrote in *Miranda vs. Arizona* that the Fifth Amendment's protection against self-incrimination was applicable in state as well as federal court trials.

Warren said that: "The person in custody must, prior to interrogation, be clearly informed that he has the right to remain silent, and that anything he says will be used against him in court; he must be clearly informed that he has the right to consult with a lawyer and to have the lawyer with him during interrogation, and that, if he is indigent, a lawyer will be appointed to represent him."

Even though these decisions were made by both Democratic and Republican appointees, conservative Republicans began to agitate against "judicial activism," and appointments during the Reagan and Bush Sr. administrations increasingly represented a philosophy that favored government over individuals and business over workers. Rights that had been recognized by the Warren Court were whittled away by decisions of the Rehnquist Court.

Ironically, the ultimate judicial activism occurred in the election of 2000, when the U.S. Supreme Court reversed a decision of the Florida Supreme Court that had upheld the rights of Florida voters to express their clear intention and choice for president.

The United States Supreme Court in an opinion joined in by Chief Justice Rehnquist (appointed by Reagan) and Justices Scalia (appointed by Reagan), Thomas (appointed by Bush Senior), Kennedy (appointed by Reagan), and O'Connor (appointed by Reagan) ruled in *Bush v. Gore* in favor of the Republican candidate George W. Bush.

In a purely political (versus constitutional) decision, the Court found that the "intent of the voter" standard may sound good in principle, but it lacked specific standards to ensure equal application. The legal tawdriness of the decision was demonstrated by the Court's order that the ruling was to have no effect as precedent in the future.

Four of the majority justices were members or affiliates of the Federalist Society, which was also instrumental in the appointment and confirmation of Justice O'Connor, the fifth member of the majority.

Justice Scalia, one of the founders of the Society, declared in 2002 that "government . . . derives its moral authority from God" and acts as the "minister of God." He went on to say, "The reaction of people of faith to this tendency of democracy to obscure the divine authority behind government should not be resignation to it, but the resolution to combat it as effectively as possible."

Under the leadership of Chief Justice John Roberts, a majority of the Supreme Court is now composed of individuals whose backgrounds are in government, business, or academia and who have never represented a criminal defendant.

The Roberts Court has narrowed *Mapp* and *Miranda* protections and recently eliminated the First Amendment rights of government employee whistle-blowers. In another series of decisions, the Court has made it difficult or impossible for individuals to sue businesses and corporations involved in financial schemes that harm consumers.

The Court has expanded Scalia's "divine authority behind government" in supporting statutes, primarily based on religious grounds, that limit or eliminate the freedom of choice by women, while at the same time allowing the government to spend taxes in support of religious "faith-based" programs.

The U.S. Attorney General takes an oath to "defend the Constitution of the United States," and the office has traditionally acted to defend individual civil rights; however, the current Bush administration has almost entirely politicized the Justice Department.

Bush's Justice Department does not protect voting rights—it actively works to interfere with the rights of individuals to vote, particularly the poor and disenfranchised. It no longer protects civil rights—it now issues secret opinions allowing the government to confine prisoners without trial and to subject them to torture during unlawful interrogations. It no longer protects workers and the environment—it now aggressively acts to eliminate statutory and regulatory protections in favor of businesses, whose interests are contrary to very statutes enacted to protect the citizens of America and their society.

The United States was once a world leader in securing civil and human rights. As a founding member of the United Nations, it was a signatory to the treaties and international agreements that established the postwar Geneva Conventions and the Universal Declaration of Human Rights in 1948.

The Declaration included the provision that "if man is not to be compelled to have recourse, as a last resort, to rebellion against tyranny and oppression, that human rights should be protected by the rule of law." It says that everyone "has the right to recognition everywhere as a person before the law," and no one "shall be subjected to torture or to cruel, inhuman or degrading treatment or punishment."

The United States no longer leads. To the contrary, it no longer follows international law or the norms of civilized society. The International Court of Justice was established in 1945 as the primary judicial organ of the United Nations. The United States relied upon the Court in 1979 to sue Iran for seizing American hostages; however, it withdrew from compulsory jurisdiction in 1986.

Until recently, the U.S. acknowledged the court's jurisdiction only when it opted to do so, including a ruling in 2005 in favor of Mexico on behalf of 50 of its citizens on death row in the United States, who were denied access to Mexican consular officials as required by international law.

Although the Court's verdict was accepted by the U.S., it used the case as an excuse for withdrawing from even optional jurisdiction in the future. The Bush II administration did so because it wanted to end the Court's meddling in the American judicial system.

The United States is now violating with impunity many of the very treaties and international agreements it originally shaped. Although the War Crimes Act of 1996 was passed unanimously by Congress, its definition of war crimes relied upon "breaches of the Geneva Conventions."

Because of fears that American officials, including President George W. Bush, could be prosecuted for their criminal acts committed in the Iraq War, presidential counsel and later attorney general Alberto Gonzales labeled the conventions as "quaint" in a memo denying protection to prisoners of the war on terrorism.

President Bush also "unsigned" the United States' participation in the Rome treaty of 1998 establishing The International Criminal Court in the Netherlands. The authority of the Court is based on the principles of the World War II war crime trials and is intended to try individuals accused of mass murders, war crimes, and other gross human rights violations.

Bush announced the United States would not provide information to or cooperate with the Court. Moreover, Bush stated the United States was no longer bound by the Vienna Convention on the Law of Treaties, that establishes an obligation to conform to treaties that have been signed, but not yet ratified.

In its pursuit of homeland security, the United States now arrogantly stands alone among nations in its defiance of international law and is unrepentant in the abrogation of the constitutional rights of its own citizens.

The words of Benjamin Franklin have never been more apt, "Any society that would give up a little liberty to gain a little security will deserve neither and lose both."

The Disease of Crime

Sam had some unique observations about the nature of crime and the justice system.

Deception, greed, hatred, and violence are diseases that infect the inherently peaceful and cooperative nature of human society and its members.

The effects of crime are felt not only by its immediate victims, but also by everyone whose rights are diminished by law enforcement activities or whose taxes have to pay for them.

One of the most debilitating effects of crime is the fear of it we all come to experience to one degree or another. To the extent we install additional locks or lighting, that we worry about leaving our property unattended, or are afraid to freely walk at night in our neighborhoods, the fear of crime affects our health and the quality of our lives.

Whether we live in gated communities or behind barred windows, the fear of crime gnaws at the very core of our existence. We ignore that unease—that ancient internal warning deep inside of us—at our peril.

Even simple property crimes such as vandalism, theft, and burglary cause us to feel violated and to distrust others.

Child beatings and molestations often result in the victims becoming future offenders, as the contagion is spread from generation to generation.

Violent crimes, such as assault, robbery, and rape, cause lifelong emotional problems in its victims. Homicide—whether the result of passion between acquaintances or the randomness of serial killers—leaves emotional wounds in surviving families that can never be healed.

To truly contemplate crime, to imagine its real-life consequences, and to effectively control it requires us to empathize with its victims and the emotional and physical horror of their experiences. We must dispassionately find practical solutions that balance the instincts of vengeance with the benefits of rehabilitation, and the rights of individuals with the duty of government to maintain a safe environment for us to live.

Although violent crime decreased in the United States after 1991 at about the same time that President Clinton began to use federal RICO statutes against gang leaders, funded an additional 100,000 local police officers, and signed legislation banning assault rifles, it is now on the rise again.

While other forms of crime continue to decrease, probably as the result of changes in demographics and improvements in law enforcement, there has been a dramatic increase in the numbers of street-level crimes, such as murder, robbery, and gun assaults over the past two years, particularly in medium-sized cities and the Midwest.

Even though the United States continues to incarcerate more criminal violators for longer terms than any other nation, the spread of methamphetamine use and violent street gangs are fueling the flames of violent crime across the nation.

The primary problem, however, according to law enforcement officers, is the easy access to guns and their ready use to settle disputes.

Particularly among young people raised on media violence and trained on violent video and computer games, there is a predisposition to use deadly force to resolve disputes. In the past, arguments between young people were usually resolved with fists, sticks, or knives. Today, young people often act out their violent fantasies with automatic weapons that can fire dozens of rounds in seconds.

The reduction of crime in every category and overcoming the debilitating fear of crime requires widespread citizen participation at the local level and a lasting commitment at the national level.

One of the first things the federal government should do is to acknowledge as a matter of policy that law enforcement is just as important to protecting national security internally as the military is to protecting it externally.

Just as we determined early on in our history that military officers required the specialized education provided by the service academies at West Point, Annapolis, Colorado Springs, and New London, we should establish a national Justice Academy on the same premise.

Admission could be by congressional appointment, and all students would receive a basic course of study in the nature and values of a free society before majoring in law enforcement, prosecution, defense, judiciary, or corrections.

Professional administrators must be educated for all elements of the justice system to ensure there is individual justice in every case and that freedom is enhanced, rather than diminished, by the administration of justice.

Once they gain practical field experience following graduation, students should be encouraged to return for graduate studies, including degrees in law. The expectation would be that the graduates would serve out their careers in the public administration of justice at the local, state, and federal levels.

While recognizing its responsibility to train administrators for the local and state elements of the justice system, the federal government must reaffirm that neither the military, nor the national intelligence agencies, can ever be allowed to participate in the internal enforcement of criminal laws.

The role of the federal government in criminal law enforcement should return to its historic place of being restricted to those offenses clearly having a national effect. The present trend to federalize crimes must be reversed, with the emphasis on law enforcement reduced to the most local level possible.

People should police themselves to the greatest extent achievable, for when we give up the policing power to our "big brother" in Washington, we are truly lost—forever.

Militarization of the Police

Aileana said, "As a former military officer, one of the more unsettling trends I've seen in recent years has been the increasing militarization of local police forces in response to protest activities. While we have become accustomed to seeing specialized units, such as SWAT teams outfitted in black coveralls and other combat gear, regular police officers are now appearing as robocops with military weapons at political demonstrations, such as the anti-globalization protests in 1999 in Seattle against the World Trade Organization and in 2003 in Miami against the Free Trade Area of the Americas."

In what has become known as the "Miami Model," the aggressive deployment is characterized by a violent police response to nonviolent demonstrators, the arrest and harassment of journalists among the protestors, and mass preventive arrests.

Acting under the aegis of the Department of Homeland Security, as many as 40 different law enforcement agencies blanketed Miami, and unidentifiable police "extraction teams" in full body armor and wearing ski masks were deployed in unmarked vans to haul away protestors.

The New York City police used similar tactics in 2004 at the Republican National Convention, where there was a "zero tolerance" of protest. Hundreds of peaceful demonstrators and innocent bystanders were illegally arrested, fingerprinted, photographed, and subjected to prolonged detention in wire cages before being released without prosecution.

Repressive tactics were also used the same year as a counter-terrorism measure at the Democratic National Convention, where Boston police established a designated fenced enclosure topped by razor wire as the "free speech zone." Protestors could demonstrate only in the zone, which was well away from the convention and beyond the view of participants and the news media.

Another full-court press against protest occurred in 2004 at the G8 Summit on Sea Island just off the coast from Brunswick, Georgia. The governor declared a month-long state of emergency along the coast and more than 25,000 local, state, and federal police officers and military units in armored assault vehicles were deployed in or near the small coastal town, that has a population of only 15,000 residents.

Local businesses closed up for the week and boarded up their windows. The federal government spent more than $25 million to protect the summit against terrorism; however, fewer than 250 activists showed up to demonstrate, including three who protested that pigeons had more freedom than they did.

Sam responded to Aileana and expressed a fear now being felt by many people.

Although it is alarming that our government is so willing to curtail First Amendment free speech rights and to have police officers dressed in black with ski masks jump out of unmarked vans and haul protestors off to jail, it is particularly chilling to be unable to distinguish local police officers from military soldiers.

Particularly, when the local officers are acting under the control of the federal government in concert with the military and are armed with military weapons, there is no real difference in the impact they have on our civil liberties.

With our economy in collapse, and with the possibility of widespread unemployment and hunger, I have a recurring fear that the day will come when our police will mount machine guns in their surveillance helicopters and will begin to shoot into masses of protestors, whom they can no longer control on the ground.

The same ultraconservative forces that want to arm citizens with automatic pistols and assault rifles as a matter of right are also willing to allow police officers to subvert other rights and to unleash military weaponry, all in the name of liberty. It is an insane cycle that must be halted if our free society is to survive.

Aileana cautioned that there may be times when the use of the military is appropriate, "The mayor of Little Rock asked President Eisenhower to protect young black children, who were enrolled in previously all-white schools. Eisenhower federalized the Arkansas National Guard—after the governor used them to block the students, and he deployed Army soldiers to escort the children."

Although we had prepared much of our research in advance, it had been a long day, and we decided to call it quits. Heather had to get ready to go to the movies with her friends, and it was time for Sam and Aileana to go watch the sunset. To continue where we left off, we agreed I would look into the question of firearms.

Gun Control

There are few political issues so emotionally charged in America as gun control. Representing less than 5 percent of the world population, the people of the United States own one-third of all guns in the world. There are as many as 300,000,000 guns in the hands of Americans, one for every man, woman, and child.

Were it not for a single sentence in the Bill of Rights, guns would be like any other consumer product, which could and should be regulated for the public good. The Second Amendment simply says: "A well regulated militia being necessary to the security of a free State, the right of the People to keep and bear arms shall not be infringed." It all comes down to the comma. Did it divide the Amendment into prefatory and operative clauses?

The question is whether the Amendment provides the states with a right to maintain militias, or for individuals to personally own firearms. At the time it was enacted, and ever since, the Amendment has been viewed as a restriction on the federal government, and not upon the states.

Many states originally required every adult male to own a gun, powder, and bullets and to "bear arms" if called up as a member of a local militia. All states have now evolved their militias into formal National Guard units that serve under the command of their governors and are subject to federalization in time of war.

Many, if not all, states have passed laws denying the right to own certain types of firearms, such as sawed-off shotguns and machine guns. Generally, most people, except convicted felons and non citizens, can own guns in their own homes.

Most states have laws that deny the right to carry concealed weapons; however, some states are now permitting more people to carry guns concealed on their persons or in their cars. For example, for the past 20 years, Florida has allowed "law abiding" citizens to carry concealed guns by simply declaring they are doing so for self-defense. The list of those who carry is a state secret and the numbers have increased from fewer than 25,000 to more than 410,000.

The Florida law is so permissive that felons can easily obtain gun licenses despite registration as child molesters, or convictions for burglary, armed assault, and homicide. Individuals can obtain licenses even if they have outstanding criminal warrants, or if they are subject to domestic violence injunctions. Is there any surprise that Miami police officers now have the option of carrying assault rifles on patrol?

The essential question is whether a state confronted with a wave of gun terror can enact reasonable laws that restrict the ownership and carrying of firearms, much as they all do with motor vehicles?

Specifically, can a state require guns to be registered and individuals to be licensed to own and carry them? Or, does an insane person with a history of extreme violence have the constitutional right to own and carry a concealed machine gun while stalking the target of his delusions?

Even though the Bush administration Justice Department interpreted the Second Amendment to allow individual ownership of weapons, gun control laws are widely supported by most local, state, and federal law enforcement officers. Nonetheless, laws are advancing that protect gun manufacturers and dealers from civil liability for selling firearms to individuals, even if they knowingly sell weapons to dangerous individuals on government watch lists of terrorists and criminal gangs.

By law, records of individuals who purchase weapons are quickly destroyed or kept secret, even from law enforcement agencies, and members of terror groups can easily purchase assault weapons at gun stores. A federal "relief from disability" program, supported by the National Rifle Association, has allowed thousands of convicted felons to rearm themselves.

Law enforcement officers support gun control laws because they are so easily used to kill during acts of violence, either self-inflicted or against others. More than a million Americans have died from gunshot wounds since 1960, more from suicide than homicide.

Worldwide, more than 86 percent of all children under the age of 15 who die from firearms are in the United States, and guns are the second most frequent cause of death overall for Americans between the ages of 15 and 24.

Only motor vehicles surpass guns in causing death and injury in America, most from accidents rather than intentional suicide and homicide.

Although the overall crime rate in England exceeds that of the United States in several categories, including an assault rate that is almost double that of the U.S., violent crimes are far less likely to result in death, since guns are used in only five percent of robberies and seven percent of murders in England.

In the United States, guns are used in 41 percent of robberies and 68 percent of the murders. The overall rate of firearm deaths in American is eight times that of the combined death rates in the 25 other industrialized nations.

For children, the firearms death rate is 12 times higher. In just one year, no children were killed by guns in Japan, 19 in Great Britain, 57 in Germany, 109 in France, 153 in Canada, and 5,285 in the United States.

We were at this point in our discussion when the Supreme Court decided that the Second Amendment provides individuals with the personal right to keep and bear arms, rather than that the states have the right to maintain militias.

Nine law enforcement groups had joined in a friend of the court brief to the Supreme Court asking it to reverse the federal appeals court ruling striking down the District of Columbia gun control law. These groups, representing thousands of police executives and working police officers, wanted to retain laws that reduce the danger of gun violence, with "demonstrable public safety benefits."

Writing for the Federalist majority and ignoring the brief of the law enforcement professionals, Justice Scalia said "the District's ban on handgun possession in the home violates the Second Amendment." However, the Court did seem to leave the door open to reasonable regulation of the personal possession of firearms such as licensing and registration.

"It's no surprise," Sam observed. "Justice Scalia likes to brag about how he used to carry a rifle to target practice on the New York subways, and he recently accompanied Vice President Cheney on a duck hunting trip. And, Justice Alito once wrote that he would even strike down a federal law regulating the possession of machine guns."

A Safe, Just, and Civil Society

If we are to ever achieve a peaceful society, people will have to decide they want to give up their guns and that they do not want their police officers to be armed.

I dream the day will come when there will be a metal sculpture at the entrance to every police station and court house across America welded together with the guns that have been lawfully seized, that have been purchased for destruction, or that local citizens have voluntarily surrendered.

As the decades pass and rust from the guns runs down the concrete, the time will come when people will wonder why anyone had ever wanted to own a machine designed to kill other people, including children.

We must recognize violent crime as a deadly threat to society and take steps immediately to reduce its impact, including gun registration and licensing owners. Gun ownership and shooting are at least as dangerous as owning and driving a car.

Personal ownership of firearms may never be entirely prohibited, but we need legal and civic responsibility for licensing and registration. State and local statutes that balance reasonable purposes and individual rights with community protection must be established.

In every society placing a supreme value on life, the final responsibility forever rests, at law and in conscience, upon each who elects to possess or use a firearm in detriment of the rights of others and who either pulls the trigger or chooses not to.

Ultimately, we the people have to rely on those we most trust to enforce our laws in our communities. First, we have to take steps to ensure that guns are only in the hands of the most responsible, who will in time find them to be unnecessary, before we will be able to trust that our police can and will defend us.

Then, we will place our firearms on the scrap heap of history and will live in the kind of society we all want to share and bequeath to our children and their children.

Peers For Peace

Since Sam was saying that gun control ultimately depended upon our trust in law enforcement, I asked him what he thought about the relationship between the people and their police at the local level, and what could be done to better prevent and deter crime.

As Davis and Fisk both said, the primary responsibility for law enforcement must continue to be borne by the people in local communities working as peers with those they appoint to exercise the restraint of police authority and empower to legitimately lay hands on those who violate the freedoms and rights of others.

The willingness of ordinary people to report crimes and to appear as witnesses requires they have the ability to influence and restrain the use of force against themselves.

Some jurisdictions have established independent civilian review boards where people can complain about police disrespect, harassment, or brutality and can express other concerns about local law enforcement or make policy recommendations. Some boards have the power to investigate complaints and make discipline recommendations, and they are often staffed by political activists.

These boards are often viewed with distrust by law enforcement officers, who fear an increase in their personal risk during arrests and other contacts, and by administrators, who resent any interference with their management and disciplinary responsibilties.

The emphasis and composition of these boards should be changed to one that is more reflective of the true nature of the people and their police and to one that is more beneficial to that relationship. Peer Review Councils should be established in every jurisdiction that deploys law enforcement officers.

To avoid the undue influence of activists with an ax to grind, panels could be composed of an attorney-advisor performing pro bono services on behalf of the local bar association, a responsible citizen chosen at random from the local list of registered voters, and by working police officers with good conduct records assigned by their administrators.

Multiple councils should be established and advertised, as needed, throughout the jurisdiction and should meet in publicly-accessible locations, such as schools and churches. To encourage a full airing of complaints or disclosure of recommendations, panels meetings should not be open to the public; however, all proceedings should be tape-recorded.

Complainants and other witnesses should be placed under oath and should provide narrative testimony followed by questions by panel members. Efforts should be made to identify other witnesses to be contacted in follow-up investigations, and any physical evidence should be received and booked by the law enforcement member. The council should make a finding as to the nature and extent of the complaint, whether it appears to be founded or unfounded, and, in more serious matters, whether further investigation should be conducted.

While the findings of Peer Review Councils should result in a legal presumption of misconduct, final disciplinary decisions necessarily have to be made by the appropriate law enforcement administrators.

The Exclusionary Rule

The widespread use of Peer Review could also result in other benefits in the administration of justice. The Supreme Court and justice system administrators and commentators have long searched for an effective alternative to the Exclusionary Rule that avoids having to allow guilty parties, even in serious violent crimes, to go free because of unlawful searches and seizures or other law enforcement misconduct.

Combined with an effective civil remedy providing for minimum damages, the use of Peer Review Councils in those states that enact enabling statutes could lead to judicial decisions overruling the judicial exclusion of relevant evidence as a constitutional remedy for Fourth Amendment search and seizure violations by law enforcement officers.

Statutes providing councils with the power to summon registered voter members, to subpoena witnesses, to administer oaths, and to give a presumptive effect to council findings could provide a basis for replacing the Exclusionary Rule in jurisdictions that establish Peer Review Councils.

Consisting of public and police members, these councils could peacefully act together as peers to resolve complaints of police misconduct and to help formulate the policies that guide the actions of their local officers.

The overall effect would be to improve the effectiveness of law enforcement, especially in serious matters, while at the same time ensuring that law enforcement is more responsive to and respectful of the constitutional rights of everyone.

Voluntary Confessions and Eyewitness Identifications

As we learned earlier, courts will exclude admissions and confessions that have been illegally obtained, particularly as the result of force, duress, and torture. The recurring question in all cases is whether the statement was in fact freely and voluntarily made—all of which goes to the reliability of the statement as evidence.

With the advent of DNA testing and other more reliable forms of forensic evidence, we are learning that many people have been convicted by their own confessions, when in fact, it was impossible for them to have committed the crime.

In just one Florida county, Broward, at least 28 confessions have been excluded in murder cases by county courts, disbelieved by juries, or abandoned by the police or prosecutors since 1990. In some cases, completely innocent defendants were held in custody while the real killers went free.

More than 200 wrongfully convicted prisoners have been exonerated by DNA evidence in recent years, some who have served as many as 25 years in prison. These false convictions were primarily based on faulty eyewitness identifications or coerced confessions.

Research has shown that human memories are highly suggestible and that the use of false statements by interrogators can convince even completely innocent individuals to confess to crimes they could not have committed.

Particularly, if false accusations are combined with threats of incarceration and promises of leniency, innocent persons may knowingly make false statements they believe are in their best interest. Once false confessions are made, defense attorneys often find it almost impossible to exclude or overcome them at trial, irrespective of evidence of deception and coercion by law enforcement officers.

Sam said, "It no longer appears that the question is whether or not statements obtained without the *Miranda* warning should be allowed. That seems to have become accepted police procedure."

The real issue is whether any statement should be allowed unless the entire interview is tape recorded. With the ready availability of sophisticated audio and video recording facilities in police stations and inexpensive portable, pocket-sized digital recorders, there is no reason why interviews should not be completely recorded, from beginning to end, if the statements are to be used as evidence.

In other words, there should be a presumption that unrecorded statements are involuntary. That should be the law in every jurisdiction!

The Fifth Amendment is different from the Fourth Amendment. The Fourth excludes illegally seized evidence whether or not it was seized from an accused; the Fifth Amendment prevents our own words from being used against us.

Illegally obtained admissions and confessions must be excluded from prosecutions, given the fact that our government is increasingly willing to allow even evidence obtained by torture. There are no alternatives. Otherwise, the Fifth Amendment has no meaning.

In its *Miranda* decision, the Supreme Court tied the Fifth Amendment to the Sixth in finding that whenever a person becomes a potential criminal defendant, he or she has to be made aware of the right to counsel.

In addition to a speedy and public trial, the Sixth Amendment also guarantees the rights "to be informed of the nature and cause of the accusation; to be confronted with the witnesses against him; to have compulsory process for obtaining witnesses in his favor, and to have the Assistance of Counsel for his defense."

In 1963, the Supreme Court ruled unanimously in *Gideon vs. Wainwright* that the Fourteenth Amendment prohibition against depriving any person of life, liberty or property without due process of law is violated if an indigent person is not provided free legal counsel in a felony proceeding.

Four years later the right was extended to children in juvenile delinquency proceedings, and subsequently to all stages of a criminal proceeding including lineups, arraignments, plea negotiations, preliminary hearings, sentencing, and appeals.

The National Advisory Commission on Criminal Justice Standards and Goals established a basic set of standards for the defense of indigents in 1973, which were followed in 1976 by the *Guidelines for Legal Defense Systems in the United States*. Although most local, state, and federal court systems attempt to follow these guidelines, the actual quality of representation, because of inexperience, incompetence, funding and heavy workloads, often leaves much to be desired by everyone involved in the system.

Former Attorney General Janet Reno concluded that the lack of competent, vigorous legal representation for indigent defendants calls into question the legitimacy of criminal convictions and the integrity of the criminal justice system as a whole.

The right to the *effective* assistance of counsel was considered by the Supreme Court in two decisions in 2002. In *Burdine vs. Texas*, the Court found that Burdine was denied the effective assistance of counsel when his attorney slept through critical portions of his trial which led to his death sentence. The same Court ruled in *Cone vs. Tennessee* that an attorney, who was mentally ill, erratic, and failed to offer any mitigating evidence or closing argument, however, was effective, even though his client was sentenced to death.

At Sam's request, Aileana printed out reports of some recent major trials, and he offered a few observations after reading them.

In the O. J. Simpson media-circus murder trial, we all saw that it is possible for a wealthy defendant to purchase a subversion of justice.

The question is not whether every person accused of a crime is entitled to a "dream team," but whether an indigent, presumptively innocent, defendant is to be provided with a defense adequate to confront the charges against him or her, without leading to a failure of justice.

Even a person with middle-class income may not be able to afford to effectively defend against a death penalty case involving dozens of witnesses. The defense must be able to reasonably respond to the accusation, and if an accused cannot afford the representation, it must be provided.

If a local jurisdiction cannot afford to investigate, prosecute, or provide an adequate defense in a complex case, the matter should be undertaken by the state as a matter of law. There cannot be a disparity between the resources available to the prosecution and the defense.

The system works fairly well, except in death penalty cases where high costs lead to inequities that result in innocent persons being condemned to death. Given the great expense of providing a balanced defense, consideration should be given to eliminating the death penalty altogether as a practical matter. There is much more than economics, however, involved in the imposition of the death penalty.

The Death Penalty

Some economists, whose science relies upon the concept that there is always a reduction in an activity as its costs increases believe that capital punishment does, or should act as a deterrent to murder; however, there are several problems with the theory. One is the very high financial costs of death penalty cases, and another is a failure to consider the effect of investing the same amount of money in crime prevention. Moreover, only a small percentage of capital cases ultimately result in the imposition of the death penalty.

Legal fees in death penalty cases are four times that of other murder trials and often exceed $2 million each; each automatic appeal following conviction costs up to $700,000 in legal fees; and actual executions can cost up to $1.2 million each.

California spends more than $114 million a year on the death penalty, not including the cost of life imprisonment cases, and it spends on average a quarter of a billion dollars on each person it ultimately puts to death. Florida spends about $24 million for each execution, while Texas is the most efficient at only $2.3 million per death. Texas executes more prisoners than any other state; however, its murder rate actually increased in 2003 and was above the national average.

Less than one percent of all murderers are condemned to death, and only two percent of those condemned are ever executed. Sixty-eight percent of all convictions are reversed upon appeal, and more than 113 death row inmates have been exonerated since 1973.

Still, the United States has thousands of prisoners awaiting execution. It put 42 to death in 2007, until a moratorium on lethal injections was declared, while the Supreme Court considered whether or not the practice constitutes cruel and unusual punishment.

The United States is the only democracy that carries out executions—more than a thousand since 1976, including 224 juvenile offenders. It also voted against a United Nations General Assembly resolution in December 2007 that called for a global moratorium on the death penalty.

Together, the United States, Iran, China, and Saudi Arabia execute 94 percent of all death sentences, worldwide, each year. Even Russia has now abolished the death penalty.

A Safe, Just, and Civil Society

In 2000, Republican Governor George Ryan imposed a death penalty moratorium in Illinois, because the state was exonerating more death row inmates than it was putting to death, 13 versus 12 since 1977. He created a Commission on Capital Punishment that issued a report in 2002 calling for substantial limitations on the death penalty.

A majority of its members would have recommended eliminating the death penalty altogether, yet the Commission was unanimous in concluding that the penalty should be considered only in cases "where the defendant has murdered two or more persons; or where the victim was either a police officer or a firefighter; or an officer or inmate of a correctional institution; or was murdered to obstruct the justice system; or was tortured in the course of the murder."

The Illinois commission also recommended that the death penalty be barred "when a conviction is based solely upon the testimony of a single eyewitnesses, or of an in-custody informant, or of an uncorroborated accomplice, or when the defendant is mentally retarded."

Sam said he was reminded of the words of the French writer, Albert Camus who wrote in 1957, "Crimes by the government are more significant by far than crimes committed by individuals."

Although more than half of us think we should do away with the death penalty when there is an option of life imprisonment without the possibility of parole, the majority of our states continue to engage in the most barbaric act known to humanity—in the name of all of us, human beings are deliberately killed as a warning to others.

We must remember that in the days of public hangings in England for all felonies, pickpockets, who would be put to death if caught, had a field day. We continue to engage in public vengeance, which is the worst possible example we can set for our children. The practice is without any demonstrable benefit, and it only serves to brutalize our society.

We would be better off without the death penalty, especially if we used the money we spend on it to prevent crime before it occurs.

Aileana, who had been quietly listening and knitting during our discussion, said the stupidest thing she ever heard was Justice Scalia's observation about "How enviable a quiet death by lethal injection."

She was not entirely convinced the death penalty was ineffective as a deterrent; however, she would defer to the professionals: "Only one percent of police chiefs surveyed in 1995 thought the death penalty should be expanded as a primary focus to reduce violent crime."

The War on Drugs

Aileana went on to say, "My greatest concern is what can be done to reduce crime overall and to create a more effective criminal justice system. The police chiefs really believed the best way to reduce crime was to prevent drug abuse, improve the economy, and provide more jobs. It appears we are wasting money and resources on the so-called war on drugs."

Aileana wanted to do a little computer research on the subject before we continued. The next time we met, she reported, "What we've learned is that drug addiction is a brain disease, rather than a moral weakness. It has been proven that as many as half of addicts have a genetic deficiency of dopamine receptors in their brain that causes highly impulsive behavior, including the use of drugs. In addition, drug use causes chemical changes in the brain's communication system that disrupts the way nerve cells send, receive, and process information."

Based upon social, economic and family circumstances, many individuals begin to use drugs as a form of self-medication, as they seek relief from depression, anxiety, or more severe psychological problems.

Once the reward circuit in an individual's brain begins to process the false information that the drug is good for you, strong memories of the pleasurable effect are established that are very difficult to overcome and that may last forever. The greatest risk occurs in young people, whose brains are still developing judgment and self control.

Brain changes result in poor judgment and behavioral problems, including poor performance at school and jobs, accidents, unplanned sexual activity, unwanted pregnancy, violence, and criminal conduct,

In addition to all other indirect consequences, more than 25,000 people are dying each year in the United States as a direct result of drug use. Addiction itself is a very preventable disease; treating it with criminal sanctions has been a complete failure.

The War on Drugs that was declared by President Nixon in 1973, and continued by every president since, has been a very expensive failure. The U.S. has spent more than $500 billion and has locked up thousands and thousands of users, all to no avail.

We are spending nearly $50 billion a year to confine more drug users today than the entire prison population in 1980, approximately 40 percent of the state prison population growth.

Despite this draconian remedy, there is no difference today from 1975 in the percentage of children who use illegal drugs. Drug use among adults is also unchanged, even though more are dying from overdoses than ever. Worldwide, almost a half-trillion dollars a year is spent for illegal narcotics, leading to massive profits for those who produce and distribute them, including criminal syndicates and terrorist organizations.

The only scholarly consensus resulting from all of the studies on drug programs is one done by the RAND Corporation 13 years ago that compared "supply-side" programs, such as drug interdiction and arrest of traffickers and "demand-side" programs, such as drug treatment designed to reduce the market for drugs.

RAND found that overseas military efforts and the imprisonment of users were the least effective ways to reduce drug use. Overall, the most cost-effective way was drug treatment. Major gains were best realized by concentrating on the comparatively small group of hard-core addicts and getting as many as possible to abstain forever.

Although the federal government has continued to emphasize punishment of users—even of those who use marijuana by medical prescription for the treatment of cancer—local and state law enforcement officers are increasingly concentrating on the drug-related violence associated with its trade.

Officers have learned that only 15 percent of federal drug convictions involved actual traffickers; the rest were street-level user-dealers who were easily replaced.

In 2000, California voters established a statewide program to divert non-violent drug offenders from prison to treatment programs. Those who complete the program have a good chance of avoiding drugs and future crimes; however, the main problem is that many do not attend the sessions and there are insufficient enforcement mechanisms to compel attendance.

I was particularly impressed with the efforts of Law Enforcement Against Prohibition, an organization composed of active and retired police officers and judges. LEAP believes the "War on Drugs" should be ended and that drug laws should be decriminalized.

Members do not support drug use, but believe that reasonable regulation would be far more effective. LEAP points to the experience of Portugal, which experienced a significant reduction in crime when it decriminalized its drug laws.

One of the "blowback" effects of the War on Drugs has been the explosion of methamphetamine use. Drug cartels have adjusted to enforcement efforts by branching out from cocaine and heroin—which require harvesting, refinement, importation, and redistribution—to the manufacture of methamphetamine, that only requires the combination of readily available chemicals into a potent product.

Mexican gangs are now relying on the legal importation of these chemicals from China and the creation of precursors from raw materials to supply the epidemic that is sweeping the United States. One Chinese pharmaceutical executive was recently found to have $206 million in cash stashed in his home in Mexico.

A consequence of the War on Terrorism has been the staggering increase in Afghan opium production, that increased 57 percent in 2006 and an additional 15 percent in 2007. Afghanistan is now supplying 95 percent of the world's opium.

The Taliban, who had virtually eliminated the production of opium, are now supporting and taxing the opium trade to expand their operations and to purchase better weapons to fight NATO and American troops.

"It is not that the criminal justice system has failed in its mission in the War on Drugs—it should never have been involved in the first place," Sam said. "The criminalization of non-violent drug possession and use was as just as misguided as was the prohibition of alcohol in the Twenties."

Whenever legislators do not know what to do about a social problem, they simply make it a crime and dump the responsibility on law enforcement officers to solve it. When we criminalize personal and social problems, we turn people into criminals and eliminate their inhibition against committing other crimes, including the use of violence to obtain drugs.

As the diseases of deceit and hatred can never be completely eliminated from all who have become infected, personal violence and other serious crimes will continue to be inflicted upon innocent victims.

The criminal justice system must be more finely focused on the most serious and threatening crimes, with alternative family courts having the primary responsibility for resolving most cases resulting from alcoholism, drug addiction, and other situational offenses.

To eliminate the gigantic profits that feed terrorists, organized crime, and public corruption—and to end the "War on Drugs" against our own society—the possession and use of drugs must be decriminalized and alternative methods found to reduce the demand for drugs and to provide effective treatment for those who become habituated and addicted to them.

Medical doctors should be authorized to prescribe low-cost drugs for those who become addicted and who agree to participate in educational recovery and treatment programs. Prescription drugs could be filled by licensed pharmacists at a cost far lower than illegal drugs on the street.

The illegal distribution and sale of drugs would necessarily remain a crime; however, the federal government could obtain sufficient supplies for all pharmaceutically distributed drugs at a fraction of the cost currently expended for eradication and interdiction programs.

Combined with education and treatment programs, the availability of low-cost drugs would largely eliminate the criminal organizations that rely on and encourage the "War on Drugs" to stay in business.

Although the federal government has spent billions on convincing Americans that marijuana is a "gateway" drug, studies by the Institute of Medicine and the RAND Corporation dispute the theory.

There is no reason why states should not be able to legislatively allow medical doctors to prescribe medical marijuana to patients who would benefit from it. Moreover, states might want to allow the cultivation of marijuana for personal use pursuant to authorization by local communities, which could collect fees and issue permits for the growing of a few marijuana plants for personal use.

Marijuana growing permits could be taken away for the sale of marijuana, or if its use results in unsafe conditions, such as child neglect or other socially undesirable conduct.

The only way to stop the supply of drugs is to eliminate the profit motive and the demand. Drug use is a public health problem, not a criminal justice problem. If we treat it the same way as we have alcohol and tobacco use, we will see the same decline in use and associated problems.

Aileana agreed.

By treating drug use as a criminal offense, the United States presently confines almost a half million people for nonviolent drug convictions, more than the entire population of prisoners in all of Western Europe. More than 1.5 million people are arrested each year on drug charges—40 percent just for marijuana possession.

Most troubling is that while African-Americans are only 15 percent of all drug users, they are 37 percent of everyone arrested for drug charges; they are 50 percent of all drug convictions; and they are 74 percent of all drug convictions sentenced to prison. More than 70 percent of the 260,000 prisoners now confined in state prisons for nonviolent drug offenses are African or Hispanic Americans.

Locking up nonviolent drug offenders is but one example of how the criminal justice system has been misused to warehouse individuals who should be treated with other alternatives to better protect society.

Criminalization in a Punitive Society

More than just drug laws, the federal and state governments have been on a legal binge for the past couple of decades passing thousands of laws that criminalize every conceivable form of deviant or defiant behavior. Concern about this excess of criminalization is finally uniting conservatives and liberals to reverse the trend.

Edwin Meese, who served as attorney general in the Reagan administration, criticizes this astounding number and vagueness of federal criminal laws. "It's a violation of federal law to give a false weather report, and people get put in jail for importing lobsters."

The U.S. Chamber of Commerce recently filed an *amicus* brief about a law used to prosecute corporate executives and politicians in which it is a crime to defraud an employer of "honest services." The

Chamber called the law unintelligible and complained it was "used to target a staggeringly broad swath of behavior."

A book by a Boston lawyer, *Three Felonies a Day*, argues that all Americans violate the thousands of vague federal criminal laws every day, allowing the prosecution of anyone targeted by law enforcement.

Sam said, "It's all well and good that conservatives are concerned about the legal exposure of corporate executives, but I fear our punitive society is permanently harming large populations of our young people."

Zero-tolerance laws in our schools that penalize and suspend students for minor infractions disproportionately target young people of color. These young people are pushed out of school, which may be their only hope for success in life, and into the criminal justice system where they are marked for failure. Critically, even in minor matters, they lose their inhibition against committing crimes.

Once they are in the system, it is very difficult for these young people to get back into school, and even if they do, the school staff and the local police make it difficult for them to remain there. These kids drop out of school, and the street corner is a way station for their return to the justice system.

Once they are marked as a failure in school and as a criminal in the punishment system, they find it almost impossible ever to get to college or a job.

All too often, our schools neither educate nor train students to succeed in life or the workplace. They come to look like prisons, with detention rooms and campus police officers. Those who drop out quickly find that the next step is to experience the real thing. Almost one in four African American youths are locked up on any given day.

It matters not whether one is a student or a corporate executive—when everything is against the law—everyone is a criminal. Most of the time, the rich and powerful escape the clutches of the law, while the poor and disadvantaged suffer the most.

Prison Reform

It had been another long day, and we were all tired. Sam asked if it might be possible to interview some corrections professionals and perhaps to visit some prisons before going on with the chapter. I told him I'd look into it.

The next morning, I telephoned a source who had provided valuable insider information several years before for a series I was writing at the time on California's prison system.

The Department of Corrections is headed by a political appointee; however, its day-to-day operations are conducted by a cadre of career professionals. My source is one of those anonymous hardworking bureaucrats who provide continuity in such agencies. He readily agreed to speak with Sam under conditions of confidentiality and offered to make some introductory telephone calls on our behalf.

Several days later, Sam and I flew up to Sacramento, rented a car, and met our source for lunch. He was more than pleased to participate in our research, as he had followed the coverage of Sam's ordeal in the various media.

Although we continued to shun all interviews, Sam's last statement of his ordeal had become one of the most frequently viewed videos on YouTube, and there had been follow-up productions on several television magazine shows. We had already experienced Sam's fame that morning, as several people recognized him as we passed through the airports.

Our source brought some data with him to illustrate the scope of the problems facing correctional professionals today. The United States now has the highest incarceration rate in the world—higher than any other nation.

The United States locks up 714 of every 100,000 inhabitants, with Russia a distant second with 550 prisoners per 100,000 inhabitants. Today, 22 percent, or almost one quarter, of all prisoners in the world are confined in American jails and prisons. Thirteen and one-half million adults pass through more than 5,000 jails and prisons in the United States every year, and 60 percent go on to commit other crimes.

More than 1.6 million American adults, or about one in every 100, is in prison or a local jail. The United States imprisons its citizens at a rate that is five to ten times that of Western European democracies. The incarceration rate has been increasing every year for 35 years, and it is now five times higher than it was in 1972.

Although Americans have largely eliminated official racial prejudice in most of its institutions, there is wide disparity of sentencing according to race. Nearly 60 percent of all jail and prison inmates are racial or ethnic minorities.

On any given day, less than two percent of young white men, aged 22 to 30 are in jail or prison. At the same time, 13.5 percent of all young African American men are confined. Almost one quarter of blacks who have never attended college, and one third of high school drop outs are locked up. Overall, African Americans are seven to eight times more likely to be locked up than whites.

California, an otherwise progressive state, is the most egregious example of a criminal justice system gone completely off track. In 1977, California's "corrections" system had only 20,000 prisoners, but now confines more than 173,000.

Its legislature increased mandatory sentences more than 1,000 times in the 1980s, and in 1994 the voters passed a rigid "three strikes" proposition giving life sentences to even nonviolent offenders.

California built 21 new prisons between 1980 and 2005 and is presently spending $35,000 on every prisoner every year, compared to an average of $7,000 for each public school student and $4,000 per college and university student.

Even with all of this, California has the highest recidivism rate in the country, with more than 70 percent of its parolees returning to prison within three years.

Every prison is overcrowded—far beyond capacity—and most are in a state of permanent lockdown, with prisoners caged for 22 to 23 hours every day. The governor declared a state of emergency and is making plans to move thousands of inmates to out-of-state private prisons.

As we were discussing these dismal statistics and wondering if there were any alternatives to prisons, our source talked about his experience 35 years earlier when, as a recent graduate, he served on the staff of the National Advisory Commission on Criminal Justice Standards and Goals.

He recalled, "One night after a Commission meeting in Los Angeles, some Police and Corrections Task Force staff members got together at a late-night dinner. After a few drinks, we talked about what we would recommend to the Commission, if politics were not in issue.

> Using paper napkins, we drew plans for a Free Town, where most prisoners would be sentenced to simply live, work, and obey the law. Those who couldn't make it would be isolated and treated as patients in a high-rise Treatment Facility in the middle of Free Town that could be reached only through a tunnel from outside.
> We wrote up the idea and circulated it privately, and still talk about it from time to time when we get together at conferences. So far as I know, no one has ever published on the subject.

Sam was intrigued by the idea, and our source said he would dig out a copy of the working paper and send it to us.

As we were finishing up our coffee, our source told us he had spoken with the wardens of three prisons who had agreed to talk about their facilities on a non-attribution basis and to allow informal tours. Because of inmate confidentiality and other regulations, we would not be able to talk with any of the prisoners without prior approval of their attorneys and other arrangements.

After lunch, we drove 20 miles east to Folsom Prison, which is California's second oldest prison. It was built by prisoners, starting in 1867, on 350 acres deeded to the state by a private company in exchange for prisoner labor to build a dam on the American River, a sawmill, and an electric generating plant for the city of Sacramento. Today, in the prison made famous by singer Johnny Cash, the prisoners only make license plates.

Although there is a New Folsom next door that primarily houses drug offenders, we toured Old Folsom, which is constructed of the native granite quarried on the site. By tradition, the whistle still sounds each day at noon for the 4,200 inmates.

Folsom earned a tough reputation over the years and was known as the "end of the line." Some prisoners are still kept in the original 4x8 foot stone cells behind a boiler plate door, with a viewing slot and air holes.

Even though we were unable to talk with prisoners, the tour gave us a sense of how it would be to do "hard time" in an old-fashioned "slammer." Sam was quiet as we later drove over to San Francisco to spend the night—his only comment was, "so many, so young, and so lost."

We awoke early the next morning and drove across the Golden Gate Bridge to the San Quentin State Prison, which is located on 432 acres of prime real estate on San Francisco Bay. Because of the value of the land, San Quentin is believed to be the most expensive prison in the world.

San Quentin is California's oldest prison, having been constructed in 1851 by prisoners who were confined on a prison ship anchored in the Bay. Recent construction uncovered the original dungeon in the basement with niches for wooden pegs to secure chains and shackles, and iron-latticed oak doors.

San Quentin has California's only death row, and it now holds more than 669 condemned prisoners for an average of 16 years pending

A Safe, Just, and Civil Society

appeals. California progressed from hanging, to the electric chair, to the gas chamber in 1938, and now uses lethal injections to carry out executions.

The Schwarzenegger administration has been secretly constructing a new execution room without legislative approval; however, the old gas chamber is still the place of death, and current inmates can chose either gas or injections. The chamber, a green metal octagonal box with an airtight door and a 30-foot chimney, is located in the basement of the prison.

Sam stood looking into the chamber, as the assistant warden recounted how difficult the last execution was. It took more than 12 minutes for a sweating medical technician to find a suitable vein to insert an IV into "Tookie" Williams' arm, as he lay strapped down on a green padded medical table, commenting on the fumbling attempts.

An observer reported that, after the three drugs were administered, Williams "gulps several times. He appears to pass out as his deep quick breaths become shorter. They become quicker and shorter by the second. His large chest begins to move slower and his toes no longer move, his head no longer strains or moves."

The assistant warden said all lethal injections had been on a legal hold; however, the U.S. Supreme Court just decided they did not constitute cruel and unusual punishment.

Sam slowly shook his head from side to side.

The question is not whether the method of death is barbaric to the one being put to death, such as being burned alive, but whether any form of legal homicide is a symptom of a barbaric society.

I fear that executions will become easier with modern technology and chemistry—not more difficult. We must come to see that the condemned are symbols of our failures, and that the real harm is done to those who live in an increasingly cruel society, particularly our children.

We flew out of San Francisco that afternoon on the final leg of our tour of California prisons. We spent the night in the town of Eureka and drove up the coast the next morning in a rented car almost to the Oregon border and California's most secure prison.

The ultramodern Pelican Bay facility is typical of many such prisons being constructed around the country. In many respects, it is a return to the medieval dungeons—in that inmates in the Security Housing Unit are confined in windowless cells with poured concrete sleeping slabs, concrete writing tables and stools, and stainless steel toilets and sinks, behind steel-plate doors perforated with holes instead of bars. Eight cells are clustered into modules within which prisoners are kept isolated 24 hours a day.

After being strip searched, each prisoner is allowed out of his cell for an hour-and-a-half each day to walk in circles, alone, in a long narrow room with 20-foot-high concrete walls and no windows.

There is no education or vocational training, counseling, or any form of group activities. Television, radios, and writing materials are available only to those who can afford them, and many prisoners live in absolute silence—except when they scream.

Uncooperative prisoners are removed from their cells by extraction teams of eight guards in combat gear, including face shields and riot shields, armed with stun guns. Prisoners are chained, hog-tied, and dragged from their cells.

Sam was shaken by our tour of the isolation modules and remained silent for the rest of the tour. As we were getting in our car in the parking lot, he turned and looked back at the bleak concrete block buildings.

There is not even a hint of rehabilitation going on here, only pure punishment. This is sheer madness! This is inhumane! How can we expect these men ever to return to civil society with any hope or chance for the future?

We flew back to Los Angeles that afternoon. I made a few notes on my laptop and Sam mostly looked out the window at the clouds passing below.

Aileana was happy to see us when I dropped Sam off at the beach house, and I went home to my family. It had been a sobering trip for both of us.

We met that weekend and talked for a while to overcome our shared sense of despair. The problem was apparent as Sam struggled to find a logical solution. "If we are to determine the best way to protect public safety," Sam said, "we have to look at the real reason most prisoners are locked up.

"Only 11 percent of all federal prisoners have committed violent crimes, while 55 percent are sentenced for drug offenses. Overall, three quarters are nonviolent offenders, with no history of violence, and one-third are first time, nonviolent offenders. The odds are that many of these prisoners are factually innocent and have been wrongfully convicted."

How did the United States, the land of freedom, end up with the most punitive and repressive criminal justice system in the world? The simple answer is that politicians have to be elected and to do so, many of them encourage fear among the voters and promise to do something about it. Then, when they are elected, they chose the harshest methods available to prove how tough they are.

Legislators pass laws criminalizing misbehavior that should be and would be more effectively dealt with by non-criminal programs. They lengthen and mandate sentences, and they eliminate the sentencing discretion of judges regarding whatever particular crime happens to be in the 24-hour news cycle at the moment.

Over the past thirty years, the criminal justice system has evolved from one of rehabilitation to one of pure punishment. Parole boards have become politicized, and clemency and pardons are increasingly rare—as everyone involved in making decisions has become fearful of being labeled as "soft on crime." Education and job training programs have been eliminated as more and more prisoners are simply locked down all the time.

Juvenile Justice

"The most deplorable element of America's justice system is the manner in which it has come to treat juvenile offenders," Aileana said.

Even before adolescence, many states now consider children as young as 10 years old to be competent to stand trial in juvenile court, and more than 40 states now treat children as young as 14 as adults. As many as 150,000 children are locked up each year in adult jails and prisons.

Children sentenced to adult lockups are subject to violent assaults and are more than 36 times as likely to commit suicide. These children are neither educated nor rehabilitated and, upon release, constitute a far more dangerous threat to society. They are trained to be hardened criminals and are far more likely to commit violent crimes in the future.

Only one state, Missouri, has abandoned juvenile prisons. Twenty-five years ago, it began to construct small local centers that offer therapy, rather than punishment for juveniles. They are kept near their homes so their parents can participate in family therapy. Case loads are small, and therapists follow their patients after release to assist in continuing therapy, school problems, and job placement. Upon graduation, only about ten percent are recommitted to the system by juvenile courts.

Perhaps the sickest thing the United States is doing to its children is to sentence them to life in prison. Except for Israel, the United States is the only country to do so, with more than 2,387 children currently serving life terms in America. Fifty-one percent of these children have never before committed a crime.

Racial disparity also plays a role with African-American boys being ten times more likely than whites to be sentenced to life without possibility of parole. In California, the rate is 20 times greater, although a "reform" currently being considered would allow them to apply for parole after 25 years.

"Once upon a time Russia was criticized for the manner in which it incarcerated its citizens, but no longer, Sam said. "Now, it is the United States which is the target of human rights organizations."

Amnesty International and Human Rights Watch studied the cases of children serving life sentences in adult prisons in the United States and concluded: "There is no evidence it deters youth crime or is otherwise helpful in reducing juvenile crime rates."

The United Nations recently voted on a resolution calling for the abolition of life imprisonment without the possibility of parole for children and young teenagers. Only the United States voted against it.

Life or Death

Because of harsh sentencing laws and the absence of parole, thousands of prisoners are now serving lengthy terms that are tantamount to life sentences. In addition, the number of prisoners actually sentenced to life in prison has doubled in the last ten years, with 132,000 prisoners, or almost one in ten, serving life terms.

Because of habitual offender or other mandatory sentencing laws, including drug trafficking, less than two-thirds of prisoners sentenced to life imprisonment have committed murder.

As these thousands of prisoners grow older, they are less and less likely to ever commit crimes again should they be released, and the cost of their medical care increases with each year they are incarcerated.

The rest of the world looks aghast at the life sentences imposed in the United States. Most Western European judges would consider 10 to 12 years to be an extremely long term, and even Mexico refuses to extradite defendants who face sentences of life without possibility of parole. Such sentences are largely unknown in other criminal justice systems.

"Just think about the fate of someone sentenced to life in prison," Sam said. "There is no hope, no future. They are simply written off."

A life sentence without the possibility of parole is really a slow and painful death sentence, which is why some defendants are now begging juries to impose the death penalty instead.

With a life sentence, there are no incentives to learn a trade, gain an education, or modify behaviors. There are no rewards, only punishment, and a daily reinforcement of the most antisocial attitudes.

With no reason to engage in good behavior, prisons are dangerous places for both inmates and their guards. Without hope, there is only anger, and when there is only anger—there is always violence.

Rehabilitating Corrections

I asked Sam what he thought could be done to rehabilitate the criminal corrections system:

The first thing that has to be recognized is that a just system requires a large amount of discretion by prosecutors, juries, judges, correctional officers, parole boards, and governors if there is to be individual justice in individual cases.

Next, to avoid discrimination, discretion must be exercised according to written policy standards that ensure that individuals in identical circumstances are treated equally.

Therefore, laws have to be enacted that allow for a wide range of discretion and that require decision-making agencies and entities to research, draft, and publish the policy standards that govern the exercise of discretion.

Finally, unless we are prepared to return to the Dark Ages in which every crime resulted in the death penalty, the criminal justice policy process has to take into account that there is always a risk in confinement decisions and that the benefits to society as a whole justify the risk of deciding cases on an individual, rather than collective basis.

The trend of "mandatory minimum" sentences is destroying the justice system.

As we earlier discussed, federal criminal statutes should be restricted to those that clearly have a national, rather than a regional or state, justification. Next, every state should review its criminal statutes and eliminate those crimes that can be better handled in alternative family, drug, and traffic courts.

The presumption that children under a certain age are incapable of committing crimes should be reinstated where it has been eliminated, and juveniles should be handled only in a juvenile corrections system that emphasizes rehabilitation and education at community-based facilities, with follow-up programs.

Once there is agreement on which crimes should be handled only by the criminal justice system, sentences should be reduced to a range that anticipates that most prisoners will achieve rehabilitation during their confinement and can be released without a significant risk to society.

In addition to returning verdicts of guilt or innocence, jurors should be allowed to make sentencing recommendations. Only they know how close the verdict was and the extent that mitigation and aggravation played a part in the decision.

In all but minor matters, a comprehensive background and sentencing report must be prepared by social science professionals, and judges should have a broad range of discretion in the imposition of sentences. Judges should be encouraged to take risks by enacting a statutory presumption for probation and other alternative sentencing options for many, if not most crimes.

A sentence to prison should be the last resort and not the first choice. For all but the most horrific and violent offenses, sentences should not exceed five years. Statutes should not allow any time off for good conduct, but they should provide a procedure by which reasonable periods of time can be added for bad behavior—with a guarantee of due process.

Once it is decided that individuals must be removed from the free society, the expectation is that they will be on their best behavior while learning to rejoin those who live in freedom.

Sam: A Political Philosophy

To envision how moderate sentences would more effectively protect society, let us imagine a completely different type of correctional system, one that truly emphasizes healing and rehabilitation, rather than punishment. Rather than to treat inmates as loathsome pariahs, let us create a system that treats them as if they are personally infected with a disease that has infected society as a whole.

Rather than despising them for their illness, let us learn and work to cure them in a way that avoids a relapse and the infection of others. Imagine that the rest of society is peacefully proceeding along, and every effort is made to repair the damage done to individuals, so the vast majority of them merge seamlessly back into the free flow of society—without suffering any further legal disability, parole, or loss of rights.

Assuming a fair and compassionate sentencing process, where would we send those who require removal from the free society? I have given this question a lot of thought during and since our trip up north, and I have found no better answer than the one provided by the informal report of the corrections professionals sent to us by our contact in Sacramento.

The simple solution is that convicts should be sent to a remote Free Town surrounded by a high wall having two gates. Upon their arrival, they would enter one gate, and they would be expected to obtain a job within the town, to support themselves, and to obey the law.

Obeying the law would be the only requirement. When they completed their sentence, they would leave by the same gate and would rejoin the society of free people without the burden of parole.

Free Town would have a community court to handle civil disputes and minor violations of the criminal law. Upon being charged with a criminal offense, a prisoner would have the right to a jury trial of his peers; however, the jury would be selected from individuals who had served at least two-thirds of their terms without any disciplinary or criminal problems, and the verdict would be by a two-thirds majority.

The jury would make a recommendation for the length of term extension to the judge, who would impose the sentence, which could not exceed the sentence imposed for the same offense in the free society. Attorneys would not be allowed to practice in the town, and the community court judge would decide all civil suits.

Both prisoners and non-prisoners would be encouraged to establish businesses in the town and would be expected to pay the legal minimum and prevailing wages for the labor performed directly into each employee's bank account.

Prisoners who managed their income—without outside assistance—would be entitled to have their spouses and significant others live with them in the town; however, dependents could not be employed in the town, nor would they be allowed to come and go, except in emergencies. Of course, they could always chose to leave on a permanent basis.

Upon application, approval and supervision by the community court, minor children would be allowed to live in the town, and schools would be established for their education.

All drugs, including alcohol and tobacco, would be prohibited in the town, and attendance at addiction rehabilitation programs would be encouraged.

All prisoners would have the benefit of professional counseling, if desired, and health, dental, and vision care would be provided on the same basis as it is provided in the free society.

Individuals who refuse to be self-supporting or who commit repeated or serious crimes would be removed through the first gate and taken back inside through the second gate. The second gate would lead to a tunnel under the Free Town to a Treatment Facility, a large multi-story round building with glass walls located in the center of the town, which would have no direct connection to the Free Town.

Upon arrival in the Treatment Facility, an offender would be subjected to a community court trial by the judge to determine if he or she should be permanently removed from the Free Town and kept under treatment as a patient in the facility for the duration of his or her term or for a period of reevaluation.

The Treatment Facility would be staffed by rehabilitation, education, and mental health professionals and would be dedicated to curing its patients of their emotional and behavioral problems before their scheduled release date.

Prisoner-patients would be confined in pie-shaped rooms, with a door at the apex opening into a common area equipped as a library, recreation, and eating area. The entire curved wall would be constructed of unbreakable glass allowing patients to look down upon the Free Town, where other inmates would live and work in relative freedom.

Nonviolent prisoner-patients would be allowed into the common areas for specific purposes, such as to check out a book, read a newspaper, exercise, or eat, and would be otherwise confined to their rooms.

Violent patients would be confined to their rooms for the protection of others and would be subject to video monitoring at all times.

Other than for the preparation of meals and the laundry of uniforms in the Free Town, which would be shipped through the gates and tunnel, the entire confinement center would not have any prisoners involved in its operation.

Professional counseling and educational services, including reading and writing classes, would be available for the patients; however, television would not be allowed in the facility. Popular "G-rated" movies chosen by majority vote would be shown in the common area once a week for patients who demonstrate good citizenship.

Graduates of the rehabilitation program who commit nonviolent crimes following release would continue to be charged and sentenced the same as first offenders, until such time as they learn to live in the free society.

Violent offenders may have to be returned to the Treatment Facility for longer periods of time.

Civil Commitment of Sex Offenders

At our next meeting, Aileana said she had been thinking about Sam's ideas, "You've convinced me that the corrections proposal would allow most prisoners to be self-supporting, would be more effective at rehabilitating them, would cost less than the present system, and would provide greater protection to society. How would the program deal with psychopaths and others, such as child molesters and rapists, who are not usually amenable to psychiatric treatment?"

In the past, most states had mentally disordered sex offender statutes that provided for the treatment of such individuals in state hospitals, instead of prisons. However, over the past 30 years, as states evolved from rehabilitation to a punishment, these programs were eliminated in favor of longer prison sentences without treatment.

Following several high-profile sex crimes in the 1980's and commencing in 1990, approximately 19 states have now enacted sexually violent predator statutes allowing for the continuing detention of certain prisoners after they complete their prison sentences.

Today, more than 2,700 rapists, pedophiles and other sex offenders have been civilly committed to indefinite confinement following the expiration of their terms. Approved by the Supreme Court in 1997, these statutes provide a due process hearing, often with a jury, to determine if an individual is a sexually violent predator.

The idea is that the individuals will receive treatment until such time as it is safe to release them; however, most refuse to participate in the program on the advice of their attorneys because to do so would require them to make statements that could be used against them in future criminal trials.

In addition to a lack of participation by the most dangerous individuals, these programs are failing for a number of other reasons. Also swept up are nonviolent exhibitionists and elderly offenders, who are past the age where they are considered dangerous.

The selection process uses actuarial formulas that include factors, such as the number and age of past victims, that were already used in the past to determine the length of sentence. All too often, commitment decisions are based upon politics, publicity, and emotion—rather than the individual risk of recidivism.

Although each commitment costs more than $100,000 a year, the treatment regimens are largely unproven, and there are few standards or independent evaluations.

Sam said, "The real risk to society posed by civil commitments in criminal proceedings is the concept of preventive detention. Once we begin to lock up people to prevent them from committing crimes in the future, where do we stop?

"It's easy to target sex offenders, but what about compulsive gamblers, shoplifters, and alcoholic drunk drivers? Statistically, many of them will commit crimes in the future, but which ones?"

Even if we were able to design a completely effective selection criterion that was 100 percent effective, don't we have the duty to provide an equally effective treatment program?

How can we confine someone we believe is incapable of controlling his or her criminal behavior before that person commits a crime? Otherwise, isn't the next step to simply execute or work to death those who we decide are a risk to our orderly society? Isn't that what happened in Nazi Germany?

To preserve the rights and freedoms we consider most important in our society, we cannot confine people unless they are convicted of having committed a crime, and then only in compliance with constitutional guarantees, including the right to be aware of the charges and consequences—before the trial.

Whether or not an accused is a sexually violent predator, incapable of controlling his or her criminal behavior, should be alleged in the original criminal complaint—in addition to the issue of criminal guilt—and should be proven beyond a reasonable doubt during the trial.

Two terms would be prescribed by law, one for the basic offense, wherein rehabilitation is presumed, and a second longer term for the specific purpose of treatment.

If the allegation is found to be true, the defendant's sentence should be suspended, and he or she should be assigned to a treatment program and receive immunity for any crimes the person reveals during the course of treatment.

The program should provide for an ongoing evaluation by staff mental health professionals, regular progress reports, and recommendations to the court. Although an individual would have the right to an independent evaluation at his or her own expense, there would be a rebuttable presumption in favor of the professional staff's opinions and recommendations.

Individuals who successfully complete the program before the shorter term prescribed for the basic offense could complete the remainder of that term at a correctional facility as earlier proposed. Otherwise, individuals would be required to continue in the treatment program for the longer term.

If the longer term expires and the professional staff is still unable to certify to the court that the individual is no longer a sexually violent predator, a third civil commitment phase would take place wherein the court would determine if the suspended sentence should continue, while the individual is ordered to continue treatment indefinitely.

The court could terminate jurisdiction should it ever be determined that the individual is no longer a sexually violent predator.

Private Prisons

Given the fact that states are already spending almost $500 million a year on sexually violent predator programs and it costs as much as $40,000 a year to confine other prisoners, I looked in to whether there was any benefit in the privatization of these programs, as is being done with jails and prisons.

There is no question that private prisons have become big business and that prison and parole reform is not in the financial interests of the corporations that operate them. The two largest private prison corporations, Corrections Corporation of America (CCA) and the GEO Group regularly contribute to the campaigns of Congressional members, who oppose sentencing and parole reform, and they are investing heavily in the campaigns of all 2008 presidential candidates.

It is estimated that almost two-and-a-half-million prisoners are currently confined in the United States and the prison population will grow by 192,000 in the next five years.

Inmates are increasingly shuffled from state to state, from public to private prisons, to relieve overcrowded local conditions. To accommodate this influx of business, the Corrections Corporation of America is presently spending $213 million to build facilities to house 5,000 new prisoners.

"It requires very little research to determine that private jails and prisons are a bad idea from both a fiscal and public policy standpoint," Aileana said. "Although the availability of private prisons may provide an escape valve for overcrowded public prisons, there are no cost savings."

The investments by corporations in private prisons must return a profit, so they are operated on a cut-rate basis. CCA estimates that it earns $50.26 per day, per inmate, at a daily operating cost of $28.89 per inmate. To earn such enormous profits, private prisons employ nonunion guards with little training and provide low salaries and benefits resulting in staff turnovers that are three times that of public prisons.

There is very little competition, as only two corporations, CCA and GEO, control 70 percent of the private prison market. One study in 1997 by the United States General Accounting Office found that there was little evidence that any substantial savings occurred.

Another comprehensive study found that every single operator of private prisons, jails and detention facilities experienced "decreased security, inadequate staff training and equipment, inadequate protection of prisoner's human rights, degrading prison conditions, and poor employment standards. Newspaper reports are replete with accounts of escapes, abuse of inmates, and financial mismanagement."

Sam believed two fundamental issues involved in the operation of private prisons pose insurmountable conflicts of interest.

Forceful incarceration is one of the most drastic things we can do to our own citizens, and it requires the very highest degree of public accountability. Sound correctional practices require constant judicial, administrative, and political oversight.

Corporations exist to provide profits for their shareholders and to pay high salaries to their executives. Their bottom line should have nothing to do with public safety or the rehabilitation of inmates. Indeed, corporations are not even liable for depriving inmates of their constitutional rights.

Even as we complain about importing products from China that are produced by prison labor, private prisons in the United States are also branching out into other commercial endeavors involving manufacturing and service industries.

Private prisons are becoming sweatshops where clothing is sewn and office equipment is manufactured in competition with private industry. Prisoners can be paid as little as 45 cents an hour—if the product is to be exported.

Even when manufacturing products or providing services for the domestic market, prisoners usually receive, at best, the minimum wage for work that outside workers would receive up to $20 to $30 an hour. Most of us are unaware that when we dial directory assistance for information, we are probably talking to a convict—who is earning less than a dollar an hour.

These prison employers do not have to worry about unions, overtime, or workers' compensation, and employees who complain about unsafe working conditions can easily find themselves locked up in solitary confinement.

The most exploitive facilities are those operated by private corporations for the Immigration and Customs Enforcement arm of the Department of

Homeland Security. Since DHS guidelines prohibit non-citizen detainees from earning more than a dollar a day, the corporations dragoon their entire service staff for little or no cost.

Essentially, these corporations are using slave laborers for their own profit. We must remember than many of the Nazi concentration camps provided prisoners to work for the profit of German corporations.

Martial Law and Concentration Camps

Aileana said, "Out of curiosity, as I was just listening to you talk about concentration camps, I typed the phrase into my laptop search engine. Take a look at what came up."

As Sam and I looked over her shoulder, we saw page after page of references to martial law and the construction of concentration camps in the United States on behalf of the Department of Defense, the Department of Homeland Security, and the Federal Emergency Management Agency (FEMA).

A close examination revealed that many of these references were conspiracy theories lacking sufficient facts to support their conclusions; however, taken as a whole, there was an abundance of factual information showing an alarming trend in the deployment of federal and military forces to restrain and detain American citizens. The United States appears to be teetering on the brink of martial law, and it matters not who is the president or which party is in power.

Commencing in the late Sixties, following urban riots across America, the U.S. military initiated plans to assist local and state civil authorities during civil disorders. Planning accelerated during the Reagan administration with a Disturbance Plan that defined its targets as "disruptive elements, extremists, or dissidents perpetrating civil disorder."

An Army field manual said "if there are more detainees than civil detention facilities can handle, civil authorities may ask the [military] control forces to set up and operate temporary facilities . . . . These temporary facilities are set up on the nearest military installation or on suitable property under federal control . . . supervised and controlled by [military police] officers and [noncommissioned officers] trained and experienced in Army correctional operations."

At the same time these plans and manuals were being developed and issued, President Reagan authorized a secret program for the imposition of martial law and massive detentions. If confronted with civil disturbances, major demonstrations, and labor strikes that would affect continuity of government and/or resource mobilization, and to fight subversive activities, the military was authorized to arrest as many as 400,000 people and move them to military facilities for confinement.

As reported by the *Miami Herald* on July 5, 1987, "These camps are to be operated by FEMA should martial law need to be implemented in the United States and all it would take is a presidential signature on a proclamation and the attorney general's signature on a warrant to which a list of names is attached."

The U.S. Army has a Civilian Inmate Labor Program for establishing civilian inmate labor programs and civilian prison camps on Army installations—which allows for the use of civilian inmate labor in work camps.

The original mission of FEMA was to assure the survival of the United States government in the case of nuclear attack, with a secondary responsibility to coordinate the federal response to natural disasters. However, FEMA has come to operate as a secret government in waiting, with powers far beyond that of any other federal agency.

The John W. Warner Defense Authorization Act of 2007 authorized the president to assume local authority "if domestic violence has occurred to such an extent that the constituted authorities of the State or possession are incapable of maintaining public order."

The President now has the power, without any advance notice to Congress, to declare martial law in any city experiencing a civil disturbance or riot similar to any of those experienced in the past 40 years and to deploy the military, irrespective of the wishes or consent of local and state authorities.

President Bush has issued a Presidential Directive regarding Enduring Constitutional Government, that is to be "coordinated by the President, *as a matter of comity* with respect to the legislative and judicial branches." [emphasis added] In other words, the Enduring Constitutional Government will be run by the President, and any cooperative role played by Congress and the judiciary will be at his discretion.

Once the President declares an emergency, he or she alone controls the entire apparatus of government. The President becomes responsible for arranging for the "orderly succession" and the "appropriate transition of leadership" of the other two branches of government, and he would do all of this with the able assistance of the Vice President—who has the primary job of coordinating things.

After reading over this threat of martial law, Sam said, "Conceivably, at his or her sole discretion, existing and future presidents have the power to use any provocation, including the election of a successor president hostile to his or her existing policies, to declare a state of emergency and to seize and operate the government as a dictatorship for an indefinite period of time."

More realistically, a substantial increase in street and campus protests against the War on Terrorism, similar to those of the Sixties, could easily lead to the imposition of martial law in the United States.

Or, as the current recession deepens into a depression with widespread unemployment, hunger, and civil unrest, martial law could be imposed and military work camps established.

Irrespective of how it plays out, every scenario involves mass preventive detentions, without trial, by the military and requires federal confinement facilities.

In January 2006, the Department of Homeland Security awarded a $385 million contract to former Halliburton subsidiary, Kellogg

Brown & Root (KBR), to provide detention centers in the United States to deal with "an emergency influx of immigrants into the U.S., or *to support the rapid deployment of new programs.*" Unexplained were these new programs and why they require a major expansion of detention centers.

The KBR contract is open-ended and authorizes a payment of up to $385 million per deployment. It is administered by the U.S. Army Corps of Engineers, which envisions the development of at least four detention centers, each detaining up to 5,000 people.

Established at "unused military sites or [leased] temporary structures," each facility will be able to accommodate prisoners for extended detentions and to arrange for the "rendition" of potential terrorists to sites outside the continental United States.

In October 2006, Bush signed the Military Commissions Act which suspends habeas corpus rights for everyone deemed to be an enemy combatant and allows the president to confine such combatants indefinitely without trial or access to counsel. Once detained under the Act, "no court, justice, or judge shall have jurisdiction to hear or consider any claim or cause for action whatsoever."

"This is what fear has brought us, " Sam said. "Our own government does everything in its power to make us fearful so we will support its illegal and unconstitutional activities, and then in our fear, we begin to distrust everything our government says and does."

Cops have an old saying that you're not paranoid if someone is really following you. We cannot ignore that the presidency has already seized extraordinary dictatorial powers and that millions of dollars are being spent for the construction of detention facilities to support the rapid development of new programs.

Nor, can we ignore that, contrary to international law, the United States government is in fact detaining hundreds of unlawful combatants in prison facilities in Guantanamo Bay and at other secret locations around the world.

Finally, we have to accept that our government is abusing and torturing these detainees to obtain information that will be used against them should they ever come to trial; that they have no access to the federal courts to appeal their detentions; that they cannot consult with counsel without the presence of military monitors, who also read their legal mail; that they cannot review or challenge the classified evidence against them; and that they cannot confront or cross-examine the witnesses against them.

There's another old saying, "If you snooze, you lose." We have a very narrow window of opportunity between the time we recognize a deadly threat and when we do something about it. Given the highly-advanced technological age we live in and the ready availability of overwhelming military force, once our freedoms are lost, they will be gone forever—whether or not every single one of us is "bearing arms."

In February 2008, Congress took an important first step in restricting the President's power by repealing a largely unrecognized section of the 2007 Defense Appropriations Act that had effectively transferred control over the National Guards from state governors to the President.

With the unanimous support of the National Governors Association, the National Sheriffs' Association, and other law enforcement agencies, Congress restricted the power of the President to order the National Guard of any state to be used within that state or in any other state without the consent of the states' governors.

The federal government must immediately stop the deployment of National Guard troops to fight the illegal war in Iraq and bring them all home where they belong. Remaining under the control of state governors, and given time to rest and the resources to re-equip, a well-trained and properly deployed National Guard, acting in support of local law enforcement, will be able to maintain order in most, if not all, domestic disturbances, natural disasters and terrorists attacks.

If we survived the assassinations, bombings, and riots of the Sixties and 9-11 without martial law, we should be able to get by today without military intervention or the President's help.

There is no time to lose. Congress must hold hearings on the power of the President to declare martial law, to deploy the military within the United States, and to detain American citizens without trial or the benefit of habeas corpus. Congress must establish the constitutional limits of presidential power by statute—rather than allow the President to do so by his own executive orders.

Big Brother is Watching

"The incursions on civil liberties in the United States in the past 25 years, and particularly since 9-11, are mind boggling," Aileana said. "It matters not whether you are a Democrat or a Republican, rich or poor, or liberal or conservative, we have all been deprived of substantial freedoms guaranteed by the Bill of Rights, unnecessarily, in the War on Terrorism. The year may be 2008, but it might as well be *1984*."

Within days of 9-11 and with little debate or dissent, Congress passed the USA Patriot Act that allows government agents to engage in a number of previously prohibited activities.

Agents can define any criminal law violation as domestic terrorism—if it aims to "influence [government policy] by intimidation or coercion [or] intimidate or coerce a civilian population," including illegal civil disobedience, anti-war protests or environmental demonstrations.

Agents can obtain a warrant, sneak into your home, peek at your computer files, copy your computer hard drive, and, if they say the magic words, that notice would "seriously jeopardize an investigation or unduly delay a trial," they don't even have to tell you they've been there.

Agents can obtain blank search warrants for electronic surveillance, without probable cause, as long as the magic words, "relevant to an ongoing criminal investigation" are spoken. Agents can then trap and trace the telephone numbers you call, your emails, and Internet usage.

Agents can review business records, including those of libraries, bookstores and Internet service providers, without establishing probable cause sufficient to show a connection to terrorism, espionage or another crime, and they can forbid any notification to the patron, buyer, or user.

Agents can issue National Security Letters to force production of records and information, without having to obtain a court order; and they can demand, without a court order, the production of confidential education records, based only on their declaration that the records are needed for a terrorism-related investigation.

Agents can require a variety of businesses, including insurance companies, car dealers, real estate brokers, and the U.S. Postal Service, to respond to search requests by federal law enforcement agencies and to file suspicious activity reports when they detect unusual activities by their customers.

The enlistment of businesses to report on their customers has now gone well beyond that required by the Patriot Act. Without any authorization of law, the FBI has gathered more than 23,000 representatives of private industry into an organization known as InfraGard to provide information to the government and to participate in the imposition of martial law.

In case of martial law, InfraGard members are expected to share their resources with the government and to protect their portion of the infrastructure. In turn, members receive legal immunity and cannot be prosecuted, even for the use of deadly force.

This is not the only time the government has secretly enlisted businesses to participate in extralegal endeavors contrary to the interests of their customers. Commencing as early as February 2001—well before 9-11—the National Security Agency (NSA) solicited customer calling records from the major telecommunications companies. AT&T, Verizon, and Bellsouth consented, and their records were incorporated into a NSA database.

The billions of telephone call records provide information such as the names, addresses, and other personal information of domestic customers and can be quickly cross-referenced by computer to identify the numbers of incoming and outgoing calls. Using its ever-expanding cache of information, the government is able to use data mining technology to establish links between disparate bits of information.

Subsequently and pursuant to presidential, rather than congressional, authorization, the NSA obtained even more direct access to all telephonic and Internet traffic passing through the American-based gateway switches of the largest telephone and Internet companies, including AT&T, Sprint, and MCI.

With the globalization of communication, these switches are the routing intersections between many international to international communications, in addition to most domestic traffic. NSA access allows the government to vacuum up enormous amounts of data.

President Bush re-authorized the illegal program more than 30 times since its inception, even though the Foreign Intelligence Surveillance Act provides the legal, exclusively statutory framework for the electronic surveillance of foreign intelligence. FISA prohibits the monitoring within the United States of any communication to or from any person in the United States unless authorized by the statute.

In July 2008, Congress not only weakened the law against electronic surveillance; it also effectively immunized the telecommunication companies that had violated the earlier law. Presidential candidate Obama voted in favor of the law, even though he had earlier promised to filibuster it if it came up in the Senate.

Without any warrant, the NSA can look at every email sent, monitor every Internet site visited, track every telephone call, *receive information about every bank account and credit card use, and every airline passenger file.*

This is not everything. Under its secret 1948 Echelon agreement with Canada, Great Britain, Australia, and New Zealand, the United States captures virtually all satellite, microwave, cellular and fiber-optic communications traffic—worldwide. Using advanced voice and optical character recognition software, NSA computers immediately identifies code words or phrases in targeting specific messages for further processing, analysis, and action.

In addition to other government data bases, the Department of Homeland Security has created the Directorate of Information Analysis and Infrastructure Protection to contain all available public and private information on everyone in the United States. Included in its data base are the memberships, purchases, books read, financial transactions, and medical records of millions of Americans.

The massive volume of statutes and presidential directives that violate the Bill of Rights is simply unbelievable, and most Americans are unaware of them. Otherwise, they approve, because they believe the restrictions are directed only at international terrorists; however, there have been many changes that directly affect every one of us.

Although almost half of the states have passed legislation opposing it, the Real ID Act of 2005, which will be effective in May of 2008, requires all states to provide identification cards that meet federal standards. Under the law, every citizen and legal resident will have a national identification card, that in most cases will be a state driver's license. The card will contain personal information and will be required in order to vote, fly, or open a bank account.

"All of this is pure fascism by any definition." Sam said. "It subordinates the interests of individuals to the government, and it's contrary to the Constitution, the Bill of Rights, and the historical liberties of the American people."

Shortly after he was first elected, President Bush stated, "If this were a dictatorship, it'd be a heck of a lot easier, just so long as I'm the dictator." At the time, most people thought it was a joke.

The truth is that Bush and Cheney seized greater executive power than Franklin Roosevelt ever held during World War II, and even more than Abraham Lincoln had during the Civil War.

Where is all of this leading us? The government has already deployed private Blackwater mercenaries in New Orleans following Hurricane Katrina—whose only mission was to control, rather than to help residents. Equipped with automatic weapons and driving unmarked vehicles without license plates, they acted as government appointed vigilantes to terrorize vulnerable American citizens. One bragged: "We can make arrests and use lethal force if we deem it necessary."

For all this, the American people paid Blackwater almost a quarter million dollars a day for these services.

The government is organizing private defense contractors to conduct broad surveillance using spy satellites and to gather other electronic data within the United States for domestic law enforcement purposes. Today, approximately 70 percent of the intelligence budget goes to private contractors. To whom are they accountable, those whose constitutional rights they violate or those who contract for their services?

U.S. military forces in Iraq are scheduled to receive equipment in the near future that will allow them to quickly evaluate a suspected insurgent's biometric data, such as iris scans and fingerprints, and to electronically query a data base to see if the person is on a terrorist watch list. If so, the suspect can be immediately executed—without detention or trial. Once these devices are in common use in Iraq, what is to keep the military from adopting their use against Americans in the case of martial law?

James Madison once wrote, "It is a universal truth that the loss of liberty at home is to be charged to the provisions against danger, real or pretended, from abroad." The thing I fear the most is another terrorism incident in the United States, real or contrived. I fear that the government will use the opportunity to further expand its powers at the expense of individual citizens.

One out of every one hundred American adults is now behind bars, and our economy is in a tailspin. What if hunger and homelessness drive thousands, if not millions to commit crimes to survive, or to feed their families? How many more prisoners can we incarcerate before some bright bureaucrat comes up with the idea to declare many of them to be walking dead anyway and start executing those with long sentences. Would there be any shortage of corporations prepared to build the gas chambers and supply the chemicals?

Or, how long will it take for some fat politician to offer legislation requiring everyone receiving food assistance to work in public work gangs?

And what if all this takes place no matter who the president is?

I fear that liberties lost will never be regained. I fear our government, and I fear for the future of our children for whom freedom may be only a distant racial memory, no longer a part of our daily lives.

What Can Be Done?

Probing his thinking further, I asked Sam what he would do about America's justice system if he were the president.

The Justice Department must be kept directly under the President's control. I would consider the Attorney General to be one of the most important appointments I would ever make as president.

The appointment should be based upon nonpartisan competence, rather than political favoritism or compromise. Candidates should have an outstanding national legal reputation and should be dedicated to the preservation of the Constitution and the Bill of Rights.

In the appointment of federal judges, including Supreme Court justices, I would follow the same standard set by President Eisenhower and would select the most outstanding candidates based on character and ability, rather than any ideological or religious grounds or membership in any legal society or political party.

Politics, such as the mass firing of U.S. Attorneys during the Bush Junior administration, should play no role in the administration of justice in the United States. All appointments in the Justice Department should be based on legal ability and adherence to the rule of law and professional ethics.

Evenhanded enforcement of all laws, including those that protect the environment, employment, voting, and civil rights, would be a top priority of the Justice Department.

The Department should concentrate its criminal law enforcement efforts on those crimes that most threaten the entire United States and should support the enforcement of all other criminal laws by state governments.

The threat of terrorism cannot be denied; however, the threat of domestic crime more directly impacts the lives of Americans on a daily basis, and it must be a top priority of the Justice Department—both from an enforcement and a funding standpoint.

The Department should resist the use of military forces in the enforcement of domestic criminal laws and should require all federal law enforcement agencies to adhere to guidelines that respect and encourage the civil rights of all Americans.

The Department should willingly provide its legal support to Congress and should commit itself to seeking enforcement of all contempt proceedings voted upon by Congress, even as against other elements of the executive branch.

All advice provided by the Department to other agencies of the executive branch, including the president, should be based upon the law and the Constitution, rather than on political, religious, or emotional grounds, and should be a matter of public record.

As for the prisoners of the War on Terrorism illegally detained at Guantanamo Bay, I would do as former Secretary of State Colin Powell recommended: "I would close Guantanamo—not tomorrow, this afternoon .... I would simply move them to the United States and put them into our federal legal system. The concern has been that the prisoners will have access to lawyers and writs of habeas corpus. So what?"

With equal access to a fair and impartial justice system, a more civil society will emerge, one in which people are more likely to respect the rights of others and to treat them with dignity, and one in which individuals are less likely to respond with violence and anger when their own sensibilities are offended.

To best ensure a safe, just and civil society, my overriding policy would be that the Attorney General and the Department of Justice simply follow the law, all of the time, and in all regards.

The law must become the political religion of the nation, the courts should be its place of worship, and their proceedings and decisions should be rituals of justice.

The Most Valuable Rights

The 2008 election was coming down to the wire, and I was en route to watch the final presidential debate with Heather, Xiomara, Sam, Aileana, and Naomi Washington, our literary agent.

With the delivery of the justice system manuscript to the publisher for editing, we felt we were nearing the end of the book project, as it was unlikely that any of the remaining chapters would be as lengthy as the ones on peace and justice.

Naomi had called to tell us that the publisher was very pleased and suggested we all meet to discuss our progress, as she was in town on other business. I invited her to a celebration dinner we had planned at the beach house.

Xiomara had been promising Sam and Aileana a traditional Mexican meal for some time, and she and Heather were busily getting it ready, including preparing the secret family tamale recipe from scratch. Starting with grinding the hominy corn by hand, and loading the rolled dough with pork, beef, chicken, and cheese, mixed with red and green sauces, and wrapped in dry corn shucks, they finished with a variety of sweet tamales. And, if this was not enough, there was caramel flan for dessert.

Xiomara had prepared so much food that we had to take two cars on Saturday. I stopped on the way for cold Mexican beer, limes, and tequila, plus mix and Grand Marnier for Cadillac margaritas. I was also detailed to pick up several pounds of thinly sliced and highly seasoned *carne asada* at a downtown *carniceria*.

I made a frosty pitcher of blended margaritas, and we gathered in the patio to toast our work and salute the glorious day. Aileana, with her pregnancy, and Heather toasted with sparkling water. I was assigned the task of searing the *carne asada* on the barbeque while the others set the large patio table and laid out the feast.

We all ate too much, and after we collapsed into patio chairs to recuperate and enjoy the beach scene, Naomi brought us up to date. There was no bad news, and the good news was that the publisher was increasing the hardbound print run. The book was to be marketed as a standard library selection and moved through all the major book sellers and discount retailers. In addition, the publisher planned electronic and audio versions of the book.

Naomi was optimistic the paperback auction she had scheduled would meet or exceed the value of the hardbound contract, and she was confident about the sale of translations in other countries.

Then she dropped the bombshell and another reason for her visit. Oprah Winfrey's producers had contacted her for Sam to appear on Oprah's talk show, and Naomi had stopped in Chicago to meet with them.

Naomi said Oprah was deeply touched by Sam's ordeal and wanted to share his story with her audience. Even though Sam had declined all media requests, Naomi believed Oprah would conduct an empathetic interview, and there was a good chance that she would select Sam's political philosophy for her book club.

Aileana was an Oprah fan and encouraged Sam to accept the invitation. She said she and K.D. would accompany him and that it would be a nice time of the year to visit Chicago. Naomi said the Oprah Show would provide first-class air travel, limousine services, and hotel accommodations.

The Most Valuable Rights

The room was positively glowing as we settled in to watch the last faceoff between the two candidates. During the next 90 minutes, we watched an energized McCain struggle to seize the initiative from Obama. He didn't pull it off.

Most pundits had awarded the first two debates to Obama, and the public believed he was more directly addressing the economic crisis that was sweeping around the world. That afternoon, the stock market had closed at 8,578, down 733 points for the day.

Many voters thought McCain had more experience with foreign affairs; however, Obama highlighted the many mistakes of the Bush II administration and directly tied them to McCain's having voted with the administration "90 percent of the time."

McCain had also lost public respect by not looking at his opponent during the debates, by referring to Obama as "that one" when discussing energy policy, and by wandering around the back of the stage while Obama was speaking.

McCain was the oldest first-time presidential nominee in history, and the much younger Obama's lead in the polls was increasing every day. Not only were people growing increasingly fearful of an economic collapse after eight years of George W. Bush, but even many die-hard Republicans were appalled by McCain's selection of Sarah Palin as his running mate.

I was able to add some background and color from my interviews with the candidates.

Obama's message of hopeful change was resonating with many voters, particularly young people, and many Democrats were dreaming of the party controlling both the White House and Congress.

McCain was better prepared this time, as he spoke about free trade, education and defense issues. He appeared tight-jawed and angry, however, as he lashed out about Obama's tenuous relationship with a Sixties radical and seemed to make fun of women's issues, such as equal pay and abortion rights.

Perhaps the greatest theater was McCain's repeated references to "Joe the Plumber." Earlier in the week, Obama had been confronted by a plumber in Ohio who claimed Obama's tax policy would make it difficult for him to buy and operate a business. After the candidate tried to reassure the man there would be no additional taxes at the man's expected levels of income and that any actual tax increases would be limited to three percent, Obama went off message and said, "I think when you spread the wealth around, it's good for everybody."

After Sam, Aileana, and K.D. departed the next week to tape the Oprah Show, and Sam had a chance to exercise his free speech rights, I stayed behind to research the next chapter.

Freedom of Speech

The Constitution of the United States of America drafted in 1787 established the federal government and defined the relationship between its executive, legislative, and judicial branches; however, it did not specify how the power of the government was to be balanced against the rights of its individual citizens.

Ratification of the Constitution by the states was resisted by those who wanted it to include a better definition of what the government could not do. Thomas Jefferson argued that "A bill of rights is what the people are entitled to against every government on earth, general or particular, and what no just government should refuse, or rest on inference."

The Bill of Rights consisting of the first ten amendments was primarily drafted by James Madison, whom Jefferson called "the greatest man in the world." It was adopted in 1791. The First Amendment states,

> Congress shall make no law respecting an establishment of religion, or prohibiting the free exercise thereof; or abridging the

freedom of speech, or of the press; or the right of the people peacefully to assemble, and to petition the government for a redress of grievances.

As a foundation of all other rights, Madison considered the freedoms of conscience and press to be the "most valuable amendment on the whole list." He believed, "Knowledge will forever govern ignorance; and a people who mean to be their own governors must arm themselves with the power which knowledge gives." And, he thought, "A popular government without popular information or the means of acquiring it, is but a prologue to a farce, or a tragedy, or perhaps both."

Jefferson said, "a democracy cannot be both ignorant and free," and George Washington wrote, "If the freedom of speech is taken away then dumb and silent we may be led, like sheep to the slaughter."

There were, however, immediate efforts to place limitations on political speech. President John Adams signed the Sedition Act of 1798 making it a crime to bring the President or Congress "into contempt or disrepute" by speech or writing.

The Sedition Act expired with the election of Jefferson in 1800, and reparations were made to those who had been prosecuted under the Act. It was not the last governmental effort, however, to stifle dissent.

Inasmuch as the First Amendment said, "*Congress* shall make no law," the individual slave states felt free to enact laws restricting the speech and writings of abolitionists. Once the Civil War started, President Lincoln authorized censorship of newspapers and the opening of mail believing that "the ends justified the means" to preserve the Union.

Acting on a "clear and present danger," the Espionage Act of 1917 prohibited saying or writing anything that encouraged disloyalty or interfered with the draft, and the Sedition Act of 1918 criminalized "disloyal, profane, scurrilous or abusive language" about the United States flag, government, or armed forces.

The Sedition Act was repealed in 1921; however, major portions of the Espionage Act remained on the books and were supplemented by provisions of the Smith Act in 1939 that prohibited attempts to undermine the morale of the armed forces. In addition, the Smith Act penalized anyone who "advocates, abets, advises, or teaches" the violent overthrow of the government or who organized, joined, or conspired with any society for the purpose.

Based on these laws, there was widespread censorship during World War II, and during the subsequent McCarthy Era, leftist and communist speeches, writings, and activities were targeted by the government for prosecution.

Through a number of decisions, the Supreme Court restricted the government's ability to censor and punish such activities, ruling "the constitutional guarantees of free speech and free press do not permit a State to forbid or proscribe advocacy of the use of force or of law violation except where such advocacy is directed to inciting or producing imminent lawless action and is likely to incite or produce such action."

Regarding flag burning, the Court ruled that "if there is a bedrock principle underlying the First Amendment, it is that government may not prohibit the expression of an idea simply because society finds the idea offensive or disagreeable."

Citizens now have a First Amendment right to collect information and to be free from prior restraint in distributing information to all members of the public without interference from the government or from private groups operating outside the law.

Freedom of Religion

Upon Sam's return from Chicago, we discussed my research on the First Amendment. Sam said he had found an amazing little book in the airport bookstore and had read it during the trip. "In the *Revolutionary*

Spirits, Gary Kowlaski reviews the religious beliefs of the 'founding fathers' and identifies the basis of their democratic faith."

Benjamin Franklin, George Washington, Thomas Paine, John Adams, Thomas Jefferson, and James Madison all believed that political freedom required a freedom of the mind and that political dissent and religious dissent were one in the same.

They dreamed of "a land where strangers were welcome and differences could thrive."

They were "children of the Enlightenment" and few of them "believed in the literal accuracy of the Bible or in the traditional creeds of Christendom. Most regarded dogmas like the Trinity, the Incarnation, and the Atonement as nonsensical or, at best, irrelevant to achieving a virtuous life."

The founding fathers agreed that "spiritual health was better measured by character and conduct than by formal catechism. How an individual lived was ultimately more important than which church he or she happened to attend, or whether they went to church at all. Deeds mattered more than creeds."

They were not, however, religious skeptics. "They spoke warmly of a Creator and a moral law that governed the universe."

The founders "believed in reason and in the power of unfettered inquiry to cast of ignorance and prejudice, coming closer to the edge of truth . . . . Disciples of tolerance, freedom, and scientific thinking, they affirmed that faith could be a progressive force in human affairs, uniting people of varying beliefs in allegiance to a shared quest for justice and the common good."

They were "religious men, who believed that human liberty, including the rights of conscience, had been divinely ordained."

As Deists, the founding fathers "worshiped in the cathedral of Creation," and they "sensed the sacred in the laws and harmonies of nature" as "revealed in the workings of earth and sky."

Even though most believed in a natural God, "their intent was never to establish a godly commonwealth or Christian nation." To the contrary,

Madison believed that "Religion flourishes in greater purity without, than with the aid of Government."

In a discussion with Madison, Jefferson imagined that "by bringing the sects together and mixing them . . . we shall soften their asperities, liberalize and neutralize their prejudices, and make the general religion a religion of peace, reason and morality."

On another occasion, Jefferson said, "The legitimate powers of government extend to such acts only as are injurious to others. But it does me no injury for my neighbor to say there are twenty gods, or no God. It neither picks my pocket nor breaks my leg."

Jefferson's ultimate challenge to established religion is chiseled in the stone of his memorial: "I have sworn eternal warfare against all forms of superstition over the minds of men."

Fortified by the Constitution and armed with the Bill of Rights, soldiers of conscience have fought Jefferson's war for intellectual freedom in the United States for more than 200 years.

Today, all of us are in grave danger, as religious fundamentalists are gaining political supremacy in furtherance of their various religious causes. Islamic fundamentalists are creating theocratic governments in the Middle East, Jewish fundamentalists have seized the domestic functions of the Israeli government, Catholic fundamentalists have seized control of the papacy, and Protestant fundamentalists are politically imposing their religious beliefs upon the government of the United States.

Seeking to redefine America as a Christian Nation, evangelical Christians are attempting to rewrite the Nation's history. If they succeed, they will destroy the very freedoms that allow them to speak freely, and they will shut down the intellectual engine that propelled the United States into a great nation.

As a "born-again" Christian (and implementing the cynical political strategy of Karl Rove), George W. Bush pandered to and received the support of the Christian evangelicals in the 2000 election, in which he lost the popular vote.

The Most Valuable Rights

Faced with another close election in 2004, Bush Junior visited with Pope John Paul II and asked the Vatican to pressure American bishops to be more active in opposing abortion and gay marriage during his campaign.

A week later, Cardinal Joseph Ratzinger (now Pope Benedict) sent a letter to Catholic bishops mentioning "the case of a Catholic politician [John Kerry] consistently campaigning and voting for permissive abortion and euthanasia laws" and reminding them that pro-choice Catholics were committing a "grave sin." The Cardinal went on to say that Catholics who voted for the Catholic politician "would be guilty of formal cooperation in evil and so unworthy to present himself for Holy Communion."

Through these efforts, Bush increased his Catholic support in the election by six points, and Catholic voters allowed him to barely carry the states of Ohio, Iowa, and New Mexico.

Bush has repaid his political debt to the evangelicals and the Vatican by providing federal financing of "faith-based" activities and "abstinence only" birth control programs, blocking federal financing of embryonic stem-cell research, and appointing ideologically compatible judges to the federal bench. In turn, his activist judges reversed decisions protecting individual rights, including the freedom of choice.

Bush was convinced he was leading a modern Christian crusade against the terrorism of the "Islamofascists," who "hate us for our freedoms." Bush said that "God speaks through me." He believed, "We are in a conflict between good and evil. And America will call evil by its name." Bush started the War on Terrorism because, "God told me to strike at al-Qaeda and I struck them, and then he instructed me to strike at Saddam, which I did."

It is troubling that Bush's foreign policy in the Middle-East appears to be based more on his belief in an imminent Apocalypse as foretold by the Book of Revelations than on real politics or what is actually in the best interests of the United States. He frequently refers to the "evil one" and may really believe the "Antichrist" is physically present on the earth.

Many evangelicals believe the "end times" are near because of the establishment of the nation of Israel and the prophesy that the final battle will occur in Israel's Jezreel valley at Megiddo (Armageddon).

Shortly after his election, Bush abandoned America's long-term policy of even-handedness between Israel and the Palestinians, saying, "I'm not going to be supportive of my father and all his Arab buddies!"

If the foreign policy of the United States is based on the President's religious belief that the Apocalypse is imminent, we can better understand why he so willingly went to war against Iraq and now wants to destroy Iran—these are the enemies of Israel. However, we do not have a defense treaty with Israel, and these actions appear to be contrary to the interests of the United States.

If the world is coming to an end, it matters not whether we protect the environment or show any concern for air or water quality. Moreover, if the domestic policy of the United States is based on an apocalyptic belief, then who cares if the country is plunging into an economic depression, its currency is becoming worthless, and millions are at risk of being homeless and starving. It is simply the end times, the few true believers will be swept up to Heaven in the rapture, and the rest will be "left behind."

"Bush's belief is shared by almost 70 percent of white evangelicals, who believe that God gave Israel to the Jewish people and that Israel is the fulfillment of biblical prophecy," Aileana said, "even though most American mainstream Christians do not agree."

Most American people are religious. As many as 82 percent believe in the Christian God; 70 percent believe in Heaven, the survival of the soul after death, and that Jesus is God or the son of God; and 73 percent believe in miracles. These beliefs are shared by more women than men, by more Republicans than Democrats, and by the least educated.

Just 26 percent of the public believe the Democratic Party is friendly to religion; however, the percentage who believe the

The Most Valuable Rights

Republican party accommodates religion has dropped from 55 to 47 percent.

The difference today from 200 years ago is that a minority of these American Christians want to impose their religious beliefs on others who do not share their views, including other Christians. White evangelical Christians make up only 24 percent of the population; however, many of them see the conversion of all others to their religious belief as a divine mission. Most share the same zeal for proselytization. They believe the Bible should be the guiding principle in making law, even if it conflicts with the will of the people, and they consistently vote their conservative political attitudes.

At the other end of the Christian spectrum, 32 percent define themselves as "liberal or progressive Christians"; however, they are disorganized and tend to disagree on most political and social issues.

It's easy to see why politicians, particularly Republicans, seek the endorsement of the fundamentalists. Even so, 16 percent of religious Americans say they are unaffiliated with any particular religion, and the number is growing, particularly among men and those under 50 years of age.

Sam said, "The attempts by the religious right to take over the government, to write Bible-based laws, and to incorporate their religious beliefs into our public schools and other government activities would be the same as if the Deists, who created the United States government, had written their minority beliefs into the Constitution and the Bill of Rights"

"There is one place where fundamentalist Christians have forced a substantial breech in the wall separating church and state," said Aileana, "and that's in the military."

When I was first commissioned, we had only a couple of chaplains assigned to each installation, usually a nondenominational

Sam: A Political Philosophy

Protestant and a Catholic priest. Primarily they conducted religious services and provided spiritual and pastoral support and counseling to military personnel and patients.

Over the years, I saw and heard that some of the new Protestant chaplains were aggressively seeking out new converts, rather than administering to the spiritual needs of those who sought comfort.

In recent years, the religious activities and statements of some chaplains and line officers have created a dangerous situation in the military. George Washington worried that chaplains might "compel men to a mode of worship they do not profess." Today, there is no doubt that pressure is being brought on individual service members to accept evangelical teachings.

When he retired in 2007, Lt. General William G. Boykin was serving as the United States Deputy Undersecretary of Defense for Intelligence. A former commander of the top secret Delta Force, Boykin toured the country appearing in his military uniform speaking to numerous evangelical groups about his religious beliefs. He preached that "we in the army of God, in the house of God, kingdom of God have been raised for such a time as this. Our spiritual enemy will only be defeated if we come against them in the name of Jesus."

Speaking of a Muslim warlord, Boykin bragged that he "knew that my God was a real God and his was an idol." He told the congregations that George Bush was "in the White House because God put him there."

The Military Ministry, a subsidiary of the Campus Crusade for Christ, has targeted military basic training facilities as "gateways" and boasts that it has converted thousands of soldiers to evangelical Christianity. The Ministry says it works "with Chaplains and Military personnel to bring lost soldiers closer to Christ, build them in their faith and send them out into the world as Government paid missionaries."

The Most Valuable Rights

On its Internet web site, the Ministry admits that "Young recruits are under great pressure as they enter the military at their initial training gateways . . ." and new recruits and cadets are pushed "to the edge. This is why they are most open to the 'good news.'" Recruits are taught that "government authorities, policy and the military—God's Ministers."

Retired Army Major General Bob Dees serves as the executive director of the Military Ministry. He says, "We must pursue our particular means for transforming the nation—through the military. And the military may well be the most influential way to affect that spiritual superstructure. Militaries exercise, generally speaking, the most intensive and purposeful indoctrination program of citizens . . . ."

In a recent book, "With God on Their Side," Michael Weinstein documents the fundamentalist takeover of the U.S. military by Christian soldiers on a mission from God. Weinstein, a lifelong Republican, graduated from the Air Force Academy and later served as an assistant general counsel in the Reagan administration. Weinstein believes that, "The Christian Taliban is running the Department of Defense."

"The conversion of our military personnel to Christian fundamentalism is beyond frightening," Sam said, "It represents a threat to all of humanity."

We have to imagine the harm to our freedoms and to other nations by a military dominated by officers who place allegiance to their personal version of God before their ethical and honor codes, before their commissioning oaths, and before the Constitution they have sworn to protect.

We have to foresee the destruction and devastation that can and will result if these modern Christian crusaders achieve effective command over the most powerful military force in the world.

We are worried that Muslim militants might get control of a nuclear device. What about Christian militants in control of thousands of missiles with atomic warheads? The answer is Armageddon.

It is difficult to imagine any change as long as President Bush is the Commander-in-Chief of the military; however, orders to comply with the Constitution, law, and military regulations prohibiting commanders from coercively influencing the religious views of subordinates must come from the top.

If nothing else, the Constitutional doctrine of separation of church and state surely means that the armed forces of the state cannot be deployed in the service of any church or religious belief.

Freedom of the Press

I received an email confirming the date and time for the airing of the Oprah Show, which had been taped earlier. Xiomara and I invited Sam and Aileana to our house to watch. Sam had stayed with us after he was first released from the hospital, but he hadn't visited since taking up residence in the beach house.

We had a large-screen television in the family room and were all looking forward to the interview. K.D. was introduced to Heather's Rat Terrier, Buster, for the first time and they got along famously—once Buster asserted his right to a cushion in front of the screen.

Sam looked very distinguished in his tailor-made dark blue suit, and K.D. accompanied him onto the stage wearing her regal gold coat and lay down at his feet. Other guests included Medea Benjamin, one of the founders of Code Pink—the women's anti-war movement and Amy Goodman, host of the Democracy Now! daily radio show.

During the first segment, Oprah and her guests discussed the horror of war generally and the illegality of the Iraq War specifically. With Oprah's empathic encouragement, Sam talked about his ordeal and why and how he endured it.

The second half of the show was directed toward efforts to end war and to how to reform government in order to prevent it.

The Most Valuable Rights

Oprah asked Sam about his book and where he was going with it. After he shared his thoughts on a peaceful political evolution and the outlawing of war, she suggested that Sam should run for president. The audience spontaneously took up the chant, "Sam for President," as the show ended. With great dignity, Sam stood and bowed his head respectfully to the audience—as his image slowly faded from the screen.

We were all encouraged and energized by Sam's appearance, and we resolved to move quickly on the remaining First Amendment issues.

"Underlying our freedom to think for ourselves is the right to obtain the unbiased information we need to arrive at valid conclusions and to make good decisions." Sam said. I recalled that Madison believed that, "knowledge will forever govern ignorance; and a people who mean to be their own governors must arms themselves with the power which knowledge gives." He also said, "A popular government without popular information or the means of acquiring it, is but a prologue to a farce, or a tragedy, or perhaps both."

Sam asked me for my opinion of the industry in which I have earned my living for more than 20 years.

The Illiberal Media

One of the great political myths is that the American news media is liberal. Perhaps it once was; however, two things have changed all of that. The first is that a tremendous amount of right-wing money has been invested in the funding of neo-conservative think tanks that have come to dominate the opinions expressed by the media. The second is that the news media has been largely purchased and merged into gigantic corporate conglomerates that largely reflect the attitudes and bias of Corporate America.

Most sadly, the independent local newspaper no longer exists in America.

The "liberal enemy" is the unrelenting target of the conservative opinion mills. The attack is unrelenting, it is dirty, and its object is to associate liberalism and Democrats with socialism.

Day after day, the primary message one hears and reads in America's news media is conservative. While most individual journalists would define their personal politics as centrists, their employers and managers—and advertisers—are unabashedly conservative, and they are the ones who control content.

Millions of Americans listen to AM talk radio each day to a message that is almost exclusively right wing. It is here, and not on the op-ed pages, that the opinion of working Americans is most influenced.

Talk radio feeds on the displaced anger in our society—anger over loss of employment or business opportunities, over our increasingly multicultural society, over changes in the role of women, over illegal immigration, and over perceived defeats or slights in daily life. It is a place where one can vicariously punch the boss or kick the dog, but it is not a very good place to obtain unbiased news or political opinion.

Once upon a time, the Federal Communication Commission's Fairness Doctrine required broadcasters to provide a balance of political opinion in their programming, and the FCC would not have allowed the present monopoly of conservative opinion on radio and television. The doctrine was repealed by the Reagan-appointed FCC in 1987, and Reagan vetoed attempts by Congress to reinstate it.

"Now that they are in control," Sam commented, "the same conservatives who once relied upon the access doctrine believe it would be an unwarranted imposition on the First Amendment to allow today's dissenters an equal opportunity to exercise their freedom of speech."

Certainly, since radio and television frequencies are scarce public commodities which broadcasters, as trustees, are only allowed to use for the public good, the Fairness Doctrine must be reinstated. In addition, the "personal attack" and *"political editorial"* rules that were killed in 2000 must also be reinstated.

How can democracy survive it the voters are only exposed to one side of political issues? How secret has our government become?

Freedom of Information

American voters have also been cut off from essential information by the increased secrecy of government. The Freedom of Information Act was enacted to compel government agencies to make public information available, and it empowered the Justice Department to "encourage agency compliance."

Clinton's Attorney General, Janet Reno, imposed a presumption in favor of all disclosure decisions; however, Bush's Attorney General, John Ashcroft, reversed the process. He urged federal agencies to deny most requests and added the protection of "sensitive business information" to the disclosure criteria. He reassured agencies that the Justice Department would defend their decisions to refuse disclosure.

Immediately after taking office, President George W. Bush signed an executive order that effectively reversed the Presidential Records Act of 1978. Under the Act, President Reagan's records, including those of his vice president, George H. W. Bush, were due to become public 12 years after Reagan's term ended.

The executive order allows Bush, or any other sitting President, to exercise a veto over the release of the records of former presidents, even over the former President's objection. The order essentially creates a property right in a President's privilege to refuse disclosure of records and allows the right to be passed to his heirs.

Former President Ford once said he firmly believed "that after X period of time, president papers, except for the most highly sensitive documents involving our national security, should be made available to the public, and the sooner the better."

Former President Carter thinks that "Powerful leaders in order to stay in office deprive their citizens of the right to know. Access to information can change the landscape of the entire society." Carter believes the Bush administration violated American's basic rights by blocking access to information and created more government secrets than at any other time in U.S. history.

Among the many executive orders signed by President Bush was one that substantially allows the government to classify many more records, to reclassify documents that have already been declassified, and to keep records classified for longer periods of time.

Bush gave the Cheney the power to classify records, and in yet another executive order, the president exempted his own office and the vice president's office from any oversight regarding the handling of classified documents.

It is not only the voters who are being deprived of essential information. The minority staff of the House of Representatives' Committee on Government Reform issued a report in 2004 that found "The collective impact of the actions of the Bush Administration has resulted in an extraordinary expansion of government secrecy." And "external watchdogs, including the US Congress, the media and nongovernmental organizations, have consistently been hindered, indeed thwarted in their ability to monitor government activities. These actions have serious implications for the nature of our democratic government. When our government operates in secret, the ability of the public to hold the government accountable is seriously threatened."

The report concluded "The Bush Administration has systematically limited disclosure of government information and records while expanding its authority to operate in secret. Taken together, the Administration's actions represent an unparalleled assault on the principles of open government."

State Secrets Privilege

Sam added, "Even the courts are being deprived of the information they need to make decisions in cases where the government has something to hide."

The State Secrets Privilege was first invoked in a case in 1953 in which the government was being sued for the deaths of nine airman resulting from the crash of a military airplane. The Air Force refused to turn over certain files, claiming they contained national security secrets. The court accepted the government's representations and dismissed the case.

When the records were finally made public 50 years later, no national security secrets were found, only overwhelming evidence of government stupidity and military incompetence.

Although it was originally based on an outright lie, the privilege has been asserted by the government in a number of subsequent cases, and most recently by the Bush administration. Without actually reviewing the evidence, the courts have dismissed cases involving the illegal rendition of a German citizen and the warrantless electronic eavesdropping on the communications of American citizens.

The New York Times editorialized: "To avoid accountability, [the Bush] administration has repeatedly sought early dismissal of lawsuits that might finally expose government misconduct, brandishing flimsy claims that going forward would put national security at risk."

Open government requires that information be shared, and that only the most sensitive information be kept secret. Government cannot be allowed to suppress information that simply reveals its own incompetence or criminal conduct. The voters have a right to know what their government is or is not doing on their behalf.

Political Censorship

Aileana, who hadn't said anything for a while, commented that, "The flip side of governmental deprivation of access to information is governmental deprivation of the right to use information. One of the most fundamental free speech rights we have is the ability to tell the world just how stupid our government is acting and what an idiot we have as its President."

A most disturbing sight is the establishment of "free speech zones" to restrict political activists from being seen or heard in the vicinity of the President whenever he appears in public. The zones are set up by the Secret Service in any area where the President is to speak or even to pass by.

Protestors who display signs are escorted to the zone before and during the event, and reporters are not allowed to display the protestors on camera or to interview them within the zone. Protestors who decline the opportunity to express their free speech in the established zone can be arrested for "entering a restricted area around the President of the United States."

What does it hurt for the President to see that there are some people who do not support him or his policies and practices? Is there any harm in allowing the public to see on the news that there are those who disagree with the President?

Obviously, we can still write and publish our opinions, as we are doing, but it makes me very angry that I can't go stand by the roadside with a sign telling the President that I think he's an idiot, as he passes by. What possible harm can that cause except to his ego?

And, there's another thing that really tees me off! Last year, Verizon took it upon itself to block abortion-rights text messages by Naral Pro-Choice America from its networks. Verizon claimed it had the right to block "controversial or unsavory" text messages, and that it "does not accept issue-oriented (abortion, war, etc.) programs—only basic, general politician-related campaigns."

What business does a telephone company have censoring legal messages on its system, no matter what they say? What are they going to do next? Install filters on voice lines to bleep out profanity?

Sam said, "While I agree with you on all of these issues, there are other situations where the government has a responsibility and duty to regulate what might be otherwise considered free speech. One example is a person who yells "fire!" in a crowded theater, resulting in deaths and injuries as people are trampled in a rush to the exits."

If false speech is not protected, then who determines if it is true or false? What about someone saying that our government is illegally spying, or that it is building camps to illegally confine thousands of us, or that it does not allow us to hold up a sign saying the President is a fool? Who decides what should and should not be protected? Clearly, in the area of political speech, the bar against restraint must be set very high.

Advertising Inherently Harmful Products and Services

Sam said, "This leads us to a very delicate question, how do we balance the public's right to know with protecting it from false, misleading, and inherently harmful advertising of otherwise legal products and services?"

Answering Sam's question, my own research had found that, as late as 1942, a unanimous Supreme Court ruled that the First Amendment posed no "restraint on Government as respects purely commercial advertising." In doing so, the Court said there was a difference between ideological and commercial speech.

The issue was reconsidered by the Court in 1976 when it overruled a Virginia statute that restricted pharmacies from advertising their prices as being unprofessional conduct. The Court stated, "If there is a right to advertise there is a reciprocal right to receive such advertising." However, the opinion allowed that there could be some circumstances, such as false and deceptive advertising, in which commercial speech was not protected.

Four years later, the Court decided that commercial speech could be protected "from unwarranted governmental regulation" if it "protects not only the speaker but also assists consumers and furthers the societal interest in the fullest possible dissemination of information." The Court found that "the State interest must be substantial" and that the regulation could be no more extensive than necessary.

Aileana had just read that British doctors were seeking a ban on all advertising for alcohol products saying, "Our society is awash with pro-alcohol messaging and marketing."

She went on to say she had real problems with government advertising of legalized gambling, which she called a "tax on stupidity." Americans spend more than $60 billion each year on government lotteries, with the lowest-income household spending almost 10 percent of all income on lottery tickets.

Although the Supreme Court has found that the Commonwealth of Puerto Rico can prohibit casino gambling advertising (while allowing gambling to legally exist), it subsequently decided that the federal government could not restrict beer manufacturers from displaying the alcohol strength of their beer on its labels and that Rhode Island could not entirely ban liquor price advertising.

Later, however, the Court recognized a "strong presumption of validity that we accord to other policy judgments made by Congress" in allowing the Department of Agriculture to assess a fee from fruit producers against their wishes to produce collective advertising.

Sam listened and wondered, "Assuming this to be the state of the law today, my question is whether Congress could or should enact a constitutionally valid statute prohibiting the advertising of inherently harmful products and services without actually outlawing the actual product or service."

Let's assume that Congress first decided that it was not in the best interest of society to prohibit the sale, purchase, possession, or use of alcohol and nicotine products because of the burden on the criminal justice system.

Further, let's assume that Congress held hearings and concluded that the use and consumption of these products is inherently harmful to both users and society.

Finally, let's assume that Congress found the political courage to resist the massive and inevitable lobbying campaign by the industries involved and that the President recognized the great value of the legislation and actually signed it.

Wouldn't such a statute benefit our society? Government would not punish you for your personal choice to indulge in potential or likely harmful substances—it would just stop the producer of the product from inducing you to do it.

Essentially, the advertising of harmful products or services is inherently false and misleading. Once we established the concept that it is better to disallow all advertising of alcohol and nicotine products rather than to criminalize their sale, purchase, possession, or consumption, there are other issues Congress might want to consider.

Should video games, movies, and music containing adult-level violence be marketed to children? Should hard-core, particularly violent, pornography be advertised at all? Should gambling, including state-sponsored lotteries, be advertised to compulsive gamblers and the poor, who can least afford the risk? Should prescription drugs be directly marketed to patients, especially for off-label use?

It remains to be seen whether corporations should be entitled to any First Amendment protection or other constitutional rights. But for now, a good first step would be to eliminate inherently harmful advertising from all sources.

Internet Neutrality

I asked Sam what could best be done to protect the public and its freedom of expression.

Assuming the great difficulty of reversing the corporate takeover of the news media, the Internet is the last best hope for democracy and constitutional freedoms. Since its activation in 1969, "web surfing" has become a part of the daily lives of most people in the developed world and has revolutionized human society.

Success of the Internet has been built on its open access; however, that access is being threatened more and more by the commercial service providers who control gateway access for most individual users.

Instead of "net neutrality," they want to reserve the highest speed limits for their own content and services and for the major corporations who can afford to pay additional tolls, and they demand the right to intentionally slow down or restrict small business or individual users who can't pay the higher fees.

These major providers want to be able to decide for themselves which Web sites load fast, which go slowly, or which cannot be loaded at all. They want to impose their own search engines or services on their customers and to slow down or entirely block those of competitors.

These major Internet providers are spending a lot of money to block any legislation or regulation that ensures net neutrality; however, Internet users have mounted a spirited grassroots campaign to preserve their access rights.

Net neutrality is perhaps the most important battle that individual consumers and voters have to fight in the corporate and big government war against individual freedoms.

The Internet will be the salvation of our freedoms. It is truly the "Fifth Estate" of modern democracy along with the Congress, the Judiciary, the Executive, and the Media, and it must be protected at all costs.

Soldiers of conscience must continue to band together to fight the war for intellectual freedom, holding the shield of our most valuable right before them as they march against ignorance, deceit, and greed. There is no alternative to victory!

Hope for Change

It was ten o'clock Saturday morning in the carpool lane of the 405 Freeway; we were late, and there wasn't anything to do but creep along at five mph waiting to get past the traffic accident up ahead that had half of the southbound lanes blocked.

Heather and I were driving down for breakfast with Sam and Aileana, and KNX all-news radio was telling us it was going to take 30 more minutes to clear the SigAlert.

We used the time to talk about the upcoming election, which was to be the subject of discussion this morning. Heather was telling me about the political atmosphere on the UCLA campus and the work she had been doing for the election, "I've been helping Rock the Vote register young voters before it is too late for them to vote next month."

> It doesn't matter which party they support, Rock the Vote has been using music and community organizing for more than 20 years to turn out the youth vote. In total, Rock the Vote has registered more than five million young voters since it started. But, we've gone over the top this year with more than two and a half million downloads from our website.
> Like everyone else, we're worried about the economy, but we're also concerned about the environment. To us, the issues are one and the same, and we're not real happy about what we're

hearing from both of the candidates. It mostly sounds like rhetoric, instead of reality.

Most of us also have some pretty strong views about the War. Because McCain is coming across as a "kill, baby kill" as well as a "drill, baby drill" candidate, we're finding that voters under 30 prefer Obama over him 68 percent to 24 percent. It doesn't help that McCain looks tired and Obama has a lot of energy.

Sam and Aileana were waiting in the kitchen when we arrived and five places were set for breakfast—four at the table and one on the floor for K.D. We all sat down to a country breakfast and began to critique the election and the candidates. We talked and K.D. listened, with one ear cocked.

Everyone had read the columns and editorials resulting from my interviews with both candidates, and they were interested in any additional insights I might have.

The bottom line was that Obama was going to win, and the only question was by how much? McCain's staff was demoralized and had basically given up. His aides were already talking about the campaign in the past tense. They were political pros and could read the writing on the wall—which is why they were already sending out resumes.

There is a lot of finger pointing as well as excuses, including Bush's failed presidency and the crashed economy, but the choice of Sarah Palin was an unmitigated disaster. As a political decision, it ranked somewhere between simple stupidity and total idiocy.

Naturally, Aileana had been following the money. She found that Obama had collected nearly twice as much money as McCain—from some interesting sources.

This will be, easily, the most expensive presidential election in history. Total spending will exceed $1.7 billion dollars, more than twice that spent in 2004.

Hope for Change

As the first major party candidate ever to reject federal funding in the general election, Barack Obama will spend almost $741 million dollars—more than that spent by both President Bush and John Kerry in 2004.

Although it is true that Obama has received a lot of small contributions, the big money has come from sources usually associated with the Republican Party. He collected $9.5 million from Wall Street, whereas McCain only got $5.3 million.

Top money came from contributors associated with Goldman Sachs, JP Morgan Chase & Co, Citigroup, Time Warner, UBS AG, General Electric, and Morgan Stanley.

Although Obama has said that he wouldn't accept money from lobbyists, he got huge sums from lobbying legal firms, including Sidley Austin and Latham & Watkins.

Wall Street is betting on Senator Obama. He voted in favor the bailout of the U.S. financial system a couple of weeks ago, and the bankers will be able to use the $700 billion cash infusion to recover from their gambling losses. They will have plenty of money left over to pay themselves top bonuses for having led the system into its worse crisis since the crash of 1929.

Bush Junior may have said, "This sucker could go down," but it was Senator Obama who sided with the Congressional leaders of both parties in their backroom discussions to engage in a massive corporate bailout.

Is it any surprise that Wall Street has contributed more than $1.2 billion dollars to congressional candidates since 2002? Or, that nine of the top ten House recipients, who each received an average of $1.5 million, serve on the financial oversight and taxation committees?

Deregulation started under President Clinton and came to fruition under President Bush, but it's going to cost taxpayers trillions of dollars to recover from the consequences of what the legal bribery of Congress and several presidents have purchased.

Do you think Wall Street is worried about a President Obama? Just look at who's advising him. Timothy Geithner, a Kissinger protégé, will most likely be his Secretary of Treasury. Geithner is the president of the Federal Reserve Bank of New York which arranged the rescue and sale of Bear Stearns.

He also made the decision not to rescue Lehman Brothers, yet he helped Treasury Secretary Paulson bail out AIG a couple of days later. Geithner is so tight with Wall Street that he will probably get the job even if, by some miracle, McCain is elected.

Another of Obama's chief advisors is Lawrence Summers, who as Clinton's Treasury Secretary played a major role in financial deregulation. He will probably get the chair of Obama's National Economic Council.

Barack Obama speaks well and has a beautiful family, but make no mistake, he's a member of the elite, and he will dance with those who "brung" him.

Sam agreed that it probably didn't make much difference who is elected president in terms of the economy, but peace and justice remain as his primary concerns.

I want to believe Obama when he says he will bring the troops home from Iraq, but if I do, I also have to believe him when he says he will increase the troops in Afghanistan and that he will "take action within Pakistan's borders, even without their permission."

What I fear is the wimp factor in which Democrats try to prove how tough they are by outshooting the Republicans. So far this year, Bush has authorized 30 drone missile attacks in Pakistan; we'll soon see what Obama will do.

He has promised to close the prison at Guantanamo Bay and that he will bring the prisoners to trial in the United States. We will soon know if he will keep that promise, but we may not know if he continues to operate other secret prisons overseas.

What will Obama do when the Patriot Act comes up for renewal? Will he continue the unwarranted blanket interception of private communications in the United States? Will he rely on the State Secrecy Privilege in the future to cover up government misconduct, or will he operate an open administration? How will he treat whistle blowers who reveal secret government corruption?

As president, will Obama investigate and prosecute those whose lies and corruption caused the illegal wars of aggression which have cost the lives of thousands of our sons and daughters and which have bankrupted the future of all of us?

We will wait and see, but I do not have great hope for the change he has promised.

It's good we will have a President who can speak in complete sentences, but will he tell us the truth? Or will he continue to tell the same lies that have become the vocabulary of our presidents? Will he just turn out to be a more articulate liar?

Money Matters

The wedding party gathered at the surf line in front of the Five-Corners lifeguard stand as sunset approached. The scene was framed by the Manhattan Beach pier on the north, and the Hermosa Beach pier on the south. It was a clear and warm evening for early November, and there were a few billowy clouds in the sky.

Aileana, who had begun to show, was wearing a beautiful cream-colored dress and Sam was wearing the conservative blue suit he had worn on the Oprah show, sans tie. The rest of us were dressed for the weather, with Heather in sneakers, dress jeans, and a warm top. We were all wearing orchid leis, including K.D., who sat at attention next to Sam.

As the bottom of the sun touched the horizon, Judge Judi asked the couple if they had something to say to each other.

Sam faced Aileana and took both of her hands in his, looked in her eyes and said, "Ana, during all the time I wandered about, lost and lonely, I dreamed of the loving touch, the comfort of an embrace, and unconditional love. Then we found each other, and you have given me this and more.

"Before I met you, I dreamed of meeting a woman along the way who would share my dreams about the universe that surrounds us and my vision of a peaceful eternity. Then we met.

"You have merged into my imagination and, together, we have gazed at the future. In Scottish Gaelic, Aileana means "bearer of the light," and you have become the light of my life.

Money Matters

"I shall hold you by my side for so long as I can walk the path, and when that is no longer possible, my spirit will abide with you and I will embrace you forever. During the quiet times when you are alone, listen carefully for the beat of my heart, and you will feel the comfort of my love."

Aileana said, "Samuel, when you became my friend, my life took on a deep happiness. This is the happiest day of my life! Here and now, in the presence of the Creator and our dearest friends, you and I and our child become a family. No matter where we are, together we are at home. I am honored to become your wife, I am privileged to declare you my husband, and I am blessed to bear your child."

Judge Judi asked if they wanted to exchange tokens of their love, and Heather and I produced the wrist watches they had chosen for each other. Aileana's was a high-tech runner's watch, and Sam's was a gold open-faced "skeleton" watch with a crystal back that allowed him to see its movement. As they fastened the watches on the wrist of the other, they promised to frequently mark the passage of time, so as to slow the moments they had together.

As the sun disappeared below the horizon, Judge Judi officially pronounced them legally married—Sam kissed his bride, and K.D. began to bark at the sandpipers.

If there was a green flash that evening, we missed it in the radiant glow of the magical moment when Sam and Aileana became one.

We walked back across the sand to the beach house where a catered dinner was waiting in the dining room. In my groom's toast, I acknowledged Sam as my best friend and the brother I had always wanted. I also took credit for having the foresight to accept Aileana's offer to nurse Sam during his ordeal. Heather toasted Aileana for her wisdom and support, as my daughter took another step into womanhood. Now, as a sister, Heather wished Aileana, Sam, and their child all the best that life had to offer. Xiomara raised her glass and predicted the child will bring Aileana and Sam as much happiness as Heather has brought the two of us.

K.D. shared in the feast by licking the plates.

They had decided to be married on election day. We had all voted that morning, and after dinner we gathered around the television in the living room to watch the returns. Given the opinion polls and the mood of the nation, there was little doubt about who would be elected, short of another electoral outrage. Barack Obama's election represented a historic event, and we all wanted to share the experience.

It was an amazing scene, as almost a quarter million Chicagoans converged on Grant Park to hear Obama's acceptance speech. We could see they were mostly young, but Oprah was there, as well as Jesse Jackson and other celebrities. Here and there were elderly black people—who undoubtedly never thought they would live to see the day an African American was elected President of the United States.

I was still a teenager in 1968 when, during the Democratic National Convention, Grant Park was occupied by thousands of young people protesting the Viet Nam War. They were chanting, "The whole world is watching" as they were beaten and gassed by the Chicago police. The times have changed in so many ways over the past 40 years. I am no longer young, and my remaining hair is no longer long. The political left is now the middle, and the right has become more radical and powerful.

When the networks called the election for Obama, the crowd went wild. There was an explosion of relief and joy. People were screaming, jumping, dancing, and even crying. Spontaneous street parties broke out in cities across the United States and in other major cities around the world. Change—and hope—was in the air.

President-elect Obama acknowledged the enormity of the task that lies ahead and the greatest challenges in our lifetime: "two wars, a planet in peril, the worst financial crisis in a century." He said, "tonight we proved once again that the true strength of our nation comes not from the might of our arms or the scale of our wealth, but from the enduring power of our ideals: democracy, liberty, opportunity, and unyielding hope." Over and over, he repeated the mantra of his campaign, "Yes, we can."

As the young president-elect stood alone on the stage and wowed the world with his eloquence, millions shared his dream for a hopeful future.

Reality struck the next morning as I was en route to take Sam and Aileana to the airport for their honeymoon: KNX reported that a U.S. airstrike had mistakenly bombed yet another wedding party in Afghanistan and killed 40 civilians, including women and children. Although the stock market had rallied a bit on election day, October had been one of the worse months in history. The decline of the S&P on Monday had surpassed even Black Thursday on October 29, 1929.

Commodity prices, profits, and credit were being driven downward and extinguished by the collapse of the housing market. There was no good financial news. One of Obama's advisors, Jared Bernstein, said, "A combination of negative outlook and uncertainly is toxic for stock markets, and you've got both of those factors on steroids right now."

On our way to the airport, we talked about the financial crisis and what was required to put it into context. We agreed I would research the history of the financial markets, the regulations that came out of the Great Depression, and the history of the current recession.

While I was tied down with money matters, Sam and Aileana were off to enjoy a late autumn in the mountains of Vermont. They had rented a log cabin on a lake and were looking forward to doing nothing but celebrating their marriage for the next two weeks.

What is Money?

We tend to look at money as an object. Something we can hold in our hand and exchange for something we want; however, that is an illusion. Money is simply an expression of credit, something we either have faith in or we don't.

Sam: A Political Philosophy

Once upon a time money consisted of metal coins—gold, silver, copper, bronze or brass—but today our paper money is just a promissory note, and our coins are laminated junk. However, even before there were coins, there was an accounting system consisting of clay objects impressed with symbols setting forth numbers and standards of measure for exchange with distant customers or suppliers.

Today, if we are going to talk about money, we have to stop thinking about it as a thing and see it as a symbol of credit.

A Brief History of American Finance

Writing at the beginning of the Revolutionary War, Adam Smith, a Scottish philosopher and economist, wrote in *The Wealth of Nations* that the free market is guided by an "invisible hand" to produce the right amount and variety of goods at the right time and place. He believed the market economy worked best for both the seller and the buyer and allowed for the optimum allocation of resources.

At the same time, Smith also believed that monopolies distorted the market's ability to provide a fair return for labor, as well as land and capital, and he was concerned about the severity of laws against workers' actions and the "collusions of masters" to defeat workers' associations.

Smith's "enlightened self interest" influenced America's founding fathers, including Thomas Jefferson, who wrote in the Declaration of Independence that the "unalienable Rights" included "Life, Liberty and the pursuit of Happiness." Encouraged by Benjamin Franklin, Jefferson had substituted "happiness" for protection of "property" as a goal of government.

Franklin believed the economic success of the colonies was because "we issue our own money. It is called Colonial Script. We issue it in proper proportion to the demands of trade and industry to make the products pass easily from the producers to the consumers. In this manner, creating for ourselves our own paper money, we control its purchasing power, and we have no interest to pay to no one." The economic depression resulting from the prohibition of colonial script by Parliament in 1764 was one of the causes of the Revolution.

The question of national banks was one of the original political issues that split American politics into factions and parties. Using the Bank of England as a model to establish a debt-based monetary system, Congress established the First Bank of the United States in 1791 and the Second Bank in 1816.

Jefferson believed "banking institutions are more dangerous to our liberties than standing armies. Already they have raised up a moneyed aristocracy that has set the government at defiance. The issuing power [of money] should be taken away from the banks and restored to the people to whom it properly belongs." As President, Jefferson refused to borrow money from the First Bank and was able to balance the federal budget throughout his administration.

President James Madison allowed the First Bank's charter to expire in 1811. He said, "History records that the money changers have used every form of abuse, intrigue, deceit, and violent means possible to maintain their control over governments by controlling money and it's issuance."

Following the War of 1812, during which the country experienced severe inflation and the government had difficulty raising money for military operations, the Second Bank was chartered by Congress in 1816. Even though it was privately owned and controlled, the bank was the depository for government funds and paid no interest; it was allowed to freely issue paper money and to avoid state taxes. The bank provided a source of great wealth for its investors and became politically powerful.

President Andrew Jackson believed that giving power and control to a single bank caused inflation and other economic evils, including exposing the government to control by foreign interests, corrupting the election of Congress, increasing the wealth of the rich, and favoring commercial and industrial interests at the expense of farmers and laborers.

Jackson opposed renewing the Bank's charter and attracted the Bank's wrath. He told Martin Van Buren that the Bank "is trying to kill me, but I will kill it!" Jackson vetoed renewal of the charter in 1832, and the next year, he removed the government's funds from the bank and deposited them in state banks.

The power of international bankers to manipulate political events for financial advantage was demonstrated by Nathan Rothschild—who misled English investors into believing Napoleon had defeated British troops at Waterloo. As the bond market crashed, Rothschild purchased government bonds for pennies on the dollar providing him with the capital to establish the largest bank in the world. His father, Mayer Rothschild famously said, "Let me issue and control a nation's money, and I care not who writes its laws."

Abraham Lincoln refused to borrow money from the banks to fight the Civil War. He said, "The money powers prey upon the nation in times of peace and conspire against it in times of adversity. It is more despotic than a monarchy, more insolent than autocracy, and more selfish than bureaucracy. It denounces as public enemies all who question its methods or throw light upon its crimes. I have two great enemies, the Southern Army in front of me and the bankers in the rear. Of the two, the one at my rear is my greatest foe."

Instead of leading the country into debt, Lincoln paid for the war by relying on income and excise taxes and the direct issuance of paper "Greenbacks" by the government. As late as 1900, Greenbacks continued to make up a third of the money in circulation; however, the bankers were not sitting idly by twiddling their thumbs.

Congress passed the National Banking Acts in 1863 and 1864, which ultimately shut down the extensive system of state-chartered banks, including some that were state owned. The resulting scarcity of capital led to the establishment of powerful banking trusts in New York City, including the one created by John Pierpont Morgan.

Morgan was able to funnel surplus capital from European countries into the United States to fund factories and railroads and to make a profit on every transaction. As he said, "I am not in Wall Street for my health."

Taking a page from the Rothschild playbook, Morgan caused a panic in 1907 by circulating false rumors that two banks were about to become insolvent. As the public began a "run" on the banks, Morgan magnanimously stepped in with $100 million in European gold, creating the perception that America needed a strong central bank to avert future panics.

Acting as a secret agent of the Rothschilds, Morgan allied with the dynasty's American representatives to push the Federal Reserve Act through Congress in 1913. One of the Act's authors, Robert Owens, came to believe bankers had conspired to create the panics resulting in "reforms" that primarily served the banker's interests. After President Wilson signed the Act, he said he had "unwittingly ruined my nation."

The Federal Reserve System failed to live up to its promise by failing to avoid a major financial bubble during World War I and the resulting depression. Following World War I, normalcy returned as people struggled to rebuild the war's devastation in Europe and to obtain the goods and services they had foregone during the conflict. Inventions, discoveries, and rapid industrial growth drove a housing bubble that peaked in 1925 and a bullish stock market that seemed unlimited in its growth potential. Wealth and excess funded a flowering of art, music, and cultural change. Automobiles, radios, and motion pictures changed the way people lived and perceived the world they lived in.

Beneath the surface and invisible to the ordinary small investors, who were borrowing nine dollars to purchase stocks for every dollar they had on deposit, was a decline in the money and credit supply. The amount of credit the Federal Reserve could issue was limited by laws that required partial gold-backing of the credit. As the redemption of demand notes for gold increased, particularly by foreign investors, the amount of available credit was reduced, creating a downward spiral in credit and the money supply.

Banks had led the wave of speculation in the Twenties by forming "securities affiliates" in which they invested their own assets and purchased new stock issues for resale to the public. Banks had encouraged their depositors to invest in the speculative issues they were trying to sell, and they had made unsound loans to the companies in which they had invested. In expectation of ever increasing returns, banks took ever increasing risks. Then, the bubble popped and depositors began to line up to withdraw their money.

On "Black Thursday," October 29, 1929, it all came crashing down—for the United States and for the rest of the world. Stock prices continued to fall for the next month and, although there was a partial recovery in November and December and early 1930, the market continued to slide down until July 8, 1932 when it finally hit bottom. The market did not return to its pre-1929 levels until 1954.

The Great Depression

Originating in the United States, the depression spread around the world causing international trade to fall by half to two-thirds, and reducing prices, profits, personal income, and tax revenues in every economy. Building slowed or stopped, manufacturing fell by half, and farmers were devastated as crop prices fell by 60 percent.

More than a quarter of all workers were unemployed in the United States, and in other countries more than a third could not find work. With reduced tax revenues, governments were unable or unwilling to provide relief.

Even though the interest rate continued to fall, people did not or could not take on new debt to make purchases. A deflationary spiral commenced in 1930, leading to even lower prices and wages, and did not stop until March 1933. The knockout blow was delivered as the banks began to fail, wiping out deposits representing billions of dollars of hard-earned wages.

The Federal Reserve System did nothing, as bank runs—resulting from debtor defaults and the withdrawal of savings by depositors—increased. Prices and income fell by up to 50 percent, increasing the burden of outstanding debts, which remained fixed at the borrowed level. With the dollar increasing in value, every attempt by a debtor to reduce his debt actually increased it. The more debtors repaid, the more they owed.

Banks failed when loans were not or could not be repaid—744 banks closed their doors during the first ten months of 1930, and 9,000 failed over the next ten years. Capital investment and construction funding virtually ceased as banks became increasingly tight-fisted in lending. To preserve profits, banks hoarded their remaining reserves and refused most loans—all of which accelerated the downward spiral.

The Federal Reserve System has been criticized for having done nothing to mediate the crisis. Some believe the Fed could have provided emergency lending to key banks or purchased government bonds on the open market to increase liquidity. The current Fed chairman, Ben Bernanke believes the Great Depression was mainly caused by monetary contraction and poor policymaking by the Fed.

Banking Reform and Regulation

Republican President Herbert Hoover ran for reelection in 1932 and was opposed by Franklin Delano Roosevelt, the Democratic candidate. Although Roosevelt called for a balanced budget and for a "sound currency to be maintained at all hazards," he expanded his views on the economy upon taking office, as he began to enact his promised "New Deal."

During the campaign, Roosevelt had said, "Throughout the nation men and women, forgotten in the political philosophy of the Government, look to us here for guidance and for more equitable opportunity to share in the distribution of national wealth . . . I pledge you, I pledge myself to a new deal for the American people . . . This is more than a political campaign. It is a call to arms."

Roosevelt had little or no respect for financiers and bankers. During his inauguration address, he blamed them for the economic crisis:

> . . . the rulers of the exchange of mankind's goods have failed, through their own stubbornness and their own incompetence, have admitted their failure, and abdicated. Practices of the unscrupulous money changers stand indicted in the court of public opinion, rejected by the hearts and minds of men.
> . . . They know only the rules of a generation of self-seekers. They have no vision, and when there is no vision the people perish.
> The money changers have fled from their high seats in the temple of our civilization. We may now restore that temple to the ancient truths. The measure of the restoration lies in the extent to which we apply social values more noble than mere monetary profit.
> Happiness lies not in the mere possession of money; it lies in the joy of achievement, in the thrill of creative effort. The joy and moral stimulation of work no longer must be forgotten in the mad chase of evanescent profits. These dark days will be worth all they cost us if they teach us that our true destiny is not to be ministered unto but to minister to ourselves and to our fellow men.

Recognition of the falsity of material wealth as the standard of success goes hand in hand with the abandonment of the false belief that public office and high political position are to be valued only by the standards of pride of place and personal profit; and there must be an end to a conduct in banking and in business which too often has given to a sacred trust the likeness of callous and selfish wrongdoing. Small wonder that confidence languishes, for it thrives only on honesty, on honor, on the sacredness of obligations, on faithful protection, on unselfish performance; without them it cannot live.

In addition to a variety of relief efforts during Roosevelt's first 100 days, Congress passed the Emergency Banking Act the day after his inauguration—declaring a "bank holiday" and a plan to allow banks to reopen. Subsequently, Roosevelt signed the Banking Act of 1933, known as the Glass-Steagall Act, that created the Federal Deposit Insurance Corporation to guarantee the bank deposits of most depositors and to effectuate other reforms.

By creating conditions for membership in FDIC, the Act forced banks to chose whether they were going to be a "commercial" bank or an "investment" bank. Both could accept deposits; however, only deposits in commercial banks were insured by the government.

Commercial banks were prohibited from underwriting or distributing securities and from purchasing shares of corporations for their own accounts. They could purchase high-quality debt securities, such as government or municipal bonds, under tightly-controlled circumstances. The Act also severed legal affiliations between member banks, both national and state, and investment banks and insurance companies.

Essentially, the Act disallowed any one company from acting in more than one area of investment banking, commercial banking, or selling insurance. It assumes that investment banking is too risky and speculative to allow the banks to accept deposits from the general public. The further assumption is that depositors who chose to put their money into accounts that are not insured by FDIC are sufficiently sophisticated to appreciate, evaluate, and accept the risks. Investment banks and insurance companies and their customers and depositors were to be disciplined by the "market."

On April 6, 1933, President Roosevelt issued an executive order prohibiting the hoarding of gold beyond a value of $100, and requiring it to be sold to the government at the set price of $20.67 an ounce in exchange for dollars. Once the government had most of the nation's gold in its vaults, it raised the price to $35 an ounce, substantially increasing the value of its reserves. That price remained in effect until President Nixon announced in 1971 that the government would no longer redeem gold certificates, effectively taking the United States off the gold standard. The nation had already stopped backing the dollar with silver in 1964.

The Glass-Steagall Act was supplemented by the Bank Holding Company Act of 1956 that prohibited bank holding companies and disallowed banks from being chartered in one state and acquiring banks in other states. It also prohibited banks from purchasing stock in non-banking companies; from owing both banking and non-banking businesses; and from engaging in most non-banking activities.

These sensible laws were the product of harsh experience, tested by time, and they existed not only to protect the public from predatory bankers, but also to inoculate bankers against the disease of their own greed. However, the Wall Street bankers, like gamblers suffering from an addition, never rested from their efforts to free themselves from the restraint of regulation.

Deploying an army of lawyers and lobbyists, provisioned by unlimited cash to pervert justice and purchase legislators, the bankers assaulted the citadel of regulation and reduced it to rubble.

Deregulation

The savings and loan industry grew out of neighborhood thrifts that accepted and paid interest on deposits and made loans for the purchase of primary residences. Following World War II, the industry flourished, as the "baby boom" fueled an expansion of home construction.

The industry chaffed under regulations limiting the types of lending savings and loan associations (S&Ls) could engage in and the interest rates they could pay on savings. When the industry was threatened in 1979 by high interest rates and inflation, Congress responded with legislation in 1980 and 1982 allowing S&Ls to expand their lending authority to include commercial loans and the issuance of credit cards, to invest limited funds in commercial real estate loans, and to relax their accounting rules.

The combination of deregulation, tax breaks, and market forces allowed the S&Ls to sell their low-interest government-guaranteed (FHA and VA) mortgages and to invest the proceeds in more profitable endeavors. Wall Street was happy to oblige. Major investment firms purchased the loans at 60-90 percent of value, bundled them as government-guaranteed bonds and sold them as securities.

All was well—as long as the real estate market boomed—there were investors interested in loaning money to S&Ls, and interest rates on loans exceed the rates on deposits; however, a drop in the real estate market caused debtor defaults and bankruptcies and the insolvency of many S&Ls.

Accounts were guaranteed by the Federal Savings and Loan Insurance Corporation (FSLIC) in the same way that FDIC insured commercial accounts. Between 1986 and 1989, FSLIC seized 296 S&Ls with assets of more than $125 billion. The rescue effort was taken over by the Resolution Trust Corporation in 1989, which "resolved" an additional 747 S&Ls. The net cost to American taxpayers was $124.6 billion, not including payments made before 1986 or after 1996.

The consequences of deregulation of the savings and loan industry should have served as a red flag for those promoting deregulation of the banking industry, but it didn't. Bankers saw the government bailout of the S&Ls as a green light for greater financial recklessness.

Wall Street lawyers forced the first breach in the protective firewalls of Glass-Steagall when the U.S. Supreme Court in 1981 allowed a bank's holding company affiliate to engage in security transactions, and in 1984, it permitted bank holding companies to engage in the discount brokerage business. Then the lobbyists took the deregulation fight to Congress.

The banking, insurance, and brokerage industries combined their forces and spent millions of dollars in a nonpartisan effort to purchase the affection of both major political parties and their politicians. They spent more than $200 million on lobbying and made more than $150 million in political contributions.

One of the primary beneficiaries was Republican Senator Phil Gramm from Texas who received more than $1.5 million from the industries in the five years before 1999. That year, all favors were repaid when the seduction climaxed with the birth of the Gramm-Leach-Bliley Act that effectively repealed the Glass-Steagall Act of 1933 and the Bank Holding Act of 1968.

The Act allowed the merger of commercial banks, investment banks, brokerage firms, and insurance companies in what became known as the Financial Services Industry.

One couple in the industry had already eloped the previous year and engaged in a common law marriage. New York's largest bank, Citibank merged with Travelers Group, Inc., an insurance and financial services powerhouse created when Travelers had earlier purchased the brokerage firm of Salomon Smith Barney. The "Citigroup" wedding was blessed by Fed Chairman Alan Greenspan, Treasury Secretary Robert Rubin, and President Clinton.

While regulations were reduced under Clinton, federal regulators were restrained by President George W. Bush from enforcing even the few remaining regulations. Acting to encourage an "ownership society" for the working class, Bush and the Fed promoted "financial innovation" as a means to create additional wealth and profits for banks and the wealthy.

The equity value of the major stock markets, especially the NASDAQ, expanded rapidly after 1993, as numerous technology startup companies quickly burned through venture capital and offered their stocks to the public through the major investment banks. The value of these companies become uncoupled from fundamental accounting techniques, such as price to earnings, as they were snapped up by investors—until the bubble reached its bursting point.

Coincident with inauguration of the Bush II administration was the "dot.com" crash of 2000 and 2001. Between March 2000 and October 2002, the crash eliminated more than $5 trillion in market value of the technology companies. The largest, WorldCom, was found to have illegally overstated its profits by billions of dollars, and its bankruptcy became the most expensive in U.S. history as of that date.

There were allegations and convictions of fraud, and the Securities and Exchange Commission fined several investment banks, including Citigroup and Merrill Lynch for having misled investors.

Aftermath of Deregulation

Never at a loss to sniff out profitable ventures and unrestrained by regulations and regulators, the banks began to experiment in new ways to make money. Indeed, it is because banks "make" money that they earn profits. The concept of "fractional reserves" allows banks to loan 80 percent of their deposits, while keeping only 20 percent on hand to accommodate those who may want to withdraw their funds. Traditionally, profits result from the spread between the interest earned on loans and the interest paid on deposits. But deregulation created whole new games of chance.

Backed up by Fannie Mae and Freddie Mac and encouraged by the Fed, banks began to make highly speculative, or subprime, high-interest real estate mortgage loans to weak or unqualified borrowers, and a new bubble began to expand.

Unlike traditional conventional loans, the subprime mortgage industry did not finance their loans from deposits, but from Wall Street investors who purchased packaged loans known as mortgage-backed securities.

Banks became even more creative by offering adjustable loans with low introductory teaser rates and interest-only loans that allowed otherwise unqualified buyers to purchase homes they would never otherwise be able to afford, once the beginning rates readjusted. Purchasers were sold on the idea that the ever-expanding market would allow them to sell or refinance, before the roulette wheel stopped spinning.

The value of housing continued to fuel the economy through most of the Bush II years, as home owners continually refinanced their homes and withdrew the equity to purchase electronic appliances, expensive cars, and other "stuff." However, the cash to pay for all this had to come from somewhere.

Money to purchase the bonded indebtedness of the federal government, allowing the soaring federal deficits during the Bush administration, primarily came from the sovereign-wealth funds of China and other exporting countries that maintained a favorable balance of payments on international trade. At the same time, individual foreign investors were dumping trillions of dollars in excess savings directly into the mortgage-based securities being peddled by American banks.

Paul Volcker, a former chairman of the Federal Reserve, worried that the United States was consuming six percent more than it was producing, "Boomers are spending like there is no tomorrow.

Homeownership has become a vehicle for borrowing and leveraging as much as a source of financial security." He said: "What holds it all together is a really massive and growing flow of capital from abroad. A flow of capital that today runs to more than $2 billion per day."

Volcker had been removed as chairman in 1987, when President Reagan decided to appoint Alan Greenspan in his place. Volcker regulated the banking industry with an even hand and effectively controlled inflation; however, Reagan wanted someone who did not believe in the regulation of financial markets. Greenspan, a literal disciple of Ayn Rand, turned on the liquidity spigot and turned off regulation. He presided over the two financial bubbles spawned by the combination—the dot.com and the housing bubbles.

Deregulation encouraged the conversion of the United States from a manufacturing and exporting economy to a financial services economy. The new financial services industry worked to manage the importation of investment capital and the distribution of goods from other nations for the consumption of those who profited from the industry and who provided services to it.

The Economic Casino

To manage the massive inflow of capital and to maximize their profits, the "smart guys" of the new industry created some really clever devices, all of which were based on the manipulation of risk and the maximization of profit. Even though the entire gross domestic product of the world was approximately $55 trillion in 2008, speculative lending—worldwide—was between $525 and $550 trillion!

These gambling devices, and their interaction, became so incredibly complex that they became disconnected from reality. They mushroomed into a massive scheme beyond the control of any regulatory agency, and they produced such fantastic wealth as to buy and sell governments.

Short of a book, or series of books, any attempt to describe these devices is inadequate; however, we can start with a subprime mortgage and try to see what happens.

Instead of holding the mortgage over its term and collecting the interest, the lender immediately sells the mortgage to an investment bank, makes a new loan with the proceeds, and books immediate and maximum profits with little risk.

The investment bank then bundles the mortgage with others and sells the bundles—or pieces or slices of the bundle called tranches—to other investors. However, these investors are also smart guys, and they also want to reduce the risk and maximize their profits. Since the underlying subprime mortgage carries a risk of foreclosure, the second-level purchasers seek guarantees against defaults.

A credit default swap (CDS) is similar to insurance in that the buyer pays a premium to the seller of the CDS to obtain a payoff if the "insured" credit instrument undergoes a "credit event," such as a default, or a "reference credit," such as a bankruptcy or a downgrade in credit rating.

Although the purchaser of a CDS is generally expected to have an insurable interest in the underlying instrument, the buyer is not required to actually own the instrument, and it is not necessary for the buyer to actually suffer a loss, only an increase in risk.

Derivatives are related to CDSs in that they are financial instruments derived from other underlying assets. Derivative traders do not own the underlying assets, but they agree to exchange cash or assets at certain points based on the underlying asset.

Derivatives are speculative and investors can profit if the value of the underlying asset moves as they predict, or, conversely, they can "hedge" their risks by betting that the asset moves in the opposite direction of their underlying position.

Hedging and derivatives are related in that two parties can agree to hedge or reduce a future risk to either or both parties by specifying an amount, price, and date certain, and by then purchasing a derivatives contract from a third party or clearing house to insure against a total loss to either party.

The smartest of the smart guys created hedge funds to borrow and invest in stock shares, debts, and commodities with the greatest risk, and they relied on a range of devices including derivatives and short selling to "hedge" their risk. Ordinarily, these funds are open only to the most professional or wealthy investors and are exempt from many of the regulations covering liquidity, derivatives, and short or long selling. The income of the top fund managers amounts to billions of dollars each year.

The slickest smart guys don't even own the investments they gamble with. "Short selling" allows investors to profit from the falling price of a stock by "borrowing" a stock from a broker and selling it under conditions where the seller will repurchase the stock at the lower "short" price, return it to the broker, and book a profit. Of course, if the price of the stock increases, the "seller" will have to repurchase the stock at the higher price and suffer a loss.

Nominally illegal, "naked" short selling allows the sale of stocks which haven't even been borrowed by "market makers."

Any residual regulation of derivatives and credit default swaps was eliminated by Senator Phil Gramm when he slipped the Commodity Futures Modernization Act into the omnibus spending bill in December 2000. Not only did the Act exempt energy trading (by companies such as Enron) from regulation, but Gramm also claimed it would "protect financial institutions from overregulation" and "position our financial services industries to be world leaders into the new century." Gramm retired in 2002 to become a vice president of UBS AG, Switzerland's largest bank, in order to support "key clients."

As early as 2002, investor Warren Buffet warned, "derivatives are financial weapons of mass destruction, carrying dangers that, while now latent, are potentially lethal." In spite of his warning, the derivatives market increased from $100 trillion to more $516 trillion over the next five years. Much like an out-of-control Ponzi scheme, it has been estimated that the worldwide derivatives bubble was ultimately inflated to a quadrillion dollars (thousand trillion).

These smart guys not only gambled with the prosperity of nations and the security of governments, but they also threatened the very existence of humanity.

The First Failures

The first foreshock of the financial earthquake that shook the world in 2008 actually occurred ten years earlier when the dice rolls of a major hedge fund began to come up snake eyes. Long-Term Capital Management was an industry leader in the use of computerized models to produce extraordinary profits, while maintaining a reserve equity of just three percent. After losses of $4.5 billion in 1998, its imminent collapse sent shockwaves through Wall Street and the government.

Fearing that the demise of Long-Term would infect the entire financial system, the Federal Reserve Bank of New York assembled a group of 14 banks to stabilize Long-Term with an infusion of $3.65 billion. The only bank which refused to contribute was Bear Stearns—the broker that handled the trades of Long-Term.

Even after the near collapse and rescue of Long-Term, then Fed Chairman Alan Greenspan testified in 2003, "What we have found over the years in the marketplace is that derivatives have been an extraordinarily useful vehicle to transfer risk from those who shouldn't be taking it to those who are willing to and are capable of doing so. We think it would be a mistake" to regulate the contracts.

Perhaps it was karma, but the failure of two Bear Stearns sponsored hedge funds in 2007, resulting from increasing subprime mortgage defaults, began to expose the bank's precarious position. With $2.5 trillion of credit default swaps on its books and with an equity-to-assets ratio of just three percent, Bear Stearns was dangerously over leveraged.

Triggered by rumors of its insolvency in March 2008, investors began to dump Bear Stearns stock and to withdraw their deposits, and the Fed again intervened to avoid a financial disaster. More than a hundred years after JP Morgan caused a panic using false rumors, his namesake, JPMorgan Chase once again benefitted from false rumors of another bank's insolvency. This time, however, it was not JP Morgan which came up with the rescue funds, but the Federal Reserve System his lies helped to create.

Bear Stearns was an investment bank and was not insured by the FDIC—therefore the Federal Reserve had to create a different kind of rescue. In a buyout deal worked out in secret over a weekend, the Fed loaned $25 billion to Bear Stearns and $30 billion to JPMorgan to finance its purchase of Bear Stearns. In actuality, since Bear Stearns ceased to exist, all of the funds ended up credited to the accounts of JPMorgan. The deal exposed U.S. taxpayers to a loss of up to $40 billion.

Since the Fed could have directly loaned the entire $55 billion to Bear Stearns and saved the bank, there is speculation that the rumors, collapse, and structured buyout were designed to allow JPMorgan Chase to avoid its own insolvency.

The situation where the banks and wealthy investors enjoy the profits and the taxpayers assume the risk has become known as the "privatization of profit and the socialization of risk." To facilitate this philosophy, the Federal Reserve commenced to lend hundreds of billions of dollars to the investment banks through its "discount window." Previously, this benefit was restricted to commercial banks only.

Black September 2008

One of the several remaining major investment banks, Lehman Brothers had been in business in New York City since the time of the Civil War. Its headquarters in the World Trade Center was destroyed on 9/11, but it was back in business at a temporary location within 48 hours. It could not, however, withstand the bursting of the housing bubble.

Lehman Brothers had more than $275 billion of assets under management in 2008; however, it was forced to retain large chunks of the subprime and low-rated mortgage it had securitized when the market collapsed. Its stock lost 73 percent of its value in the first half of 2008, and it reported losses of $2.8 billion in the second quarter.

Lehman Brothers stock lost 45 percent of its value on September 9, riding the Dow as it lost 300 points on the same day. The company announced an additional $3.9 billion loss the next day as the stock dropped another seven percent, then another 40 percent on September 11.

There were no purchasers for the firm, and the Federal Reserve Bank of New York, presided over by Timothy F. Geithner, refused to intervene. The firm filed for bankruptcy on September 14, and its stock value fell another 90 percent the next day, Bloody Monday, as the Dow dropped more than 500 points.

As was the case of Bear Stearns, there were indications that rumors and naked short selling contributed to the demise of Lehman Brothers. Fear reigned, rumors were rampant, and a perfect storm of bad news swept through the financial markets driving the Dow to rise and fall by as much as 1,000 points in a single day and to post its largest one-day losses and gains. The month became known as Black September.

Panic seized the financial markets, as credit dried up and banks stopped lending. As the panic spread to Washington, the Bush II administration contrived a solution to save the banks. In a perfect expression of the "privatization of profits and the socialization of risk," the

Treasury Department and the Federal Reserve System proposed to hand over billions of dollars to the gamblers, with little or no accountability.

The Federal National Mortgage Association (Fannie Mae) and the Federal Home Loan Mortgage Corporation (Freddie Mac) are privately-owned "Government Sponsored Enterprises" (GSE) established to encourage home ownership by guaranteeing and purchasing mortgages from lenders. They own or guarantee nearly half of the $12 trillion mortgage market in the U.S. Together, they have debts and outstanding mortgage-based securities amounting to more than $5 trillion, and by September 2008 they had suffered losses of almost $15 billion.

On September 7th, the Federal Housing Finance Agency placed the GSEs into a conservatorship run by the FHFA. The Federal Reserve and the Treasury Department committed to purchasing some of the GSE stock, debt, and outstanding mortgage-based securities. The actions increased the government's net liabilities by $238 billion.

In many respects, the bailout of the GSEs carried water for the major finance firms in that it also helped rescue the financial derivatives industry. Had the GSEs defaulted on their $5 trillion bond and mortgage-based securities portfolio, the credit default swap risks to the sellers could have amounted to payments of up to $1 trillion to the "protection buyers."

In a related action, the first actual bailout of the banks was through the backdoor of the insurance company known as American International Group. In 2008, AIG was the 18th largest public company in the world and a major peddler of credit default swaps, derivatives, and other esoteric investment guarantees. Since the amount of money AIG was required to post as collateral depended on its credit rating, the liquidity crisis caused its credit ratings to fall and its stock value to drop by 95 percent during Black September.

Deciding that AIG was "too big to fail," the Fed provided an $85 billion credit line to AIG on September 16th to meet its obligations in exchange for 79.9 percent of its equity. Subsequently, the total amount available to AIG was increased to $182.5 billion.

Not only were its shareholders and creditors at risk from a failure of AIG, but the major banks also stood to lose billions of dollars as their insured investments fell in value and their swaps declined in value or became worthless. Subsequently, AIG used $62 billion in Fed funds to pay off, at full value, its obligations to its banking counter-parties, including $14 billion to Goldman Sachs. But, the sweetest pie was yet to be baked.

Without holding any meaningful hearings or public discussions, Congress listened only to those most responsible for the economic disaster—Federal Reserve Chairman Ben Bernanke and Treasury Secretary Henry Paulson. Unless Congress passed the bank bailout "tomorrow," Paulson warned "we won't have an economy on Monday."

Although it took longer than the weekend, Congress abdicated its responsibility to the American people and voted to allow Paulson to spend at least $700 billion as he deemed necessary "to promote financial market stability."

Even though Americans were against the bailout two to one, and more than 400 top economists, including two Nobel Prize winners, voiced opposition, Congress passed the Emergency Economic Stabilization Act of 2008. The Act funded the Troubled Asset Relief Program, which provided money to the suffering banks with little or no conditions. The banks were able to use the funds to make acquisitions, pay dividends to shareholders, and pay "performance" bonuses to their executives. There were no provisions to assist workers or small businesses.

It is not difficult to show why Congress betrayed the public in favor of Wall Street bankers. The Financial Services Industry had donated more than $47 million to the campaigns of Senators Obama and McCain, "hedging" their bets no matter who won the election, and Wall Street had contributed more than $1.1 billion to congressional candidates in just six years. Nine of the top 10 recipients, who averaged $1.5 million each, served on the financial oversight and taxation committees. The four most involved in pushing the bailout through Congress, Senators Dodd and Gregg and Representatives Frank and Blunt have pocketed almost $20 million from Wall Street.

As the calendar turned on Black September, both Goldman Sachs and Morgan Stanley converted themselves into bank holding companies, accepting increased regulation for increased access to government support, and Bank of America acquired Merrill Lynch.

The Office of Thrift Supervision seized Washington Mutual Bank and placed it in the receivership of the FDIC. The bank was then sold, minus its unsecured debt and equity claims, to JPMorgan Chase for $1.9 billion.

Wachovia Bank, which had earlier purchased Prudential Securities and Golden West Financial, was on the verge of failure when the FDIC determined it was "systemically important" to the health of the economy. The FDIC decided to sell the Wachovia banking assets to Citigroup; however, Wachovia did an end run and merged with Wells Fargo in an all-stock transaction.

Twenty-five banks failed in 2008, and the expectation is that as many as 140 will fail in 2009.

Left standing were Citigroup, Bank of America, JPMorgan Chase and Wells Fargo as the largest banks in the United States. More than ever, these banks are now much "too big to fail," and they will continue to suck the life blood from the workers and small businesses of the United States.

Not only has the cost of the bailout been shifted to the tax payers, and not only has the tax burden itself been increasingly shifted to low-income earners, but workers have also become slaves to the payment of interest on the products and homes they have been enticed to purchase, and on which many of them owe more than their possessions are worth. Finally, with the Bankruptcy Abuse Prevention and Consumer

Protection Act of 2005, the ability of debtors to obtain a "fresh start" has been severely curtailed.

Recovery

Although my brief history of the U.S. financial system turned out to be longer than I expected and required more time to complete than I had planned, it seemed the minimum effort required to comprehend what has happened. I emailed a rough draft to Sam and Aileana in Vermont and looked forward to what they would have to say upon their return.

Monday rolled around and I met the couple at the baggage claim area of LAX. The two of them looked radiantly happy, and I remarked that marriage seemed to be serving them well. But as we were crossing the street on the way to the parking structure, Sam stumbled over the curb and fell to his knees on the sidewalk. He was embarrassed as I helped him up, and I caught a look of concern on Aileana's face.

Nothing more was said about the incident, but later in the day when we were alone, Aileana cryptically said that it was time to get Sam in for a checkup.

It was another boringly beautiful Southern California day, and we sat on the patio talking. Sam had read the history of the financial system I sent him and had been doing some independent research of his own.

Sam said, "Although there were a lot of stories in the mainstream media about the 'Great Recession,' the articles provided very little real information and offered even fewer solutions. The media pretty much adheres to the party line, and I had to go to the Internet to find independent thinking. I found a small group of alternative-media writers who seemed to really understand what is going on with the economy and have some sound suggestions about what to do. Some of the most insightful analysis and avant-garde ideas are being offered by these writers."

Money Matters

"Working with your history and their ideas, I believe we can talk about some changes that have to take place if the U.S. economy is to survive as a free enterprise system."

Regulation is one of those words, like socialism or liberalism, which has negative connotations for many conservatives, but no matter the word used, we cannot have a complex society without organizational controls.

As you fly into the greater Los Angeles area on a clear night you can look down on the lights of hundreds of cities connected by thousands of miles of roads and inhabited by millions of people. The skyscrapers and freeways could not have been built without specialized regulations, and there would not be reliable electricity, water, and sanitation systems without specific federal, state, and local regulations.

You wouldn't be able to safely drive a car through intersections or down a highway meeting other cars at high speeds without laws and regulations, and the confidence that others will respect and willingly comply with the rules of the road.

Regulations have been around for tens of thousands of years and can be found in the very earliest civilizations. The gates of walled towns had to be locked during the night; the walls had to be patrolled, and taxes had to be collected from the itinerant peddlers who entered during the day.

The ancient Indian, Greek, Egyptian, African, Chinese, and Roman civilizations organized guilds of craftsmen which had the authority to regulate the flow of raw materials and the products of the guild. Guilds came to exercise control over both the means of production and the capital to organize it. The word guild comes from gold, which the guilds held for the common benefit of members.

Guilds evolved into systems of trademark and patents, chambers of commerce, labor unions, institutes, corporations, insurance companies, and banks. All of these enterprises are founded upon regulation for the common good.

Following feudalism, capitalistic economies have prevailed throughout the modern world and have provided the means for economic growth and industrialization. Essentially, property, capital, and the means of production are privately owned, and the distribution of goods and services is determined by the availability of profits in the marketplace. Labor is owned by the individual who supplies it, and his or her wages are subject to the needs and demands of the market.

Greed is another word with negative connotations. Virgil said, "Curst greed of gold, what crimes thy tyrant power has caused." However, the desire for profits and the accumulation of capital and property fuel the engine of capitalism.

Just as our modern society could not exist without regulation, it could not exist without a financial system, largely based on self interest, to provide the money and credit required to allow the free enterprise system to work. The two factors must be balanced, however; otherwise the economy does not take all interests into account and will ultimately fail.

Aileana had done some research on Alan Greenspan and market regulation, which she shared.

Greenspan was the chairman of the Federal Reserve System for 18 years, from 1987 to 2006. As a young man in the early 1950s, he became a disciple of the writer Ayn Rand, who espoused a philosophy known as "Objectivism." The philosophy emphasized individual and property rights, laissez-faire capitalism, and limited government. Rand rejected altruism or self-sacrifice as a moral ideal and promoted the "Virtue of Selfishness," or a "concern with one's own interest." Others who have expressed an admiration for Rand include President Ronald Reagan, Supreme Court Justice Clarence Thomas, Congressman Ron Paul and radio personality Rush Limbaugh.

As the "Maestro" of the economy for almost two decades, Greenspan presided over the deregulation and near destruction of the financial system; however, he reluctantly admitted during Congressional testimony in 2008 that the self-correcting power of *free markets had failed to prevent the self-destruction caused by irresponsible mortgage lending practices.*

History has demonstrated that a capitalist system does a better job of distributing goods and services than any government-controlled economy, such as communism. While free markets are essential to a capitalist system, unrestrained greed will ultimately destroy the economy. The world-wide, interconnected global economy is too essential to all societies to allow the economy to be unregulated and controlled by individuals and corporations motivated by greed.

Regulations established for the public good must control the inherently destructive avarice and greed of individuals, while allowing the economy to operate as freely as possible within mandatory guidelines that are based on experience. These regulations must restrict the accumulation of excessive monopolistic power and the growth of organizations that otherwise become "too big to fail." They must require that all financial trading take place in open exchanges and that operations be transparent and reported to regulators.

In a letter to his Secretary of Treasury in 1815, Thomas Jefferson wrote, "The treasury, lacking confidence in the country, delivered itself bound hand and foot to bold and bankrupt adventurers and bankers pretending to have money . . . ." Jefferson grasped the concept that bankers create money out of nothing by providing credit and carrying the debts on their books as assets.

Sam said, "The enormous profits earned by the private banking system could go a long way toward relieving the burden of taxation, if governments, state and federal, would regain the banking function and apply the earned interest to the public good. We have to think about what states can do on their own people, and we have to see what the federal government can do for everyone."

State Banks

I had looked into state banks as a part of my research on the financial system and found the subject to be intriguing. Although many states once operated government banks, the only one left is the Bank of North Dakota, which was formed in 1919 "to promote agriculture, commerce, and industry in North Dakota." The state owns 100 percent of the bank, which is set up as a "DBA," in which the state is doing business as the Bank of North Dakota. State law requires all state funds, including those controlled by state institutions, to be deposited in the bank.

Intended to promote the state's economic and agricultural development, the North Dakota bank's subsidized loans can be as low as one percent. Interestingly enough, North Dakota is one of the only states that has remained fiscally sound during the current Great Recession, and it has a particularly strong educational system.

Between 1940 and the early 1960s, when the Bank of North Dakota began to expand its operations, it served as a depository for state funds and as a municipal bond buyer. Today, it primarily operates as a banker's bank, in that it partners with commercial banks to participate in loans and share risks, and to purchase loans, which frees up banks to loan more money.

According to Ellen Brown, an Internet writer, the North Dakota bank has almost four billion dollars in assets and a loan portfolio of $2.67 billion. It made a profit of $58.1 million in 2008, and over the past 10 years, almost $300 million in profits have been paid into the state's treasury.

The legislatures of a number of other states, including, Oregon, Idaho, Illinois, Florida, Michigan, Washington, Massachusetts, and California, are currently considering the establishment of state banks.

Because many municipalities have taken on heavy bond debt for the construction of infrastructure and have guaranteed the debt of independent authorities that construct toll roads and stadiums, there is a grave likelihood that many of local governments will consider bankruptcy as an escape from the burden of their debts. State banks might be able to step in and help manage some of these debts as an alternative to bankruptcy, or may purchase assets out of bankruptcy.

Sam said, "given the fact that all of the states, individually and collectively, control billions of dollars in assets, it is not unreasonable to assume they can and should put these funds to work for the residents and businesses of their states."

If California were an independent nation, it would have the fifth largest economy in the world. Not counting the real property and other assets it owns, the State's two main public employee retirement systems alone control more than a third of a trillion dollars in assets. Perhaps Californians should open their own state bank.

A National Bank

Clearly, states must stand up to their responsibilities and take action to protect their citizens. One very good way appears to be the establishment of state banks; however, the national private banking system will remain as the elephant in the room, which won't go away as long as it is fed by the government and until it is tamed for the public good.

There are two solutions to the problem. The first is to reregulate the out-of-control banks and other financial institutions, whose gambling addiction has brought the entire world economy to the brink of destruction.

Reasonable regulation is not unachievable. Everyone involved in the financial system, including members of Congress whose job it is to oversee it, is well aware of what needs to be done. The problem is the power and will to do it. As long as these corporations—which operate on the principle of unrestrained greed—have the ability to bribe Congress to do its biding, there is little hope.

There is another companion solution that also presents legislative problems, but which probably could ensure a more secure financial future.

Quite simply, the federal government should dissolve the Federal Reserve System and charter its own national bank, with the government—rather than banks—owning all of the shares.

Hundreds of banks have already become or will become insolvent in the near future. Instead of bailing out these banks, the government should take them over through bankruptcy proceedings and nationalize them. This is the option favored by European governments when banks fail.

The Federal Depositor Insurance Corporation has several options when it is forced to take over a bank to protect its depositors: it can entirely liquidate the bank; it can arrange its sale to and assumption by another bank; or it can take over and operate the bank, at which time the bank's stock becomes the property of the government.

Instead of the half trillion dollars paid as interest each year to bankers, the federal government could be earning interest itself, instead of collecting taxes to pay interest.

Rather than using the $700 billion bailout fund to rescue the banks, the money could have been the ten-percent reserve allowing the provision of $7 trillion in low-interest loans to American individuals and small businesses. The action would have saved the U.S. economy, instead of foreign bankers.

Clearly, the federal government has the power to establish a national bank to exist as a parallel to a system of regulating private banks, but what should be done about the Federal Reserve?

"Yes, what about the Federal Reserve?" Aileana asked. "Where did it come from, what does it do, and why do we need it? I've taken a look at it and I don't like what I see."

Although the President gets to name its chairman, the Federal Reserve System is no more "Federal" than Federal Express. The System consists of 12 regional Federal Reserve Banks, whose stock is owned by the banks they serve. Each reserve bank issues stock, which member banks are required to purchase in order to become member banks. Member banks are

required to maintain their "fractional reserves" in their regional reserve bank. Members cannot sell or pledge their shares; however, they receive a guaranteed six percent annual dividend on their deposits.

With the creation of the Federal Reserve System, the United States government ceased to print money. Instead, the Fed prints money and loans it to the government in exchange for treasury notes. So, for every dollar printed by the Federal Reserve and loaned to its member banks, the national debt of the United States is increased.

The Constitution provides that the Congress can "coin money," in addition to borrowing "money on the credit of the United States." Perhaps, the government should take back the power to print paper money.

Sam said, "The current financial crisis demonstrates one of the great failures of the Federal Reserve in that the money it created was loaned to its member banks, which then sat on the money and refused to invest it in the economic recovery. Instead, the bailout helped banks to show a profit, thereby allowing them to pay billions in obscene bonuses to their executives."

Although the Federal Reserve is not a part of the government, it is a creation of the government, and Congress has the power to change it in any way that benefits the public. To the extent it no longer serves the good of the People and exists to protect its banking members from their own greed and gambling addiction, the government should reclaim its right to print its own currency.

By legislation, the private Federal Reserve could become the People's Federal Reserve, rather than the banker's bank.

As a protector of the People's financial economy, the Reserve could also be empowered to effectively regulate the entire financial system of Wall Street firms, commercial banks, and all other nonbank financial organizations.

Just as the Union survived during the Civil War by the issuance of Greenbacks, the government can simply create the money it needs on government printing presses, or by simple accounting entries.

The fact is that a huge part of our national debt, more than $2.3 trillion, is held by foreign central banks, which use the money they print to purchase our treasury debt. Our dollars are purchased with their currency, and they then use our dollars to purchase our securities. They are doing what we ought to be doing. We should cut out the middle man and issue our own dollars to pay off the treasury debt as it comes due.

We should look at the credit created by a national bank as a public service provided by a public utility, operated for the public good, with its profits dedicated to the good of the People. If the money were spent on things like public transportation, the national infrastructure, and the reasonable reduction of "under-the-water" mortgages, there would be an increase in goods and services, which in turn would fuel both supply and demand, without increasing inflation.

Right now, we are trying to borrow ourselves out of the crisis. This is stupid! Only the banks profit.

Student Loans

Aileana suggested that one simple way to inject money into the economy—which would have an immediate impact on demand—would be for the government to simply assume and pay off all existing student loans.

Outstanding student loans now amount to more than a trillion dollars—more than the total credit card debt of the nation. This debt sits on the back of the very young people our nation depends on to work ourselves out of this horrible recession.

It's not a matter of compassion—it's a matter of self interest. Everyone would benefit from this simple action.

Naturally, forgiveness would be opposed by the banks that hold the debt. They have the best of all worlds. They earn a good rate of interest, the loan is guaranteed by the government, and the debt cannot be discharged in bankruptcy.

There's a very good test: if the banks are against it, it must be good for the nation!

Reasonable Regulation and Transparency

Sam said, "We have to stop looking at the financial system as something like a shopping center where we go to buy what we need, for now and in the future."

We have to recognize that a modern society requires a sophisticated system to deal with supply and demand; however, we, the ordinary People, have to ensure that the system works for our benefit rather than our working for the benefit of the system.

The essence of the financial system is greed—unmitigated greed. The system will lie, cheat, and steal to maintain its profits, and it will do everything in its power to benefit the few who control it, irrespective of the harm it may cause to everyone else.

The system is far too powerful to allow it to regulate itself. It must be controlled, not only for the benefit of the People, but also against its own excesses. We have seen the results of deregulation and the damage done by the casino mentality of bankers. They have a gambling addiction, and they have to be forced to attend counseling as a condition of their probation.

Reasonably regulated and operating in a transparent manner, the worldwide financial system can work for the benefit of everyone in every country. But these two things are essential: reasonable regulation and transparency. They are the sine qua non of a free enterprise system.

Free Enterprise

Shortly after Aileana and Sam returned from their honeymoon, I received a very distressing telephone call. Aileana had not wanted to discuss it in front of Sam, but he had experienced some serious health problems while they were in Vermont. One day when they had planned to hike some of the trails around the lake, he was unable to walk very far from the cabin.

It appeared to Aileana that Sam's health was failing, and she had scheduled several appointments with specialists. One of the early decisions Sam made when he signed the book deal was to establish a California corporation to administer his intellectual property rights, including the publisher advance, and to provide health care for its officers and employees—Sam and Aileana.

As a retired naval officer, Aileana was entitled to lifetime medical care through the military hospital system, and both had rights through the Veterans Administration. In perhaps their best business decision, their corporation had joined the Kaiser Permanente health care system. Kaiser has been providing high-quality nonprofit health care for more than 60 years, primarily to Californians. Sam's primary-care physician scheduled him for a round of visits with various specialists to determine the medical basis of his disability.

After undergoing a comprehensive series of blood tests, MRIs, and other tests prescribed by the specialists, Sam learned the results were both discouraging and encouraging. The doctors were unable to isolate any particular cause for Sam's condition, yet they recognized they had much to learn about the condition known as "Gulf War Syndrome" and the effects of Sam's possible exposure to nerve gas during the conflict.

The only diagnosis the doctors could agree on was chronic fatigue syndrome, which is more a description of symptoms than a diagnosis of illness. They were, however, unanimous that Sam should reduce his activities and rest as much as possible.

Christmas was approaching, and Naomi Washington arrived for a visit to talk about the book's publication schedule and bring us up to date. Because of the high level of continuing public interest in Sam and his philosophy, the publisher was eager to get a book on the shelves of libraries and retailers.

Recognizing, however, that Sam's health was suffering and Aileana was pregnant, Naomi and the publisher had worked out a contract revision that provided for the publication of the book following the chapters on economic matters. Sam's views on other subjects, such as health care, energy, and transportation, would be included as addenda in future editions, as we were able to write them. The book could be ready for release by April, followed by electronic, paperback, audio, and foreign-language editions. The title was *Sam: A Political Philosophy*.

We celebrated Christmas with good food and a continuation of the tradition we started our first year together of decorating the tree at the beach house with special and memorable ornaments. Heather made a papier-mâché baby angel, and Xiomara and I brought a hand-blown glass globe. Sam and Aileana hung the porcelain figure from the top of their wedding cake on the tree, along with hand-carved wooden ornaments they had found in Vermont for K.D. and the baby.

New Year's Day 2009 was marked by our excitement about many things, including the imminent release of the book, the pending inauguration of America's first African American President, and the expected birth of Sam and Aileana's child.

Sam: A Political Philosophy

Born of peasant stock, Aileana was the image of healthy motherhood. She no longer ran on the beach sand every day, but she did take a brisk walk each morning to the Hermosa Pier. She returned to meet Sam at the house for a slower stroll to downtown Manhattan Beach, where they often had breakfast together.

An amniocentesis had revealed no latent defects, but Aileana and Sam decided to keep the baby's sex as a surprise of birth. Heather's birthday is on April 27, and with the baby due in late April, she was confidently predicting they would share the same birthday.

We had watched the inauguration of Barack Obama as the 44th president of the United States on January 20th, followed by his signing the American Recovery and Reinvestment Act on February 17th.

We gathered a couple of weeks later to celebrate Sam's birthday and plan how we were going to wrap up the book.

Sam had just turned 41 years old and, in spite of his weariness, his spirits were good and he was looking forward to continuing work on the book. He wanted next to take a look at the concepts of capitalism, businesses, and the labor movement and talk about how the elements should work together in a free enterprise system.

We had already submitted the chapter on *Money Matters* to the publisher, and Sam, who continued to be a voracious reader, wanted to brainstorm about free enterprise before we proceeded.

In order to determine where our economy is heading and what it should be when we arrive, we have to look back in time to see how it started. Not just at the development of industrialization, corporations, and the labor movement in the last few hundred years, but thousands of years to the very beginning of human civilization.

When archeologists and paleontologists examine the physical remains of our earliest civilizations, they nearly always find evidence of trade. Materials such as red ochre, semi-precious stones, and sea shells are often found hundreds of miles from their source, which can only mean that something of abundance in one location had an increased value at another, where it was scarce or unavailable.

Evidence of trade can be found not only between cultural groups, but within cultures as well. Undoubtedly, specialization arose early in human development when skilled individuals achieved a unique ability to create stone tools and weapons, which could be traded for food. These early craftsmen could remain at home from the hunting and gathering, yet be able to earn a living for themselves and their families.

From the evidence, it also appears the elderly, who could no longer physically earn a living, were supported and cared for because of their cultural knowledge, such as medicine and the means of survival.

Written language originated with clay tokens representative of trade commodities near the end of the Fourth Millennium BCE. These evolved into account-keeping devices, before being used to depict spoken language.

As early as 2100 BCE, written language was first used to describe a system of laws, which included provisions for commerce. Almost half of the Code of Hammurabi, written around 1772 BCE in Iraq, was dedicated to the laws of contract, including matters such as wages, liability for construction defects, and the impeachment of judges who reached incorrect decisions.

Throughout recorded history, we find that peaceful fair trade of commodities and the products of labor is intrinsic to human society and is more representative of its essential nature than the violent wars of conquest—which are often about commercial issues or commodities. This includes the oil wars now being fought in the Middle East.

At the same time, we also find an ongoing concern for achieving a balance between the labor of individuals and entrepreneurs who organize and profit from the labor of others. Indeed, the tension between the two, and how it is resolved for the benefit of both, is necessarily at the heart of every economic system.

In our lifetimes, we have observed the rise and failure of communism, which attempted to shift the benefit of the surplus value of labor from the capitalist to the worker. In its place, China and Russia have replaced the dictatorship of the workers with differing forms of state capitalism.

Overly simplified, if communism is a dictatorship of the workers and fascism is a dictatorship of the capitalists, then it appears the governments of the world, including the United States, are shifting in the direction of modern fascism.

There has to be a better way to accommodate the essential economic nature of human civilization, while protecting the freedom of workers to profit from their labors and the freedom of capitalists to benefit from their investment in the production of capital goods and services through the labor of others.

As background for a continued discussion of current economic affairs, Sam had asked me to briefly review the history of capitalism, corporations, and the United States economy.

Capitalism

The word, capital has come to be equated with money or inventory, particularly where capital produces interest, or an increase in value. The meaning evolved from *caput,* the proto-Indo-European word for head, which was applied to moveable things, such as *cattle* and *chattel*.

The word, capitalist was used by a number of authors during the Seventeenth and Eighteenth Centuries in their discussions of the economy, property and taxation. It was, however, Karl Marx and Friedrich Engels who provided the modern definition in *Das Kapital,* to describe someone who privately owns capital. Writing in *The Communist Manifesto,* they believed that workers were exploited by the private ownership of the means of production in a market economy—if the government failed to protect the rights of labor.

The communist solution was the common ownership of all means of production and the central planning of the economy by a dictatorship of the working class (proletariat) and the suppression of the wealthy class (bourgeoisie).

The most common definition of modern capitalism is an economic system based on the private ownership of the means of production, which allows for the creation of goods and services for profit.

In its purest form, free-market capitalism allows the balance of supply and demand to establish the price for goods and services, without the intervention of the government. All property is privately owned, and the government is limited to ensuring property rights and protecting the life and liberty of individuals.

With the decline of communism, state ownership of all means of production no longer exists in any modern nation—North Korea can hardly be considered a modern nation. To varying degrees, national economic systems are now largely market based, with both private and public ownership of the means of production.

Also, to varying degrees, all governments influence their economic systems through the use of subsidies, taxes, patents and copyrights, tariffs, and the regulation of monopolies.

Corporate Power

In addition to protecting the life and liberty of individuals, governments also provide the legal foundation and protection for the rights of non-person corporate and business entities to conduct business and to enforce their contracts.

Early Roman law recognized a legal concept in which a body of people, or *corpus,* could legally own property and act through agents in making and enforcing contracts. By the time of Emperor Justinian in the Sixth Century, legal entities included guilds of skilled craftsmen and business traders. In addition to being able to act like individual persons, corporations were able to survive beyond the lifetimes of their members. In doing so, they were able to accumulate wealth and power, including the ability to influence and control the governments that facilitated their creation.

The modern corporation began to emerge during the colonial period with the chartering of numerous organizations, such as the Dutch and English East India Companies, by the colonizing nations. These corporations were awarded trade monopolies in their designated geographic areas and exercised the naval, military, police, and diplomatic powers usually reserved for national governments.

The profits earned by these companies were enormous, and they were able to raise huge sums of money by selling stock to the public.

The American colonies were founded by these corporations, such as the Virginia Company and the Massachusetts Bay Company. The freedoms ultimately sought by the colonies were in reaction to the power exercised over them by the companies and the British government that created them and provided them trade and taxation advantages.

America's founding fathers were influenced by the system of natural liberty espoused by Adam Smith in *The Wealth of Nations* and others, who argued for markets freed from monopolies and other restrictions imposed on the colonies. The Boston Tea Party was an attack upon the economic power of the British East India Tea Company, which was unfairly cutting into the profits of colonial merchants.

The states were united by the Constitution and by a profound distrust of corporations, which were not allowed to own other corporations or participate in politics. Initially, corporate law in the United States emphasized protection of the public interest. Corporations required a charter from a state legislature, and they were tightly regulated. Because of this control, early industrialists such as Andrew Carnegie and John D. Rockefeller avoided incorporation in favor of limited partnerships and trusts.

All of this changed early in the Nineteenth Century when the U.S. Supreme Court—in the absence of legislation and in a series of self-generated decisions—began to endow corporations with the rights of individuals. Corporate charters were deemed to be "inviolable," and they could not be arbitrarily amended or abolished by the states that issued them.

Subsequent decisions allowed corporations to enjoy many, if not most, of the constitutional protections originally intended for individuals, including the Fourteenth Amendment rights of due process and First Amendment rights of free speech. Essentially, corporations became super persons with virtually unlimited power and everlasting life.

Today, most economists would agree with University of Chicago professor Milton Friedman, who famously said the one and only responsibility of business is "to use its resources and engage in activities to increase its profits."

Sam said he had heard enough about the growing power of corporations and how they had moved from operating for the public good to compelling the public's government act for their benefit. "Many who rely on the principles of Adam Smith and who quote Friedman fail to mention that Friedman went on to say that a corporation should act without deception or fraud."

There is no doubt that trade is a basic part of human nature, and we require corporations if we are to have a modern complex society. We must also recognize that unregulated corporations with powers far beyond that of any human pose one of the greatest dangers to individual freedoms in the United States and in every nation on Earth.

As one of the seven deadly sins, greed is an excessive and selfish desire to acquire or possess more than what one needs for basic survival and comfort. In particular, as the prime motivation for corporate power and the desire of corporate officers for wealth and status, greed represents the acquisition of more than what one deserves.

Virtually every check on unbridled corporate power, including an effective labor movement, has been defeated, allowing corporations to seize unprecedented political power in the United States.

The pursuit of profit by every possible means, legal or illegal, threatens every economic system that relies on an equality of the freedom of the markets and the freedom of workers. The concept of free enterprise requires a balance between the power of capital and labor, and achieving that balance is its primary challenge and must be its ultimate goal.

To obtain and sustain the balance between business and labor required to establish a truly free enterprise system, we must take steps to ensure that constitutional guarantees are limited to individuals. Moreover, effective laws must be enacted and enforced to effectively regulate corporations and the national economy, and to guarantee the right of labor to organize and to effectively represent its members.

Industrialization and Labor

Organized labor began with the association of skilled craftsmen and artisans into guilds during the medieval period. Masons, carpenters, glass workers, carvers, and textile workers sought to control access to materials, the secrets of their trades, and prices. Essentially, they were small business owners who sold their own products and services and employed apprentices and other workers to help them. Ultimately, hundreds of trades and professions were granted patents to represent their members. The organization of guilds led to self government in towns, and guildhalls were used for the first town councils.

Skilled workers were among the first settlers in America, and guilds representing carpenters, cabinet makers, and cobblers were formed in its first cities. The Continental Congress met in the Carpenter's Hall of Philadelphia, and the Declaration of Independence was signed there in 1776.

These skilled workers were among the first to organize and withhold their labor for higher wages. Among the first to strike for higher pay and shorter hours were New York printers in 1794. The Federal

Society of Journeymen Cordwainers (shoemakers) was organized the same year in Philadelphia.

With industrialization, both skilled and unskilled workers began to organize into unions to improve their working conditions. The organization of capital to build large factories operated by water and steam power was met by the organization of unions to represent the workers. The Mechanic's Union of Trade Associations was formed in 1827 to unite the craft unions in Philadelphia, and it was followed by the International Typographical Union in 1852.

The National Labor Union was formed in 1866 as an alliance of labor unions to agitate for an eight-hour work day. This was followed by the Knights of Labor, which gained hundreds of thousands of members, but fragmented over differences between skilled and unskilled workers—who could be more easily replaced.

The movement for an eight-hour working day became known as the Great Upheaval.

Commencing in 1877, mass strikes, primarily by railroad workers, were supported by other workers and small business owners across the country. Strikers were encouraged by townspeople, local officials, and even the militia—which was dispatched by state governors to deal with strikers. Solidarity with strikers extended across disparate industries and was supported by store keepers and workers alike. Thousands assembled under the banner of the Knights of Labor, which rejected socialism and endorsed republicanism.

The American Federation of Labor was organized in 1886 as a federation of skilled labor unions by Samuel Gompers, who represented cigar makers. Efforts to organize effective strikes were frustrated by legal injunctions violently enforced by the military and police officers.

The labor movement gained strength during strikes by the United Mine Workers in 1902— which resulted in the formation of a presidential commission to study their complaints—and the tragic Triangle

Shirtwaist factory fire in 1911—which led to legislation regulating industrial safety.

At about the same time, the Industrial Workers of the World (IWW) were successfully organizing thousands of unskilled factory workers. The IWW went on strike in Lawrence, Massachusetts, when textile factory owners reduced wages by one third in response to state legislation cutting the work week from 54 to 52 hours. The strike was supported by the public, which "adopted" the hungry children of strikers, and was violently suppressed by police officers. Mothers and their children were attacked at the train station to prevent them from traveling to their adopted homes. Widespread publicity of the violence resulted in a union victory.

The U.S. Department of Labor gained presidential cabinet status in 1913 to protect the rights of workers. It was followed by the Clayton Act the next year, which specifically held that "the labor of a human being is not a commodity or article of commerce" within the meaning of antitrust laws, which had been used to obtain injunctions against strikes. The Act limited the use of injunctions against legal boycotts, strikes, and picketing.

Following World War I and the communist revolution in Russia, the National Association of Manufacturers led an attack on the trade union movement as being an un-American conspiracy. Strikebreaking and blacklisting were tolerated by the government, and many workers were forced to sign "yellow dog contracts," promising not to strike, as a condition of employment.

Newly elected President Franklin D. Roosevelt appointed Frances Perkins as his Secretary of Labor in 1933. A strong advocate of worker's rights, she had helped investigate the Triangle Shirtwaist disaster and became the first woman to receive a cabinet appointment.

A gifted administrator who served throughout Roosevelt's four terms, Secretary Perkins was responsible for much of the New

Deal legislation dealing with labor matters, including the Civilian Conservation Corps, the Public Works Administration, the National Industrial Recovery Act, the Social Security Act, and the Fair Labor Standards Act, which established minimum wage and overtime laws for all American workers.

United Mine Workers president John L. Lewis created the Committee for Industrial Organization (CIO) in 1935 to organize all workers in specific industries, irrespective of their jobs or skill levels. Because of differences, the CIO unions were expelled from the AFL. The AFL continued to represent primarily the skilled workers of specific employers, while the CIO represented the unskilled workers in entire industries.

Encouraged by the support of the Roosevelt administration, the AFL and CIO successfully organized millions of American workers. The two groups merged into the AFL-CIO in 1955. The percentage of workers represented by unions peaked at 35 percent in 1954, and total membership peaked at 21 million workers in 1979. Since that time, private sector representation has declined, while public service union membership has increased. Only 11.3 percent of American workers presently belong to a union, having declined from 20 percent in 1983. The effect of union representation is reflected in paychecks, with a median weekly income of $973 for union workers and $763 for unrepresented workers.

Sam said, "To a certain extent unions became the victims of their own success, as the corporate powers were able to inflame resentment by lower-paid and unrepresented workers against higher-paid union workers."

One of the most successful strategies of the Republican Party and its corporate base was the conversion of primarily white, blue-collar workers and their families from the Democratic Party to the Republican Party. Many of these workers, who were conservative in their support of the military and opposed racial integration and school busing were targeted for exploitation.

Nixon called them the Silent Majority, and conservative Christian evangelists said they were the Moral Majority. Workers were encouraged by the language of free enterprise, populism, religion, and family values to oppose racial, gender, social and economic equality.

Representing the corporate and wealthy elites, Ronald Reagan proclaimed a "New Right" and gained the support of former Southern Democrats, hard-hat workers, and Christian evangelicals.

The corporate propaganda campaign continues to entice millions of working people to act and vote against their own economic interests. They are willing to accept low-wage, no-benefit employment as part-time workers or independent contractors in the belief that they can get rich and live the good life—if they work hard and don't complain. They have about as much chance of winning the lottery.

The failure of organized labor affects more than the workers—it has an effect on the entire economy. If workers are forced to accept poverty level wages, they will not have the income to purchase the goods and services provided by the economy. Even the industrialist Henry Ford believed his assembly line workers should earn enough money to pay for the cars they produced.

Not only are most American workers not represented by a union, they are not represented by any political party. The "New" Democratic Party now represents the same narrow corporate interests as the Republican Party. The alternative Libertarian Party does not believe in any government support of labor or working conditions, and while the Green Party supports "social justice and equal opportunity," it does not offer specific programs to protect the rights of workers.

Every person, whether in the private or public sector, a blue or white-collar worker, a small business owner, or corporate executive, has an interest in ensuring there is a balance between the rights of labor and capital. Otherwise, a true free enterprise system cannot exist.

Free Enterprise

That balance was once provided by unions acting with the encouragement of government laws and regulations, but corporate power over both major political parties has largely eliminated fairness in the system. The ability of corporations to obtain "right to work" laws and influence regulatory agencies to abandon their responsibilities is increasingly leaving workers with little or no power or control over their own labor.

Rather than establishing a Labor Party, such as those in European countries, workers and small business owners need to organize in a bipartisan effort to eliminate the constitutional protection now being provided to nonperson entities, such as corporations and labor unions. Capitalists should have the right to organize businesses and corporations, and workers should have the right to organize labor unions, but both should be subject to reasonable regulation for the public good.

Fair employment practices, safe working conditions, and sustainable wages are in the interest of everyone, not just workers and their labor unions. Raising the level of income and leisure benefits everyone. While increased productivity may benefit the corporate bottom line in the short term, lower wages and longer hours will ultimately harm the economy.

The appropriate role of government should be the establishment of reasonable standards, legal presumptions, and minimum damages allowing workers—whether or not represented by a union—to obtain a fair and just adjudication of their claims.

There can be no effective right to pursue happiness without a free enterprise system that provides a balance between labor and capital.

The Dangers of Globalization

Aileana said events were taking place on an international scale that might render irrelevant any advances in labor legislation and regulation in the United States.

My parents were hard-working small business owners who believed in the principles of Republicanism, as represented by

Sam: A Political Philosophy

President Eisenhower. He said, "Today in America unions have a secure place in our industrial life. Only a handful of unreconstructed reactionaries harbor the ugly thought of breaking unions. Only a fool would try to deprive working men and women the right to join the union of their choice." He also said, "I have no use for those—regardless of their political party—who hold some foolish dream of spinning the clock back to the days when unorganized labor was a huddled, almost helpless mass."

Just as Eisenhower feared the Military-Industrial Complex, I believe if he were alive today, he would fear international corporations. They have created a series of international banking and trade agreements that provide them with the power to dominate all of the world's governments.

The United States has entered into a number of international agreements, such as the World Trade Organization. These powerful nongovernmental organizations are now "harmonizing" the laws of all nations through the use of Dispute Resolution Panels to review complaints by corporations against governmental organizations that "unfairly restrain trade." National laws intended to protect consumers, workers, or the environment can be overturned by these panels that act in secret. Moreover, offending countries can be ordered to reimburse corporations for their lost profits.

The Philip Morris tobacco corporation is currently in litigation with the nations of Uruguay, Norway, and Australia, alleging their anti-smoking legislation devalues its cigarette trademarks and investments and deprives it of profits. The matter will be decided by binding arbitration before the International Center for Settlement of Investment Disputes.

President Clinton obtained ratification of the North American Free Trade Agreement (NAFTA), which had been negotiated during the Bush I administration. NAFTA is a complex, rules-based trade agreement between the United States, Canada, and Mexico. Clinton said the agreement would create "American jobs, and good-paying American jobs." Following NAFTA, production was moved from the United States to Mexican factories just south of the border, where export goods are produced using low-wage workers. The AFL-CIO has documented the transfer of 700,000 well-paying American jobs to Mexico.

Two major trade agreements are presently being negotiated in great secrecy. These are the Trans-Pacific Partnership, which includes the United States and 11 other Asia-Pacific Rim nations, and the Transatlantic Trade and Investment Partnership between the European Union and the United States. If ratified, the combination of these trade agreements will govern almost all of the world's economic output.

Under the Supremacy Clause of the Constitution, federal law and treaties are the Supreme Law of the Land. Such treaties, including these trade agreements, become binding on all judges, "anything in the constitution or laws of any state to the contrary notwithstanding."

These international financial and trade agreements restrict the ability of the United States to regulate matters concerning its own society, including the taxing of corporations, in any way that violates free trade. The agreements create a shadowy unelected worldwide economic government, that is controlled by corporations, for the benefit of corporations. The people have value in the equation only as workers and consumers. Globalization has contributed to the growing inequality in the international distribution of wealth.

Sam said, "there is a lesson to be learned from a visit to a modern automobile factory where the assembly line workers have been replaced by computerized robots, which are never sick, tired, disgruntled, depressed, or on strike."

Sam: A Political Philosophy

The lesson is not that we should return to the past and re-employ human workers to do the mundane tasks that can be so easily and effectively performed by mechanical robots. The lesson is that the corporations that have taken control of our government by obtaining the constitutional rights of people are mindlessly robotic in their operations.

These corporate robots are programmed with greed and endowed with an absence of conscience, and they are at war against human workers. The weapons they deploy are mistrust, prejudice, and fear, and like a viral infection, these insatiable robots have invaded the democratic republic of the United States of America. They have deprived the people of their free will, and they feed on human energy. Unless they are identified, isolated, and inoculated against, these corporate robots will ultimately destroy their host.

There is much more to an economic system than the accumulation of wealth and the purchase of stuff. The love of our friends and family and the respect and honor we gain through honesty and hard work all have value and must be accounted for in a system of free enterprise. After leading the people of India to freedom, Mahatma Gandhi was murdered by a religious extremist. An inventory of his entire worldly possessions included a pair of sandals, a homespun loin cloth, and a pair of eyeglasses. Can it be said that he died poor?

A Smart and Simple Tax

Early on, Sam had shared his ideas about taxation. Although they were brilliant in their simplicity, we agreed the reader needed a context to understand and appreciate his thinking. Aileana and I researched some of the issues as a foundation for Sam's tax plan. The work had been largely completed, including a transcription of Sam's discussion, and we decided it should logically follow the *Free Enterprise* chapter.

Historical Background

Today, the United States government is primarily funded by a tax on the income of all individuals, businesses, and corporations. It is a crime to evade the payment of lawful taxes, random audits are used to keep us honest, and the tax is automatically deducted from most of our paychecks. The federal income tax, however, depends on voluntary compliance with the law, primarily through self reporting.

Most of us want to believe the income tax system is fair and equitable; otherwise we would not tolerate it. Once we lose faith in the fairness of the system, widespread cheating becomes the norm, and once our tax system becomes entirely confiscatory for working taxpayers, violent revolution cannot be far behind.

Commencing in 1817, Congress eliminated all internal taxes and funded the government by tariffs on imported goods. While tariffs increased the cost of goods imported from outside the country, they were largely paid by the wealthy and larger businesses. Laborers, farmers, and small business owners paid little or no taxes because the goods they consumed were primarily manufactured in the United States.

Enforced by a new Internal Revenue Service, Congress passed an income tax during the Civil War, along with sales, excise, and inheritance taxes. The income tax was progressive in that those who earned less than $10,000 paid only three percent, while those who earned more were taxed at a higher rate.

Congress eliminated the income tax in 1868, and although it later flirted with taxing income, the government mainly relied on tariffs and an internal tax on tobacco and liquor for revenue. The U.S. Supreme Court ruled in 1896 that federal taxes on income violated the Constitution—since they were not apportioned among the states.

The Sixteenth Amendment in 1913 allowed Congress to tax the incomes of both individuals and corporations. Taxes continued to increase over the years, and with the introduction of payroll withholding in 1943, most Americans were forced to pay a tax on their incomes.

Initially, the wealthy and corporations were taxed much more heavily than individuals. When Eisenhower was president, corporations paid approximately a quarter of all federal taxes, the maximum tax rate on top earners was 92 percent, excise taxes brought in 19 percent of tax revenue, and most workers paid minimum Social Security payroll taxes.

Today, corporations pay only about 12 percent of income taxes, and the maximum rate is only 35 percent for all those who earn more than $372,950—even those who receive millions or billions each year.

It gets even worse!

In August 2008, the Government Accountability Office reported that two-thirds of all U.S. corporations and 78 percent of foreign companies doing business in the United States paid no federal income taxes

A Smart and Simple Tax

between 1998 and 2005—even though they booked billions of dollars in receipts.

The Gross Domestic Product of the United States was shaping up to be almost $14.2 trillion in 2008. From this, the government took in $1.2 trillion in estimated receipts and sustained an estimated deficit of $390 billion.

Approximately 45 percent of the revenues comes from individual income taxes, 36 percent from Social Security and other payroll taxes, 12 percent from corporate income taxes, three percent from excise taxes, 1.2 percent from estate and gift taxes, 1.3 percent from customs duties, and 1.5 percent from other sources. The Tax Policy Center calculates that individual income taxes and payroll taxes now account for four out of every five federal revenue dollars.

There have been a number of tax reform initiatives, and Aileana documented some of the more interesting ones.

Some have proposed eliminating the progressive income tax in favor of a single flat rate for everyone, in hopes of shutting down the income tax industry and the IRS; however, the proposal has had little traction since it would further shift the tax burden from the wealthy to small-business owners, the middle and working classes, and the poor.

A more popular proposal is known as the Fair Tax. Essentially, the Fair Tax is a national sales tax designed to entirely eliminate the income tax and individual tax filings.

Proponents, including Libertarians at the Cato Institute, envision a tax of 18 percent to 23 percent on the final sales of all goods and services. There would be no tax on exports, intermediate business transactions, or security transactions.

To help counteract the inherently regressive effect of sales taxes on the poor, everyone, including the wealthy, would receive monthly rebates allowing the annual expenditure of an amount equal to the federal poverty level to be tax free.

The current collapse of the banking industry has caused several commentators to propose a tax on financial transactions not only to raise tax revenues, but also to put a damper on the outrageous trading of securities that caused the crash.

Considering that, this year alone, the annual trading of over-the-counter derivatives amounted to $743 trillion globally, the imposition of a .5 percent tax on the short-term speculation in currency transactions, commodities, stocks, and derivatives would produce $371.5 billion.

Currently, these transactions are not taxed at all, allowing banks, such as Goldman Sachs, to pay an income tax of only one percent. This is so, even though Goldman Sachs is gambling with sophisticated trading software that allows it to place high-speed bets that cheat ordinary investors.

The idea of a financial transaction tax is based on the 1972 proposal by James Tobin, a Yale professor who won the Nobel Prize for economics.

Tobin viewed the world economy as being disrupted by currency speculation, in which money moved around the world as bets on the fluctuations in exchange rates. Tobin believed that the imposition of a small tax on every currency transaction would disrupt the currency gamblers, while imposing a trivial burden on those legitimately engaged in foreign trade or long-term investment.

Replacing the Income Tax

Sam believed Plato was right when he said, "When there is an income tax, the just man will pay more and the unjust less on the same amount of income."

The burden of taxation in the United States has been shifted from those who most benefit from our government to those who work the hardest and earn the least. This shrugging of responsibility is not only unfair, but it also

A Smart and Simple Tax

fails to accomplish public policy goals required to move the economy out of recession and the environment out of crisis.

Uncorrected, the heavy burden of taxation borne by workers and small business owners today for the benefit of corporations and the wealthy elite will certainly lead to chaos and violence tomorrow.

It is time to discard our stupid and complex system of unfair taxation and replace it with a smart and simple tax that balances the burden of taxation with the benefits of government.

Wouldn't it be more sensible and much fairer to simply tax the movement of all money in our economy? Not a sales tax, not a value-added tax, not a flat income tax, not a speculation tax, but rather a simple toll on every single financial transaction that occurs within our economic system. Not just every time you buy a loaf of bread, but every time stocks and bonds are bought and sold, every time currencies are traded, and every time Exxon-Mobil invests in a new oil rig.

Since the working-, middle-, and small-business-classes have far fewer and much smaller financial transactions, the wealthy and the multinational corporations, who spend a lot of money to avoid having any "taxable income," would have to share proportionally in paying the toll for their traffic on our economic highway and their use of our courts and institutions to enforce their contracts and facilitate their profits.

Why should so many of our largest corporations completely escape the payment of any taxes?

It is likely the federal government could operate on the revenues produced by a simple transaction tax of much less than 10 percent on the movement of money. It could be as little as two percent. In addition, the payment of taxes would shift to those who benefit the most from the services of our government—from individuals to the corporations and from the laboring poor to the wealthy elite.

Envision the effect of a slight touch every time money moves, a tiny "ka-ching" in the U.S. Treasury's cash register, which in the aggregate would quickly add up to more than a trillion dollars each year.

Think about the debate in Congress as to whether the tax rate should be 2.25 percent or 2.27 percent for the next year. The difference could produce billions, and the government's books could be honestly balanced every year.

Imagine that most of us would only have to pay an annual tax rate of less than five percent on the amount of money we spend, which in most cases is close to the amount we earn.

Yes, the transaction tax would result in an increase in the overall cost of the goods and services we purchase; however, the toll would apply to every single financial transaction, including the purchase of limousines and spas by the wealthy—who now rely on every imaginable scheme to avoid having any "income" upon which to pay taxes.

Those who enjoy luxuries would pay more for them, and those who gamble in the money markets would have to pay to play in the economic casino.

A tax on all financial transactions would be far more equitable than a flat income tax, which would eliminate the progressive tax rates that exact a greater contribution from those who profit the most from our economy. A flat income tax would further shift the burden of taxation from corporations and the wealthy, who manipulate the system to avoid income, to the rest of us whose taxes are withheld from our salaries.

There would also be a benefit for the wealthy, in that a transaction tax would eliminate the progressive income tax rates to the extent they still exist. The rich would simply pay their fair share based on what they spend on luxuries and on their financial manipulations.

A transaction tax would be similar in some respects to a value-added tax; however, it would apply to all financial transactions, including those intermediate sales involved in the production of all goods and services—not just in manufacturing—and it would be paid at every stage, not just at the end.

A transaction tax was believed to pose impossible accounting problems when first proposed by James Tobin 40 years ago; however, computer technology now allows for instantaneous posting of all financial transactions.

A Smart and Simple Tax

Just as workers' income tax contributions are withheld from their payroll check and sent to IRS each month by employers, computerized banking might allow the tax on corporate and banking financial transactions to be transmitted every single day at the close of business.

Aileana asked it there should be any consideration of policy issues in establishing the transaction tax and, on a practical basis, how the tax would be administered. Sam had apparently given these issues a great deal of thought.

To encourage savings, money invested in Social Security, federally-insured savings accounts, 401(k)s, IRAs, and the earned interest should not be taxed until it is withdrawn and spent. To encourage these safe investments, capital gains on them should not be taxed until they are realized and spent.

To encourage giving, donors should not be taxed; however, the recipient should pay a tax when the gift is received and the money is spent. A gift of property would be considered a completed transaction and taxed as such.

Administration of a smart and simple tax would operate somewhat like the income tax, in that individuals and corporations would still have to prepare an annual tax report documenting money received—rather than as a sales tax where the revenue is collected at the time of the transaction. For most individuals, businesses, and corporations the preparation of tax returns would be greatly simplified. The system of withholding estimated taxes from salaries and refunds, and the prefiling of estimated taxes by businesses would remain intact.

Let's say a married couple earns $100,000 of joint income. Their employers would still prepare and file 1099 and W2 forms, and the couple would file a return setting forth their "income." They would then deduct the amount paid for their own health insurance, including Medicare payments, and further reduce their transactions by the amount paid into social security, IRAs, 401(k) plans, and into federally insured savings accounts.

Essentially, from a policy standpoint, these disbursements are not being "spent." Another example might be that tax payers could further reduce the amount spent by what they give away. Charity would be encouraged, and the recipient would pay the tax when the funds were spent.

Since the tax on "income" would be no longer exist, elimination of the tax-free status of non-profit organizations should be seriously reconsidered as a policy matters. There is no good reason for allowing many of these multi-millionaire organizations and religions to continue to accumulate great wealth and avoid paying reasonable taxes on what they spend.

When all of the deductions are added up and credited against their income, the difference would be what the couple had actually spent for the year. That would be the actual amount taxed—at a very low rate.

There would also be great benefits to businesses and corporations. To the extent they are owned by U.S. citizens and salaries are paid to citizens, businesses, corporations, and other organizations should not have to pay a transaction tax on their payroll, as salaries would be directly passed through to their employees to spend (and to be taxed).

Thus, if 100 percent of a corporation's stock is owned by American citizens, or by other businesses or corporations that are owned entirely by American citizens, the corporation should not have to pay any taxes on the salaries paid to American workers. Or if 50 percent is owned by citizens, the corporation should only have to pay half of the payroll transaction tax.

The transaction tax would be paid on payrolls to American workers by foreign owners as the price of the owner's access to the services of our healthy and well-educated workers and to our free-market economy and system of justice.

Payrolls paid to foreign workers by American corporations would also be subject to the transaction tax, as the money would not pass through into our economy. This policy would reverse the current trend of outsourcing American jobs offshore to other countries?

Inasmuch as there is a movement of money when foreign imports cross our borders, tariffs could be replaced by the up-front collection of the transaction tax when foreign corporations transfer their products to their American subsidiaries or when they sell to American businesses. The *movement of goods into and out of the United States would represent a taxable transaction.*

Foreign registration and ownership of U.S. patents, copyrights, and other legal protections should also carry a toll on all protected transactions, requiring non-citizens to share the cost of our courts to enforce their rights.

While a good case might be made for a few public policy tax deductions or exemptions, such as the interest on home mortgages, child care for workers, and other state and local taxes, the final result should be a very broad-based, smart and simple tax that is fairly administered and benefits everyone.

Should Taxation Be Used to Redistribute Income?

Following their national tour and as a result of our many discussions, Aileana had been slowly moderating her Republican leanings; however, her Scottish roots and basic conservatism showed when she told Sam he was overlooking a huge problem—the earned income tax credit (EITC) and the related Child Tax Credit.

The EITC has nothing to do with taxes! Rather, it's the type of redistribution scheme that concerns people like Joe the Plumber during the election. Although the EITC "refunded" more than $36 billion to low income people in 2004, the potential for fraud is high, it consumes audit resources, and many who may qualify don't apply. All of these are good reasons to question whether it should continue to be a part of the tax code.

Since its creation in 1975, the EITC has been continually expanded, even under President Reagan, to provide tax "refunds"(primarily to families with three or more children and married couples) to people who are not required to pay income taxes. It is currently transferring around $44 billion in cash each year to more than 23 million claimants.

The process is so complicated that tax preparers may be required, even for poor families. This may be why as many as 30 percent of those who claim the EITC on their returns do not actually qualify for it. At the same time, as many as 25 percent of the households which actually qualify for the credit do not apply for it.

Many poor families rely on storefront tax preparers, who fill out the paperwork and make Refund Anticipation Loans to the "tax payers," at very high interest rates.

Another area for concern is the fact that many illegal immigrants are encouraged to establish a basis for achieving legal status by filing income tax returns using individual taxpayer identification numbers. While this may be a good thing for the individual and the U.S. Treasury, there is a great potential for abuse, if many or most of the claimed children live outside the United States.

Largely as a result of anti-tax pressures, the government has been steadily reducing its force of revenue agents—now down to 13,000 from its high of 17,000 in 1988. As a result of all of these factors, the IRS now audits far fewer major corporations and those who use offshore tax havens, and it increasingly targets the poor and middle class. Audits have tripled for taxpayers earning between $25,000 and $100,000, and the IRS automatically freezes the refunds of up to one-third of all poor people who are actually entitled to the "tax credits."

"To what extent should the federal government be involved in welfare and the redistribution of wealth is a question I have asked myself, and I'm not sure I have the answer," Sam said. "The people we talked to on our tour said they want a nurturing society, but what does that mean?"

I know the federal government came up with the EITC to help poor people, who have to pay social security and Medicare taxes, and to help achieve a national balance between generous and frugal states. But it doesn't seem to me that federal programs involving millions of families and billions of dollars each year are the most effective way to help people.

There is no question in my mind that we want a government that cares for those who elect it, but efforts of that government should be directed at making the system work well for most of the people who earn their own keep, who help take care of their families, and who help out in their local communities.

Support for those destitute people who cannot provide for themselves, and who are without family resources, should be borne primarily at the local and state level. This minimizes the potential for fraud and maximizes the chances that there will be a societal, rather than an institutional response.

That said, there is also no question in my mind that the disability portions of the Social Security insurance program should remain intact to provide uniform assistance to those who are physically unable to work.

So, I suppose my bottom line response to the EITC problem is not to include it under the Smart and Simple Tax. It probably did not belong in the tax code in the first place and was a Trojan Horse for a national welfare program that continues to grow without direction or limits.

We should be concentrating on making our tax revenues equal the outlays of our federal government to the greatest extent possible. If we carefully budget and use those revenues wisely to effectively provide for the most basic needs of families, such as education, health care, and transportation, and allow people to earn their own food, clothing, and housing, we will probably find that most people will be able to take care of themselves and their responsibilities.

Those who cannot care for themselves, and who are not covered by Social Security, should primarily look to their families, their local communities, and their state governments for assistance.

Tax Fraud and Cheating

Aileana said, "Samuel, you're sounding more like a conservative than a socialist, but how would your Smart and Simple Tax deal with scofflaws who flout the tax laws?"

Tax cheating has become so widespread that ordinary taxpayers are made to feel like fools if they pay what they owe. The federal government fails to collect as much as seven percent of what it is owed each year because of intentional cheating, which is really a fraud on everyone else who pays their fair share, primarily the working and middle classes.

With less to worry about from audits, the very wealthy avoid paying taxes by establishing offshore accounts. These are so difficult to audit that, even to the small extent it does look at them, the government often fails to complete them within the three-year limit. Senator Levin said that the government "should assume that any transaction in a tax haven is a sham."

There are so many loopholes written in the tax system to protect the income of corporations and the wealthy from taxes that the working and middle classes actually subsidize the wealthy. Not only have the tax cuts primarily benefitted the elite, but the tax code also rewards companies that move jobs offshore by allowing them to avoid paying taxes as long as they keep their money offshore.

The Tax Justice Network reports that $11.5 trillion is held offshore by the wealthiest people in the world. Altogether, these wealthy individuals and corporations keep one-fourth of all U.S. stocks and nearly one-third of all of the assets in the world hidden in offshore accounts to avoid paying taxes.

The audacity and heartlessness of those who escape taxation is mind boggling. It makes me want to throw them all in jail, along with their accountants, lawyers, and bought-and-paid-for representatives in government.

"Plato may have been right about taxes," Sam responded, "but what we have to do is to create and enforce a system that is as fair as possible, so that ordinary hard-working taxpayers do not feel they are being taken advantage of."

A Smart and Simple Tax

If and when the smart and simple tax is ever implemented, it should be done in a manner that avoids moving all of the existing loopholes into the new law. Any policy exceptions to calculating the tax on individual and corporate transactions should be restricted to measures that have broad, rather than narrow, benefits. Most of the existing loopholes were placed in the code by narrow interests and work against the common good.

Aileana said there were two things about Sam's smart and simple tax that she liked the most. The first was the tiny tax on every financial transaction would serve to slow down the reckless trading by financial gamblers who had just wrecked the economy, *and* that the tax would transfer the primary burden of taxation from the people to corporations and the financial gamblers.

Paying Our Dues

Sam had some final observations about taxation:

> *The most important thing to remember is that the preamble to the Constitution holds that it was created to "promote the general welfare." We should use that as the standard when establishing tax policy. To the greatest extent possible, the smart and simple tax should be applied to the movement of all money, everywhere and all the time, with very few exceptions.*
>
> *I have been calling my proposal a smart and simple tax, or a toll tax on the movement of money on the economic highway, but if we actually succeed and enact a fair system that works for the vast majority of taxpayers, perhaps we should rethink whether it should be called a tax at all.*
>
> *An OpEd piece in The New York Times suggested we should "stop saying 'taxes' and start calling them 'dues.'"*
>
> *Tax has become a very ugly word, and perhaps we should look upon paying our fair contribution to the operation of a government*

that fairly represents our interests and looks after the health and well being of our families as a reasonable payment of dues.

In a fair system, the government would really become our government, and our membership would be just as valuable as our joining any other organization where we pay dues.

The choice is ours. We do not have to willingly endure corrupt government and unfair taxation.

We who pay the taxes must make the essential decisions about the methods of taxation and the level of payment. Otherwise, we live in slavery and our freedoms are illusory.

A Political Evolution

In the videoed statement at the end of his ordeal, Sam talked about a national policy referendum in which voters determine their own policies, rather than choosing between candidates and the policies they propose.

Sam also talked about a way for voters to protest their lack of effective representation and to personally take control of elections by writing in the name of the individual they choose as their president to effectuate their policy.

Heather joined in our discussions as often as she could find time away from her studies. She firmly believed young people were ready to do something about the threatened economy and environment they were inheriting. Aileana, who was carrying a rapidly growing future citizen, heartily agreed.

As the four of us talked about these ideas, Sam concluded, "What this country urgently needs is a peaceful political evolution, otherwise, we may find ourselves fighting a violent revolution."

How many more lies must we listen to and how many more political scandals must we endure before we become sick enough to demand effective changes in our government? Haven't we suffered enough to force a political evolution to safeguard our freedoms in this country and to avoid committing war crimes against others?

Although we are calculating the cost in thousands of lives and billions of dollars, we cannot imagine the full extent of damage that will flow from our government having misled our nation into an illegal war with Iraq and our innocent sons and daughters into the commission of war crimes.

We can perceive the extent of devastation to our economy, as our representatives waste our hard-earned money, eliminate taxes for their wealthy friends, run up debts for our children and grandchildren to pay in the future, try to destroy our Social Security, encourage the shipment of American jobs out of the country, and allow the international value of our currency to depreciate.

All of us, whether liberal, conservative, or independent are being harmed by the failures of our government and those we've allegedly elected to run it. We must anticipate there are more lies on their lips waiting to be told, even more ugly secrets waiting to be uncovered, and even worse scandals yet to unfold.

The good news is that the American people are perhaps the best, the bravest, and the brightest our human civilization has ever produced. America is the promised land—we are an amalgamation of the races and cultures of Earth.

We will survive and, ultimately, we will achieve a government that better cares for us and is less threatening to the rest of the world. The bad news is that we will have to endure conflict to get there. So, how do we brave the upheaval?

It appeared to me, as a political journalist, the most basic problem with the United States government today is that, irrespective of the party in power, it kowtows to the demands of large corporations and moneyed special interest groups, rather than encouraging the hopes and aspirations of ordinary workers and small businesses.

Every four years the two main political parties construct platforms to serve as publicity gimmicks to get their candidate elected. After the election, both parties generally ignore their platform policies and take care of themselves and their financial supporters, rather than do what they said they were going to do for the voters. The process is supposed to result in policies that reflect the interests of the voters, but it is a disappointment at best. At worst, it is a continuing political disaster.

A Political Evolution

Access by individuals to their elected officials is the foundation of a republican form of government. However, the election of representatives is now more dependent on massive expenditures of campaign contributions from their corporate sponsors, their wealthy friends, and well-funded, single-issue, special interest groups, rather than upon a meaningful vote by an informed electorate. Currently, elections are an exercise in the mass manipulation of voters.

Aileana said, "While there are allegedly some limits on campaign contributions, there are no restraints on institutional schmoozing.

In a brief Internet search, I was able to identify expenditures in just last year of well over $2 billion by special interest groups to lobby the federal government. The Tom De Lay—Jack Abramoff lobbying scandal, arrest of Bush's procurement official, illegal contributions by Freddie Mac, and Congressman Cunningham's bribery conviction are just the tip of a gigantic iceberg.

Sam said, "You're absolutely right Ana, No matter how deeply we ordinary citizens dig into our pockets, we cannot financially compete with the powerful special interests. No matter how well we organize, we cannot match the influence of the financial and political insiders. No matter how often we march and picket, they will always beat us through the side door into the corridors of power."

Not only are we are no longer represented; we have also been stripped of constitutional protections we once enjoyed. Thoughtful people of every political persuasion are increasingly alarmed about the reductions in freedom we have passively accepted in response to 9/11. Many of us, irrespective of party or political beliefs, now question whether the Bill of Rights will survive another terrorist attack, which is sure to come.

Since we have been abandoned by our government, we must collectively focus on a peaceful method to modify our government to one which more attentively considers the needs and protection of all voters, whether Republican, Democrat, Libertarian, Green, or Independent.

An intolerant, nonresponsive, and repressive government cannot endure. The choice is whether political change results from a violent revolution or a peaceful evolution—from a revolt or an evolt.

A National Policy Referendum

One way we can regain control over our government is to require it to hold a formal National Policy Referendum every four years when we vote for our president.

Such a referendum would not make law. Rather, its purpose would be to express the collective policy of the people through their answers to the major political questions that should most concern the new administration and Congress.

Individuals and organizations could recommend policy questions, and Congress would have to debate the issues in formulating the 12 most important policy questions to be listed on a national ballot. Congress can do this by a joint resolution; however, they would have to pass a law to have a uniform national ballot which included the referendum questions.

It is essential there be some way to ensure passage of the policy referendum resolution in time for the presidential election. Perhaps congressional members should be ineligible for reelection if they fail to act, or maybe all national political campaign contributions to parties and presidential candidates should be prohibited until such a resolution is passed.

Once the questions are promulgated, presidential candidates—and other elected representatives—would be forced to take positions on a wide variety of real issues. Politics has been defined as the art of not telling the truth, and politicians quickly learn to avoid telling the truth at all costs.

Because there are special interests on every side of every issue, it is impossible to please everyone, yet the politicians strive onward, lying and denying, twisting and hiding, trying to grab every vote. The best theater can be seen during the presidential debates. Trying to get a straight answer from any of the candidates is like trying to nail spit to a wall.

A Political Evolution

Most importantly, if allowed to vote in a National Policy Referendum, we the voters would be much more likely to study the issues and arrive at our own opinions, rather than to have them spoon-fed to us by AM talk radio, Fox News, and the corporate-controlled op-ed pages.

There are those who might argue that our presidential election is a referendum on the candidates' platform policies; however, the winner-take-all results do not, in any way, suggest our level of support for any of the competing issues. Far too often, the outcome turns on which of the candidates made the fewest mistakes or devised the most effective smear campaign.

A National Policy Referendum is not a national opinion poll. The very process of articulating the political questions, the more lively debate, and our thoughtful vote will validate the results far beyond that attainable by any random sampling, no matter how scientific.

We will not be expressing a snap opinion. Nor, will we be making law. We will make policy!

In a free society, we have a duty to avoid the use of force, even if we believe our existence under ineffectual government is being seriously threatened. It is our duty to peacefully petition our government, before we resort to violence.

If we are to effectively modify our government through a peaceful political evolution, we must be allowed to exercise our vote in a National Policy Referendum. Otherwise, what can we do?

Aileana said, "Although I have less confidence than you that a policy referendum will overcome existing voter apathy and will result in a higher turnout, a referendum might help solve one of the differences between us conservatives and you liberals—who tend to have too many answers and consider too many nuances. We like closure, and having simple questions about what needs to be done would allow for more straightforward answers."

It is essential that everyone hears fair comment and competing points of view. It is far more likely we will thoughtfully consider information and political analysis if we are motivated to vote in a referendum than if we respond emotionally to brief television and radio ads, most of which are designed to evoke a negative reaction. To help raise public awareness, we should resurrect Truman's Fairness Doctrine that Reagan's Federal Communication Commission eliminated.

Very few people read print newspapers anymore, as most of us get our news from local and national televisions shows. More of us are beginning to use the Internet to get information, but control of the media by corporations is a very real cause for concern.

The University of Michigan conducted an extensive study during the late 1940s which showed that the political knowledge of Americans falls into three categories: A very few have a lot of knowledge; about half can answer simple questions about politics; and the rest know next to nothing. What is disturbing is that these statistics have not changed very much over the years, and may, in fact, be getting worse.

The Internet may save us from the asinine corporate media; however, the best result of a policy referendum might be that American voters would feel empowered and would be more likely to seek out the information they need to make informed decisions about critical issues over which they have some power to decide.

A number of countries, like Canada, Sweden, and Switzerland already refer policy matters to their voters for binding decisions. The European Union itself resulted from a referendum in the participating countries. In 2004, Taiwan submitted two policy questions regarding its relations with China to voters in its presidential election. France has submitted several major police questions to its voters, most recently in 2005 regarding the European Union Constitution. No nation, however, holds a policy referendum as a matter of course in association with the routine election of representatives.

I'm basically conservative, and I believe our right to vote in a National Policy Referendum is inherent in our First Amendment right to petition our government for redress. Our right to peacefully assemble and to seek redress was intended as the bedrock of our free society. It is a safety valve to avoid violent revolution.

But a national referendum won't help unless those we elect are forced to pay attention to our interests and to actually carry out our policies. Because of party politics, we keep getting stuck with having to choose the lesser of two evils—continual "fear voting" will ultimately destroy our democracy.

We're all sick of it, but how do we cure it?

Electing the President by Write-In Ballot

Sam imagined combining a National Policy Referendum with a grassroots rebellion in which a majority of Americans actually *write in* the name of the person they want to preside over their government. He believes the people could seize the power that legitimately belongs to them, and he believes the people could peacefully evolve a far more effective and representative government.

Can we trust the current method by which we elect our president? Aren't there good reasons why we should rebel against the present system?

In 2000, more than a half million voters selected Al Gore, the Democratic candidate, over George Bush, the Republican candidate. Bush prevailed, however, in the Electoral College because a fraudulent election in Florida gave him that state's 20 electoral votes, even though the candidates were separated by only a few hundred votes. Bush had an edge, and the fix was in. His brother, Jeb, was governor, and the Florida Secretary of State chaired his election committee.

Not only were thousands of eligible—mostly Democratic—Florida voters disenfranchised before the election, but every effort to manually recount the ballots, including thousands of rejected votes, was blocked by the

Secretary of State. A phony "Brooks Brothers" riot was staged by Republican Party operatives flown in from all over the country to intimidate local election supervisors.

Finally, five Republican-appointed members of the U.S. Supreme Court contrived a politically-motivated judicial decision that reversed a far more reasoned opinion by Florida's high court, which had ordered that every voter's intention be determined as accurately as possible.

Aileana said, "The more I research the 2000 election and look at the 2004 election, the more outraged I become! I was raised to trust and believe our national elections were essentially fair and honest; however, I have come to fear for our republic."

After the 2000 election, Congress passed a $3 billion Help American Vote Act, which encouraged the States to purchase secret computerized voting systems manufactured and maintained by companies whose officers uniformly support the Republican Party.

Walden W. O'Dell was the chief executive of one of those companies, Diebold Inc. In August 2003, he sent a letter to 100 wealthy friends inviting them to a Republican Party fund-raiser at his home in Columbus, Ohio. He said, "I am committed to helping Ohio deliver its electoral votes to the president next year." It sure looks like he did just that.

Under the Digital Millennium Copyright Act, the state and local purchasers of electronic voting systems are not allowed access to any information on how voting results are recorded, nor is there any requirement that the machines provide a paper trail for recounts. One doesn't have to have a master's degree in computer science to conclude that the lack of access was a recipe for fraud, irrespective of the party that controlled the machines.

The 2004 election differed from 2000 in that George W. Bush may have actually received a higher percentage of the popular vote; however, it is becoming increasingly clear that he should

A Political Evolution

have lost in the Electoral College, except for another fraudulent election, this time in Ohio.

The Ohio Secretary of State, Kenneth Blackwell served as the chairman of Bush's Ohio reelection campaign and publicly called Senator Kerry, the Democratic candidate, a "disaster," sure to reap "terrible" and "horrible" results if elected. Not only did Blackwell cause the registrations of Democratic voters to be rejected because they were on the wrong weight of paper, an insufficient number of voting machines were allocated to poor (and largely Democratic) precincts.

When combined with a Republican Party program of aggressively issuing personal challenges to voters and the casting of provisional ballots, the vote suppression tactics led to long lines and waits of up to seven hours to vote, primarily in poor neighborhoods. Many people finally gave up and surrendered their right to vote to physical exhaustion.

Exit polls across the nation appeared to give Kerry an advantage in the popular vote, up to three percent in the swing states of Ohio, Pennsylvania, and Florida. Even before the votes were counted, however, Blackwell was bragging that he had helped deliver Ohio in announcing Bush's victory. In just these three states, the odds of the dramatic swing between the exit polls and the final tabulation have been calculated as 250 million to one!

A computer error allegedly created thousands of nonexistent Bush voters in Ohio, and one lawsuit claimed that official rolls in Ohio's most populous county omitted 170,000 registered voters. It is significant that Bush carried Ohio by fewer than 119,000 votes in an election where more than 90,000 ballots were discarded because they failed to indicate a valid choice for president and more than 23 percent of all provisional ballots were rejected.

Interestingly, the statewide hand count of "acceptable" provisional ballots and absentee ballots (after Blackwell had already declared a victory for Bush) provided Kerry with 54.46 percent of the vote. In several heavily Republican precincts, Blackwell certified election results showing more votes than registered voters—up to 124 percent more!

Attempts to conduct a recount in Ohio's election were frustrated by Blackwell's personal—rather than random—designation of the precincts to be recounted and by earlier visits to many of those same precincts by technicians of the voting machine companies, who may have tampered with the machines to ensure that the machine results matched the precinct's reported tally.

Subsequent examination of Ohio's computerized voting systems demonstrated that the locks to memory cards could be easily picked, and handheld devices could be used to plug false vote counts into machines. Several states, including Ohio and Florida, have since banned computerized voting machines, especially those relying on touch screen technology.

During the joint session of Congress on January 6, 2005, to certify the electoral vote, only one dozen Democratic House members and one Democratic senator stood up to complain about the voting irregularities in Ohio. These few objections did, however, force a debate about Electoral College results for only the second time since 1877. After a two-hour session, the Senate voted 74-1 and the House voted 267-31 to reject the protest. Can it be said that either party truly had the interests of the voters at heart?

Sam believes in voters and fair elections, not in the ability of either or both political parties to manipulate the votes.

Our democratic republic is founded upon our ability to trust the results of our collective vote. Is there any doubt that the advent of blackbox voting, systematic election fraud, and the widespread intimidation of voters dictate that we, the people, seize control of the election process before our chance is lost forever?

A Political Evolution

Each of us must find within ourselves the individual courage and initiative to perform one simple rebellious act—refuse to use the computerized voting machines or any other machine ballot.

Instead of responding like laboratory animals pushing a button or touching a screen in response to the stimulus of the latest ten-second television smear ad, we can each take a little longer to carefully consider the candidates presented on the ballot by the various political parties. Once we decide, we can demonstrate our literacy and our power by clearly writing in our personal choice for president of the United States, whether or not his or her name is on the ballot!"

Aileana said, "That sounds good, Samuel, but half of all voters don't even bother to go to the polls to vote, and less than one quarter actually elect the president for all of us." Sam replied, "Yes, Ana, but just imagine the immense power that would flow to the people if voting truly became universal."

If voter turnout were dramatically increased, and if only 15 to 25 percent of us were to write in our vote, trust that the politicians will be scrambling to ensure that all write-in votes cast for them are legally counted. We would quickly find them registering their willingness to accept every write-in vote naming them for any office of public trust.

All paid political advertising should be prohibited everywhere during the week before the election. Rather than being required by statute to vote as is done in some countries, we should all enjoy a national paid holiday to honor ourselves as voters and to celebrate the most sacred sacrament of our national political religion.

States should be required to register every eligible voter. Polling places should be located in every neighborhood, and no voter should ever be turned away from the polls.

It should become a tradition for the entire family to visit the polls together, and a part of the ritual should be a very careful and public hand count of every vote cast at every polling place.

Sam: A Political Philosophy

We should go to our polling place and thoughtfully answer the policy questions presented on the paper ballot. Then, we should carefully write in the name of the person we want to implement our policy.

Rather than wearing American flags on our lapels and displaying a phony patriotism, we should proudly wear our "I voted. Have you?" stickers and demonstrate true freedom and democracy to the world.

It could take a week or so to patiently hand count—or recount—the paper ballots. So what! It would be a refreshing change in today's world of instant gratification.

We will decide who is in charge of this country and we will chart the direction of its future. We are The Voters!

Aileana asked, "Even if everyone voted using a write-in ballot, what can be done about the likelihood of the Electoral College selecting a president who does not receive the most popular votes? Short of a constitutional amendment eliminating the College, are there other ways of voting that would result in a more accurate result? I have been researching these questions and found some interesting answers."

The plurality, or winner-take-all system we currently use allows a spoiler, such as Green Party candidate Ralph Nader in 2000, to split the vote for one candidate allowing another, who receives far fewer votes than a majority, to become president. In that election, Nader's candidacy was partially underwritten by the Republican Party specifically to split the Democratic vote. If a third party candidate draws enough Electoral College votes, the election would have to be decided by Congress.

The best solution I found is for voters to score each candidate. Instead of just selecting one or another candidate. the voter can assign a value, such as a number of stars, to all candidates.

For example, a Nader voter in 2000 would have been able to award three stars to his or her favorite candidate, but could still award two stars to Kerry, who next best represented her or his interests. Another voter could have awarded Bush two stars, Reform

A Political Evolution

Party candidate Pat Buchanan two stars, and Libertarian Party candidate Harry Browne one star. The scores of all candidates would be totaled to determine the winner in each state.

This system of "range voting" is becoming increasingly popular on the Internet where it is used to rate videos and other presentations. By adding up the total number of points for each candidate, the true favorite is easily identified. It might be possible to use optical recognition scanners to calculate the votes and avoid hand counting, except as a backup.

Had this system been in use in 2000, Gore would have won in states such as New Hampshire and Florida, where the vote was close, and the Nader effect would have been eliminated. The same system could be applied throughout the voting process to ensure that elections to Congress, as well as to state and local offices, best effectuate the voters' selections.

Range voting would lend itself to paper ballots and write-in elections as the voter could be provided with five "bubbles" after each name or blank for write-in selections to be filled in, depending upon the score the voter wanted to assign to each candidate. It might take even longer to count the ballots, but the result would be a far more accurate reflection of the voters' true choices.

Another alternative is the National Popular Vote Interstate Compact which requires all of a state's electoral votes to be cast for the candidate who receives the highest "national vote total." To date, eight states and the District of Columbia have enacted laws to join the Compact. It will become effective when the number of states possessing 270 electoral votes (enough to elect the president) agrees to the new system.

Popular voting for the president is supported by 78 percent of Democrats, 60 percent of Republicans, and 73 percent of independent voters.

Elimination of the Electoral College by constitutional amendment would allow for more than two viable political parties, who could more accurately represent the interests of their members.

Voterism

Sam said he was tired of trying to figure out if there's any real difference between Republican and Democratic politicians, and whether there's a difference between liberals and progressives, libertarians and anarchists, independents and moderates, tea partiers and neoconservatives, or occupiers and greens.

Many people are fed up with being forced to chose between the lesser of two evils, and are afraid to cast a vote of conscience because the worst of two evils might otherwise get elected?

The one thing we all have in common is that we are voters and we are sick and tired of our government being controlled by corporations and special interests groups that could not care less about our happiness, our health, our families, our jobs, or our futures.

What we need is a political philosophy that focuses on the rights and interests of all voters.

Sam said he had been thinking about whether America needed a new political party dedicated to the interests of voters and decided that it would be better if every political party recognized and honored voters as the essential basis of representative democracy. He offered a few new terms and their definitions.

Voterism *is the political belief that a legitimate government must be composed of and created by the voters who elect it, and that the primary purpose of such a government is to care for the needs, aspirations, and interests of those who elect it.*

A **votocracy** *is a government organized to sustain the environment in which its voters live, maintain the economy in which they earn a living,* and defend the rights of every individual to be secure in his or her person and property.

A **voteristic** government continually evolves by encouraging the informed opinion and participation of all potential voters in referenda to develop political policy, not law, and by the election of representatives who are an extension of the voters and who are committed to the effectuation of the policies established by the voters.

A **votercentric** government is one that is founded upon the belief that a free society depends upon the handwritten selection of representatives by voters who use hand-counted paper ballots and who celebrate all national elections with a paid voting holiday.

A **voteric** is a nation whose government is organized according to voteristic principles. It is one in which voting is a sacrament of the national political religion.

A **voterian** believes that a voteristic government can impose only minimal legal restraint on the liberties of each voter in her or his pursuit of happiness.

A **voterist** believes that a votocracy created and controlled by individual voters is the most favorable form of government.

Sam said that **voterism** should not be a new political party; rather it is a way for independent-minded and concerned voters of every political persuasion to think for themselves.

As our rapidly-changing world spins into a new millennium, and the older forms of governments are using new forms of technology to become more repressive of and less responsive to their electors, isn't it time for all of us to consider a transformation in how we organize for the common good?

A Peaceful Political Evolution

I had recently read *Washington's Crossing*, an excellent history of the near failure of the American Revolution in the winter of 1776, and was encouraged that Americans might be ready for a peaceful political evolution.

The author, David Hackett Fischer concluded that it was not Washington's leadership or the victories at Trenton and Princeton that saved the revolution following the colonials' resounding defeat in New York City. Rather, the victories resulted from the revival of spirit that arose among the ordinary people in the Delaware Valley as they began to read Thomas Paine's *American Crisis*.

According to Fischer, "This great revival grew from defeat, not from victory. The awakening was a response to a disaster. Doctor Benjamin Rush, who had a major role in the event, believed that this was the way a free public would always work, and the American republic in particular. He thought it was a national habit of the American people (maybe all free people) not to deal with a difficult problem until it was nearly impossible."

As we discussed Fischer's book, Sam said, "Our modern crisis is real; we face a disaster, and the American people have to do something about it. We, the ordinary voters of every party, must evolt against politics as usual and join in a nonviolent bipartisan evolution to transform our government."

If we simple voters are smart enough to earn a living and to figure out how to pay our taxes, and if we have the courage to fight the wars started by our government, we are also entitled to collectively establish basic policy to guide our government and to personally write in the names of the persons we consider most qualified to implement our policies.

I asked Sam what we should do if we are denied our right to vote in a national policy referendum or if our write-in votes for president are not counted.

Well, we might just have to compel a Constitutional convention as provided in the Constitution: "... on the application of the Legislatures of two thirds of the several States, [Congress] shall call a Convention."

A Political Evolution

Perhaps Abraham Lincoln said it best, "This country, with its institutions, belongs to the people who inhabit it. Whenever they shall grow weary of the existing government, they can exercise their constitutional right of amending it or their revolutionary right to dismember or overthrow it." Obviously the amendment option is the preferred choice, rather than another civil war.

Our genetic pool is the most robust and diverse of any society on earth, and the revolutionary spirit continues to run deep and true in the blood lines of all of us who yearn for freedom and the full fruits of our labor.

Let us unite together to show the world what we are really all about and what we can peacefully accomplish together.

Let us again demonstrate a new system of government that will better serve to provide freedom, justice, and prosperity to all who share this fragile planet.

Managing the Presidency

As we were coming down to the wire with the book, we added one last chapter we had been working on all along, as it serves to envelop all earlier issues. Sam believed the executive branch of government, as currently managed, is a failure and he was greatly concerned about the increased power of the "unitary executive."

The Constitution provides that "The executive Power shall be vested in a President of the United States of America" and that "the President shall take care that the laws be faithfully executed . . . ." It has been argued that these clauses create a unified executive department and that Congress cannot by statute create executive agencies outside the president's control.

President George W. Bush repeatedly asserted that his presidential power was unilateral and unchecked. He went so far as to claim his office and that of the vice president were not "agencies" of the executive branch and were not required to comply with federal laws, or even his own executive orders directed to such agencies.

Moreover, Bush issued more "signing statements" during his first term alone than all prior presidents combined. In doing so, Bush essentially nullified the statutes he signed as they relate to the executive branch. For example, although he signed the law against the use of torture, he issued a signing statement asserting that he has the authority as the Commander-in-Chief to ignore the law.

Managing the Presidency

Bush also authorized electronic surveillance without warrant outside the law prohibiting it, and he declared he had the power as a "war president" to ignore the Geneva Conventions and could indefinitely detain immigrants and American citizens as unlawful combatants without due process of law.

Sam argued that the law was the law—which brought the conversation around to what can be done if the President does not believe he is subject to the law.

As a result of Watergate, the power of Congress increased, while that of the Presidency decreased. Some checks and balances remained as long as different parties controlled Congress and the White House; however, with the elevation of George W. Bush to the presidency and with the Republican Party in control of both houses of Congress, increased power began to flow to the president.

Many neoconservatives, including Cheney, Rumsfeld, and their deputies, believed the President should control all levers of federal power.

Following 9-11 and Bush's declarations of an enduring war on terrorism and his assertion of power as the Commander-in-Chief to conduct the war in any manner he decided, the balance of the separation of powers shifted entirely to the presidency.

Ordinarily, as the final arbiter of the law, the Supreme Court should restore the balance; however, the Court is now controlled by members of the Federalist Society, for whom belief in a unified executive is a bedrock principle.

Those who founded our government feared the power of a strong executive. It is strange indeed that members of the Federalist Society endorse a shifting of power to the presidency, for if we look at the Federalist Papers we find that James Madison warned that the accumulation of all powers in the same hands is the very definition of tyranny.

Thomas Paine said it well: "In America, the law is king. For as in absolute governments the King is law, so in free countries the law ought to be king; and there ought to be none other."

Sam: A Political Philosophy

Aileana said, "As a military officer, my problem was never that I had too much power. Rather, I often found that I was responsible for a mission and that I didn't have either the resources or the authority to allocate available resources as I thought best. If the President is the Commander-in-Chief of the military and if a war is being fought, shouldn't she or he have the power to allocate the resources provided by Congress?"

Sam did not disagree in principle.

The issue is not whether the President can and should command the military, but whether he has the power to order violations of the Constitution and the laws enacted by Congress.

We elect our representatives to express our will, and we do not want our government to violate international law by illegally invading another country and locking up prisoners without due process, nor do we want our President to authorize torture in violation of our own laws.

Our government is supposed to act in our name and on our behalf. When it does not act in our best interests, it does not act in our name. When the President commits unlawful acts, he does not act as our President. He acts as a tyrant.

Keep in mind the United States did not even allow the images of its presidents to be minted on its coins until 1909 when Abraham Lincoln's face was stamped on the penny. We thought the practice was too similar to that of the kings displayed on European coins; however, in the last hundred years, we have come to look upon and treat our presidents as royalty.

The problem came to a head with Bush Junior. His qualifications were insignificant and he would never have been elected were it not for the fact that his father had been President, yet he governed as though he had a mandate from God.

Aileana wanted to know, "Given the fact that the United States is the greatest superpower in the world, how can its government be administered without a super powerful executive?"

As I had done several times before, I asked, "Sam, what would you do if you were President?"

Sam said it was an intriguing question, but that he was getting a little tired and wondered if he could sleep on it overnight. He promised an answer the next morning.

The next day was Saturday, and Heather asked if she could come visit K.D. and work on her homework at the beach. We arrived early and shared breakfast with Sam and Aileana before adjourning to the living room.

Heather took K.D. for a run down the Strand, and we listened to what President Sam would do if he were in charge.

The President of the United States cannot be all things to all people, nor can she or he embody or personify the politics of either liberals or conservatives without interfering with the rights of the other. Rather, the President should be a neutral advocate of the policy and will of the American people.

If we are to pretend the presidency is a television reality program, let's make a couple of assumptions. First, if there were a National Policy Referendum, the President would have a far better idea of just what the people want and, if she or he were elected by a massive write-in vote, she or he would be more likely to feel as a part of the people and to believe that their interests were the same.

If the people of the United States elected me to exercise the power of the presidency on their behalf, I would warn them that the modern president, no matter who is elected, cannot possibly do everything that has come to be expected of the office and to obtain, at the same time, the information necessary to make good decisions.

George W. Bush is a good example of exactly what is wrong. He was perhaps the most incurious President ever elected. He could not or did not read; he had little interest in what ordinary people thought; and he was totally controlled and manipulated by those who supplied him with the limited information required to make stupid decisions.

At the same time, much like Reagan in the past, Bush appeared before the media almost every day and read from the script provided him about whatever issue seems to be the most important at the moment. He was almost a caricature of a puppet, flapping his lips without a clue about what was really going on.

President Obama may be more articulate, but he too seems compelled to offer an opinion or statement about everything that spins through the 24-hour news cycle.

One of the first things I would do, after asking for the prayers and best wishes of everyone in the world, would be to announce a "look alike" contest requesting individuals whose appearance was most like mine including, race, age, height, weight, hair, and facial characteristics to send in videos of themselves reciting something like the Gettysburg Address. The top 10 or 20 winners would each receive a prize, including a trip to Washington, DC and an autographed photograph taken with me. The only difference between us would be that he would be wearing my well-cut suit and I would be dressed casually.

Thereafter, whenever I wanted to secretly travel around the country and someone recognized me, I could simply say I was one of the contest winners and show them an autographed photograph.

One of the primary purposes of my administration would be to reduce and bridge the vast political gulf that has come to divide the political parties and the People. The government cannot be effectively administered unless this is done.

To help unite the government, I would select two assistant presidents to help run the executive branch. My first choices would probably be the two losing candidates who received the most votes.

Although President Lincoln relied upon a cabinet of rivals to govern during the Civil War, the present enmity between political parties virtually precludes success. If they would agree to participate in a nonpartisan administration dedicated to effective governance, I would work with the two assistant presidents to determine how best to divide and delegate the responsibilities of the executive branch.

Although I would never give up direct control of the Departments of Defense and Justice and the intelligence agencies, I would delegate *authority for most other internal and external matters to the two assistants and would ask them to prepare their nominations and recommendations for all positions requiring senate confirmation, including all cabinet posts.*

The President has the authority under the Constitution to conduct the nation's foreign relations; however, the Department of Foreign Affairs and the office of Secretary of State was the first to be established. The Secretary of State should continue to have responsibility for the operation of the State Department and for the negotiation of treaties. There are, however, a host of foreign executive responsibilities, including some currently undertaken by the Department of Commerce, the Office of the United States Trade Representative, the Export-Import Bank, the United States Trade and Development Agency, and the Overseas Private Investment Corporation that are independent of diplomatic relations and could properly be administered by an assistant president. In addition, the assistant president for foreign affairs could and should represent the president at many of the current economic summits, including G8 and G20, where governmental policy can be more effectively discussed and negotiated without the decision-making power of the American President.

The Department of Homeland Security should be shorn of most of its law enforcement responsibilities, and it and other departments and agencies having internal responsibilities should be administered by the assistant president for domestic affairs.

A primary responsibility of the domestic assistant president should be the improvement in federal and state electoral procedures, such as the National Popular Vote initiative, ranked voting, and campaign finance reform.

In addition, the domestic assistant president should work with the states to reduce the current ugly partisanship and negative campaigning that is poisoning the electoral system. States should reform their primary election processes by allowing "fully open/top two" primaries, with the top two finalists running in the final election, even if they are from the same party.

Finally, the elected vice president should have a real job. His or her primary responsibility should be to serve as an effective President of the Senate; however, she or he should also be tasked with very specific executive branch responsibilities.

First, the vice president should have the primary responsibility to implement the policy and will of the people through effective legislation. Included in this would be a program of congressional reform of rules, procedures and practices that interfere with the ability of Congress to represent the People.

One of the first tasks would be to eliminate or modify Senate rules that allow a minority of senators, or even individual senators, to delay the progress of legislation and confirmation of presidential appointees. The current filibuster rule that has come to require a supermajority of 66 senators to pass any contested legislation could be eliminated by majority vote on the first day of any legislative session.

In addition, the vice president should become a super parliamentarian and effectively use congressional rules and procedures to break deadlocks and move necessary legislation forward. Procedures such as reconciliation to pass tax and spending bills and other arcane methods should be available for judicious use—if required to conduct the People's business.

Second, the vice president should press Congress to increase its membership by statute in order to obtain better representation of the People. The number of constituents for each representative has vastly expanded since 1913, when each representative represented about 200,000 people, to the present 700,000. This makes for poor representation and expensive campaigns.

The exact number of representatives would have to be carefully considered. A return to 1913 levels would require 1,500 representatives, and the House of Representatives chamber would have to undergo remodeling. Perhaps there should be rows of benches, as in the British Parliament, instead of individual desks. Nonetheless, the People deserve more effective representation than they currently receive.

Managing the Presidency

Finally, the vice president should have lead executive responsibility for the budget of the United States. He or she should work closely with all parties in Congress, the Congressional Budget Office, congressional oversight committees, and executive department audit functions to ensure the hard-earned tax dollars of voters are well spent and carefully accounted for. In the absence of an economic crisis, the budget should be balanced each year.

I would meet with the three prime administrators almost daily, either in person at a physical round table, or by video conference, to ensure the government maintains a nonpartisan course that benefits, rather than harms the People—who provide the power to the government.

It should be the role of the two assistant presidents and the vice president to hold regular press conferences and to communicate with the public, as required, about their individual areas of concern.

Except for statutory and traditional appearances, such as the State of the Union Address, and other rare and unusual occurrences, I would avoid speaking to the media or making public addresses. Instead, I would quietly travel the country meeting with voters, directly, asking how they are doing and what their government should be doing for them.

The main necessity for delegating responsibility is to free up time for the President to obtain the information required to make good decisions. I would require impartial research papers on all serious issues, and I would read them along with books and written articles on the subjects. I would continue to browse the Internet and to seek alternative opinions wherever available. Finally, I would discuss the issues with my assistants and other advisors before making final policy decisions.

Since I would be on the road so much, maybe the White House should be subdivided into a duplex for the two assistant presidents and their families. Perhaps it would help them to more closely work together for the benefit of the people, and . . . maybe they could keep an eye on each other.

As a guideline to his administration and those he selected to help him, I asked President Sam about his domestic policy.

Sam: A Political Philosophy

The constitutional oath taken by every President says, "I do solemnly swear (or affirm) that I will faithfully execute the office of President of the United States, and will to the best of my ability, preserve, protect and defend the Constitution of the United States." Adhering to that oath would be my overriding domestic policy.

Every act undertaken by me and my administration would be dedicated to ensuring that every person in the United States receives the protection of the Constitution.

Beyond that, I would dedicate my administration to ensuring that every child has equal access to nutrition, health care, and education, and that all parents receive the maximum assistance of government in securing the healthy future of their children, their family, and their society.

What about his foreign policy?

We must talk directly to the people in every society, in every nation about the dangers that confront all of us, without reference to nationality, borders, or past history. Matters such as poverty and hunger, disease, education, and threats to the environment cannot be solved by any one nation alone, even for its own citizens.

We must seek the friendship and goodwill of people everywhere by acting toward them as a good neighbor or friend should, and we must encourage them to share in the benefits of freedom and democracy, rather than trying to force them to change.

Deception and violence as a means of foreign policy are inherently defeating. To the contrary, I would seek to communicate my respect for the culture, religion, language, and rights of all others and to peacefully share with them the bounty of the planet we live on.

I would encourage everyone, everywhere, to share a vision of a world at peace, one in which we can all aspire to provide a better life for our children and hope for the future of our collective humanity.

Publication and Transition

The book was released on tax day—April 15, 2009. The publisher had done an excellent job of pre-publication marketing, and the book was reviewed in most major newspapers. Sam's Internet supporters were ecstatic, and a YouTube clip of his appearance on the Oprah Show went viral.

We all traveled back to New York City for the release. The publisher's party was subdued, as Sam's health had continued to deteriorate. Seated with Aileana, who was almost full term in her pregnancy, and K.D., he was the center of attention, as guests circulated around seeking a few words with him. Xiomara, Heather, and I enjoyed the party and the celebrities who attended. Heather fell in love a couple of times, but Xiomara had brought her own leading man. We danced as though there was no tomorrow.

Reviews were generally very favorable, with most reviewers concentrating on the content of Sam's philosophy and political policies, instead of the method he had used to gain attention. All of the major retail book chains picked up the book, and library orders were gratifying.

Given his weakened physical condition, there were no book signings; however, a large public event was organized by the journalism department of Columbia University while we were in New York. Comfortably seated on stage, Sam answered questions submitted by the audience and, holding a copy of the book, he read several selections that are central to his philosophy. The response was overwhelming. As he stood to accept the standing ovation, he had never looked so distinguished—or so frail.

As we were being driven through JFK airport on a shuttle cart to our departure gate, Heather excitedly pointed out the book prominently displayed in the Hudson News concession.

To Heather's great disappointment, Aileana's baby did not arrive on her 27th of April birthday, but a few days later on the first of May. Sam was with Aileana during the delivery, and the rest of us waited outside for the news. It was a healthy baby girl!

As we surrounded Aileana and the nursing baby, Sam, who had always dreamed of traveling to China, said he would like to name her Mei, the Chinese girl's name meaning beautiful. Aileana agreed, but wanted to add her own mother's name, Lynn. So, Mei Lynn joined us to face the world which we were all seeking to make into a better and more secure place for her.

Spiritual, but unaffiliated, Sam and Aileana had often attended sessions of chamber music on Sunday afternoons at the nondenominational Neighborhood Church during the summer in nearby Palos Verdes. Two weeks after Mei Lynn's birth, we gathered on the church patio overlooking the Pacific Ocean for her blessing and name ceremony. Xiomara, Heather, and I stood with the couple and accepted the life-long responsibility to help care for the child.

Heather graduated with honors from UCLA and accepted a job with the publisher to promote the book. Neither Sam or Aileana were in any condition to travel, and my own writing commitments made it impossible for me to do more than occasional weekend book signings. The publisher also hired Heather's BFF (best friend forever) as her assistant, and the two young women began a year's effort to travel the world in promoting the book.

Heather would typically tell the story about how the book came to be written and would play a video of Sam at the Columbia University appearance reading a few selections. Afterwards, as people lined up with their books, her friend would write the date and address the autograph as requested by the purchaser, and Heather would visit briefly with each person, then uses a rubber stamp to print Sam's large dashing signature in red ink. Thousands of books were autographed in this manner, and *Sam* remained on *The New York Times* bestseller list week after week.

Despite Aileana's excellent nursing, Sam's physical condition worsened. He was easily fatigued and lacked energy. Researchers at Georgetown University had identified a medical basis for what was commonly known as the gulf war illness. They were able to locate specific neurological damage in the areas of the brain associated with pain, which caused veterans to become easily fatigued.

Sam was admitted to the Kaiser hospital for a new battery of tests, including magnetic resonance imaging before and after exercise, to determine if the basis of his illness could be traced to his exposure to neurotoxins during the Gulf War.

Xiomara and I visited Sam and Aileana in his hospital room on Saturday after the first week. The look on their faces told us the medical results were troubling. Sam asked Aileana to explain the findings. She said the doctors had finally diagnosed amyotrophic lateral sclerosis, commonly known as Lou Gehrig's disease or ALS.

The disease is often identified only after all other alternatives have been excluded. The doctors were aided by findings of the Department of Veterans Affairs that Gulf War veterans were nearly twice as likely to develop the disease as other military personnel. The decision was based on an epidemiological study of almost 2.5 million military personnel who served in the war.

ALS attacks motor neurons in the brain and leads to a progressive loss of motor functions. Initially, muscle weakness leads to loss of balance and stumbling, as Sam had been experiencing. Ultimately, there is an inability to move the body, then speech, and ultimately swallowing. Although ALS develops at different speeds in individuals, it is ultimately fatal to everyone.

There is no loss of mental function, hearing, sight, smell, taste, or even sexual function, and some people, such as Stephen Hawking, the English physicist, have lived for decades with the disability and fathered children.

Sam not only had the best medical care available, but he and Aileana had become financially independent from book sales. They decided to remain in the Los Angeles area because of its concentration of medical facilities, and they exercised the option and purchased the beach house.

There is an opening in the boardwalk wall in front of the house leading to the sand, and Sam and Aileana purchased a motorized wheelchair equipped with balloon tires that allowed them to go down to the surf line each evening for the sunset. Sam was able to move a few steps around the house, and they had a lift chair installed on the stairway. To provide mobility away from home, they bought a van equipped with a power lift that allowed Sam to wheel onto the lift and into the van to sit next to Aileana as she drove.

Sam was the featured speaker at the largest ever gathering of veterans organized against war that was held in Los Angeles in October 2009. Vietnam and Iraq Veterans Against the War and Veterans for Peace gathered to proclaim that war is an atrocity and a crime against humanity.

Heather arranged to be in town to celebrate both Thanksgiving and Christmas with all of us at the beach house. Sam's disease had been accepted as a part of our lives, and we were dedicated to share his life to the maximum for as long as he survived. Sam realized he would have suffered the disease irrespective of his ordeal, and had he not chosen to undergo it, he would still be living on the street.

Knowing that we do not consciously remember the years of our infancy, Sam was dedicated to holding Mei Lynn in his arms and talking to her for as long as it was possible for him to do so. The two of them sat together for long periods each day as he told her about the things he had seen in life and what a magnificent future she and all of the children in the world will have. As he gazed down at her, he saw his own intelligent hazel eyes looking back at him. He had developed dexterity with his opposing finger stumps, and while he still could, he helped feed Mei Lynn solid food and changed her diapers. Fortunately, no pins are required for modern disposable diapers.

As we hung new calendars for 2010, Heather was in Europe promoting the book—which had been translated into all of the major languages. We gathered to reflect and make our resolutions for the new year.

Although the plumbing, electrical, and heating systems of the old beach house had been upgraded in the past, the exterior needed attention. The house was clad with wood siding, which had been painted black with white trim, much of which was faded and peeling. They decided to restore the original wood siding and paint it with brighter colors. We joked that it could become the Hermosa Beach White House, but then again it could be pink or purple—to be decided.

The publisher was making no demands on us under the revised contract; however, Naomi Washington advised us that future printings were being planned and the publisher would appreciate essays on other subjects. Health care, energy production, and the bailout of the automobile industry were current events that Sam was talking about. We resolved to address these issues during the year.

The last resolution was to employ full-time, live-in assistance to help Aileana care for Sam and Mei Lynn. Aileana said she would find someone.

Health Care

Networking through nursing friends, Aileana identified a young Filipina-American, who had just graduated as a registered nurse from Cal State Long Beach. Tala (whose name in Tagalog means bright star or planet) was interested in working for a few years to save money for tuition before studying to become a physician assistant. She agreed to live in one of the extra bedrooms, serve as a nanny for Mei Lynn, and help as needed with Sam. One of the goals was to allow Aileana to spend more quality time with Sam and accompany him on outings.

Sam liked to take his motorized wheelchair down to the surf line for the evening sunset, often with Mei Lynn on his lap and K.D. on a leash. He often accompanied Aileana on her morning walk, motoring along the Strand to Manhattan Beach for breakfast. He and K.D. were recognized by many people, and they struck up friendships with their neighbors.

Tackling the subject of health care, our plan was for me to provide the political background and Aileana to comment on the practice. Sam was thinking about policy and where we should go in the future.

Aileana said they were lucky the Veterans Administration had acknowledged Sam's ALS as being service connected, and she was entitled to health care as a retired officer. They were both receiving excellent health care through Kaiser, but she was concerned about the quality of health care provided to most people.

Health Care

President Truman was the first president to seek federally-funded health care for Americans. He sought legislation providing health care for seniors; however, Congress failed to act. Years later, Lyndon Johnson signed Medicare into law at the Truman Library in Independence, Missouri, and handed the first two Medicare cards to Harry and Bess Truman.

Under Medicare, health benefits are provided by private doctors and hospitals and paid for by the government, which negotiates lower, uniform costs. It covers approximately half of health care costs for seniors, with the balance borne by individuals, or by supplemental insurance plans.

In 1974, President Nixon sought a Comprehensive Health Insurance Plan to provide coverage to all Americans. For those not covered by employers, an Assisted Health Insurance plan would pay all costs beyond an individual's ability to pay. Nixon also asked Congress to enact improvements in the coverage provided by Medicare to include the costs of drugs and other out-of-pocket expenditures. Congress did not act on his proposals.

With the growing number of elderly Americans, the cost of prescription drugs became a major issue in the 2000 election. Once elected, President Bush proposed changes supported by the pharmaceutical industry that resulted in a Medicare drug benefit based on deductibles and caps. The net result was that the government was prohibited from directly negotiating lower costs with the drug companies, and substantial increased profits began to flow to the drug companies.

For good reasons, the soaring cost of the profit-based health care system was again an issue in the 2008 presidential election. Overall, medical care costs Americans 16 percent of their national output, which amounts to more than $6,000 per person, or double that of any other developed nation. At its present rate of growth, health care will consume almost half of the gross domestic product by 2050.

Sam: A Political Philosophy

Providing health coverage to its employees increases the cost of every car manufactured by General Motors by $1,500. Employers are shifting the cost of insurance to their employees, with employees paying more than 35 percent of health care coverage. Through a variety of personnel devices, including independent contractors and part-time workers, many employers are avoiding providing any health care benefits. Before the 2008 election, more than 40 percent of Americans were without health insurance.

During the presidential debates, John McCain proposed the standard Republican approach to providing health care that had been developed by the conservative Heritage Foundation and endorsed by the Business Roundtable. The proposal continued the monopoly of health insurance companies and ensured their profits by mandating that everyone have coverage and imposing fines on those who didn't. The system provides a limited subsidy by the government for low-income or unemployed people. It was the type of coverage implemented in Massachusetts by Republican Governor Mitt Romney.

Barack Obama proposed a single-payer system, like Medicare, providing a public option for people who could not otherwise obtain insurance. Following his election and with the support of almost 75 percent of the public, the Democrats introduced health care reform bills in Congress. We had all followed the debate in Congress during the Winter of 2009, and we discussed the result following passage of the Patient Protection and Affordable Care Act in June 2010.

Initially, President Obama held out for a public option, saying in July 2009, "Any plan I sign must include an insurance exchange—a one-stop-shopping marketplace where you can compare the benefits, costs and track records o a variety of plans, including a public option to increase competition and keep insurance companies honest."

The bill passed by the House of Representatives included a public option; however, passage in the Senate required the vote of Senator Joseph Lieberman, who had been Al Gore's vice presidential running mate in 2000. Lieberman, who subsequently abandoned the Democratic Party and became an Independent, had received more than $500,000 in campaign contributions from the insurance industry. He stated the public option was designed to allow the "government to take over all of health insurance" and opposed its inclusion. The option was stripped from the legislation passed by the Senate and agreed to by the House. Even so, not a single Republican voted for the bill!

Aileana was outraged, "It's clear that President Obama never actually practiced law or ever engaged in negotiations to settle a case. Ultimately, he folded his own plans for a single-payer system and accepted the Republican subsidy-penalty plan. Then, he negotiated against himself by making every single compromise in favor of the Republicans, as they refused to vote for their own plan—even those who had previously supported it. Rather than protect the public, the bill enhances the profits of the insurance industry. I'd like him to come out here and explain to me why, with a majority in Congress, he abandoned his base and passed the other side's plan over their opposition. While he's here, I could probably sell him the Hermosa Beach Pier."

Workers cannot bear the present weight of health care, much less take on more. The health care burden on the working and middle classes resulted in a 23-fold increase in bankruptcy filings from 1980 to 2001, directly as a result of medical bills. Many of those filings were by hard-working people who had medical coverage when they got sick and then lost it. Currently, about half of all bankruptcy filings in the United States occur because of health-related expenses.

Since we are spending a greater percentage of our gross domestic product on health care than any other major industrialized nation, you would think we should have the best medical care in the world, but we don't. Other countries provide more doctors, nurses, and hospital beds for their patients, and we suffer an infant mortality rate well above that of the other industrialized countries.

Sam: A Political Philosophy

Only Latvia, among the 33 industrialized nations, has a lower survival rate for infants. At the other end of life, we are in the 29th place in the World Health Organization's life expectancy rankings. We die earlier and spend more time disabled than the citizens of other developed nations.

Why is our health care system so lacking? The simple answer is that we have evolved a medical delivery system that allows the private medical care and pharmaceutical industries to rob us when we are sick and injured, when we are the most vulnerable—holding a gun to our heads while they pick our pockets. These industries are among the most profitable in our free-market economy.

Instead of this cockamamie program the Republicans are derisively calling "Obamacare" and hanging around the President's neck like a burning tire, we need to seriously consider what we could do in this country to obtain affordable health care—which would be equal to that provided anywhere else in the world. Both the military medical system I worked in throughout my career and the Veterans Administration system that has served millions of veterans, like Sam, are examples of national health care, and both are good systems. Even better is the nonprofit Kaiser system that is now taking care of us. Why would anyone want to receive profit-motivated health care?

Sam had given the matter a great deal of thought and had been dictating notes on the subject.

Let us envision a better way to provide health care, one that supports the premise that every child requires equal access to nutrition, education, and health care if we are ever to achieve our potential as a society; one that allows every worker to retain the benefits of his or her labor and every business owner the profits from her or his investment; and one in which we decide as a matter of public policy that it is just as important for us to enjoy good health as it is to be free from a terrorist attack.

Health Care

As a part of a comprehensive health care policy, we should establish a National Health Academy, whose graduates become professional officers in a National Health Corps. Although the task would be gargantuan, the Health Corps could assume responsibility for the operation of all public health, veterans and military hospitals, as well as every county hospital and ultimately most major medical centers across America.

Among its responsibilities would be negotiating and managing contracts with nonprofit health care companies to operate some, or all of the facilities. For-profit operations would continue to exist, along with health insurance companies; however, they would not be a part of the public health care system.

We would secure a right to receive world-class health care through the National Health Corps, without having to pay enormous profits to insurance companies and private hospitals and other health care facilities. Most Health Corps hospitals should be dedicated as teaching centers to ensure we have an abundant supply of highly qualified doctors, nurses, physician assistants, and medical technicians, and that we receive the very best medical care available in the world.

Aileana interrupted to agree, "Currently, U.S. medical schools produce only 17,000 graduates each year to fill 22,000 first-year residency positions. Twenty-five percent of all doctors in the United States are graduates of foreign medical schools, and 60 percent of those are from developing countries where doctors are scarce."

The Health Corps should also be responsible for the operation of medical and dental clinics in our public schools. Health, vision, and dental care should be provided at neighborhood schools during and after classes, both for students and for their families. Very importantly, preventive medicine would help ensure that every child arrives at school ready to learn.

The Health Corps should assume responsibility for providing medical care within the military and for teaching medical corpsman skills to every single military recruit. Properly trained and equipped, our military personnel could become revered lifesavers at major disasters, such as those caused by the Indian Ocean Tsunami and Hurricane Katrina.

Rather than to naysay the possibility of effective national health care, envision the liberating effect such a project would have on American businesses. They would finally be freed from the cost of providing medical benefits to their employees and from the high cost of worker's compensation insurance.

The Health Corps could even establish medical, dental, and vision clinics on the premises of larger companies. The increase in productivity attributed to a healthy workforce could be enormous, and we would become far more competitive with all other industrialized nations, particularly those that provide national health care to their workers.

The birth of a national health care system need not result in the demise of private health care. We should be able to determine the average cost of national health care on an individual basis, and those taxpayers who opt out of the national health care system should be entitled to a tax deduction equal to the per capita average cost of the national system.

Life is precious to each of us, and whether it is long or short, whether it is burdened by suffering or blessed with good health is often a matter of fate. There were tremendous advances in medical care in the Twentieth Century—indeed they are among our modern miracles. The availability of high-quality health care, however, is all too often dependent upon one's station in society.

The wealthy and those we elect to represent us, including the President and the members of Congress, have access to gold-plated medical care that many of us can only dream about. This is not right. All of us, particularly our children, must have the same opportunity to live life without pain and suffering for each of the days allotted to us.

Energy and Transportation

We celebrated the delivery of the health care paper to the publisher for inclusion in the next printing of *Sam* by throwing a Fourth of July party on the sand in front of the beach house. The Manhattan Beach Fire Department organized its annual fireworks show for 2010 on the pier, and we made a contribution to the cost. The book was selling in the millions—worldwide—and we had much to celebrate and scarce time to cherish it.

During visits between her promotional travels, Heather had become friends with Tala, as they were the same age and both were fluent in Spanish. They accepted the responsibility of organizing a neighborhood potluck party on the beach, starting in the afternoon and continuing into the evening for the fireworks display.

Looking back at the newly restored and repainted beach house, we found it to be a magnificent sight. Aileana and Sam had chosen classical simplicity, and the house reflected the red rays of the setting sun in its rich cream color, light and dark green trim, new tan roof, and low red brick walls around the front patio.

Xiomara had outdone herself with our contribution to the potluck, and there was more food than could be eaten by three times the hundreds who attended. Sam and Mei Lynn were the center of attention. The ALS was not yet seriously interfering with his speech and eating, and he rested comfortably in his motorized wheel chair, which supported a tall pole and American flag for the occasion.

Heather and Tala had invited their friends, and the young people were playing volleyball on the sand courts and dancing to their own music broadcast by a large boombox. The rest of us were less energetically entertained by a strolling Mariachi troup hired by Xiomara.

In her mother's arms, Mei Lynn was fascinated by the music and fireworks, as the rest of us oohed and aahed over her. K.D. was less impressed and sought refuge between Sam's legs. She was uncertain whether she was supposed to be protecting or being protected. Sam reassured her through the grand finale.

The Fourth of July fell on a Sunday that year, so we took Monday off to recuperate and talk about where we were going with the promised work on energy and transportation. Sam wanted to combine the two subjects—since so much energy is consumed by America's gasoline-powered cars.

Transportation

The economic crash of 2008 had a major effect on U.S. carmakers. New car sales were down by 32 percent, and the Big Three—General Motors, Ford, and Chrysler—were losing billions each quarter, as they quickly burned through their cash reserves. Ford had obtained a large line of credit in 2007, just before the crash, but General Motors and Chrysler were unable to borrow sufficient funds in the credit markets to survive.

Bankruptcy and a forced liquidation of assets not only would result in the destruction of the automobile unions and employees' retirement and healthcare benefit plans, but also in negative effects on every American worker and taxpayer. Elimination of the American automobile industry would send shock waves through the economy, causing the failure of thousands of automobile parts suppliers and car dealerships. Auto parts supply companies are among the top industrial employers in 19 states, and one out of every ten jobs in America was supported, in one way or another, by the automobile industry. It was estimated that the failure of General Motors alone could result in the loss of more than 15 million jobs.

Aileana observed, "The Big Three have a track record of making really stupid decisions."

Manufacturers have recklessly spent thousands of dollars per vehicle on advertising to convince drivers that they really want big impractical gas-guzzling cars and trucks instead of the smaller fuel-efficient vehicles they really need. The car companies have foolishly peddled financing and leasing deals far beyond the financial means of many buyers, and they have vigorously opposed realistic fuel economy standards. For the auto companies, profits have always trumped safety and economy.

As usual, Aileana was spot on. Foreign manufacturers, such as Toyota, which specialized in smaller, fuel-efficient cars, were less affected by the worldwide financial crisis. Bowing to the needs of Detroit, Congress provided an $80 billion loan to the industry, allowing General Motors and Chrysler to undergo bankruptcy reorganization, without having to liquidate. (General Motors would ultimately emerge from bankruptcy, with the U.S. treasury owning a majority interest, and Chrysler would emerge primarily owned by the United Auto Workers union and the Italian automaker Fiat.)

President-elect Obama said "we should help the auto industry, but what we should expect is that . . . any help that we provide is designed to assure a long-term, sustainable auto industry and not just kicking the can down the road." Although there has been some movement toward producing hybrid electric-gasoline vehicles, it is not yet clear whether the can was just kicked down the road. More likely than not, Americans will continue to be enticed to buy unnecessarily large, expensive, and unsafe sports utility vehicles—that provide the highest profit to the manufacturers.

Sam, who had been trained as a tank driver by the Army because of his lifelong love of cars had some creative ideas on the subject.

Given the power inherent in its bailout and ownership of auto stock, the government should impose a degree of standardization on the industry. In addition to increasing fuel economy standards, American automotive manufacturers should be required to provide a 10-year comprehensive bumper-to-bumper warranty on every vehicle sold. Once upon a time, American cars were designed to become obsolete in a very short period of time. The reliability and quality of American cars must be improved.

They must also be safe to operate. All vehicles should be manufactured around several standard "safety-cage" designs to ensure survivability in most accidents. There is no reason why race car drivers are able to walk away from 200 mph collisions but members of the motoring public are disabled and die in low-speed accidents.

Currently, each manufacturer of all-electric and hybrid vehicles has to independently design and manufacture the large batteries that provide electric power to drive the cars. These batteries are expensive to design and produce and can pose environmental disposal hazards at the end of their lifetimes.

The production of a set of standardized, interchangeable batteries for the different basic automobile designs would allow manufacturing savings for all vehicles. For example, two-passenger cars would not require the same battery power as four- and six-passenger vehicles and light trucks. Moreover, batteries could be designed for easy replacement by service stations, allowing the swapping of recharged batteries in all-electric vehicles to extend their range of travel.

The federal government should implement national tailpipe emission standards supportive of the needs of the most polluted states. In December 2007, the Bush administration's Environmental Protection Agency denied California's request to set higher emission standards than those required by the federal government. Every state should be fully supported in its effort to improve its own air quality.

Energy

Petroleum is used for more than powering internal combustion engines. It is also used to heat houses, generate electricity, and make asphalt for paving roads. Moreover, it provides the feedstock to make a wide variety of chemicals, plastics, and other synthetic materials that are widely used throughout the world. Even so, two of every three barrels of oil used in the United States is burned by cars and trucks. That basic fact must be the central focus of any American transportation policy.

Satisfying energy needs was one of the differences between the candidates in the 2008 election. John McCain called for "drill, baby, drill," while Obama wanted the country to build "wind farms and solar panels, fuel-efficient cars and the alternative energy technologies that can free us from our dependence on foreign oil and keep our economy competitive in the years ahead." Much like his rollover on health care, once Obama was elected, he encouraged the nation to drill for oil, rather than seek "alternative energy technologies that can free us from our dependence on foreign oil and keep our economy competitive in the years ahead."

Sam believed the future transportation needs of the U.S. could be met by an improvement of the Interstate Highway System and most major streets and highways in America to provide a constant source of electromagnetic energy for all vehicles that pass over them.

Space-based solar technology can provide an inexhaustible, safe, and pollution free supply of energy. It is a far more logical solution than petroleum, ethanol, or nuclear-fueled hydrogen systems. Satellites in orbit around the Earth and/or collectors on the moon's surface can be engineered to convert the sun's radiant energy into electricity 24 hours a day, which can be safely transmitted by microwave beams to receiving antennas on Earth.

Space solar power is not a new idea. NASA and the Department of Energy have been studying the issue for the past 30 years and have found it to be technically feasible. However, given the domination of the Bush II administration by the oil industry, no research and development has been done on space solar power since 2001.

If America initially dedicated space solar power to energize its national highways, the U.S. could begin to restrict the use of its remaining fossil fuels to the manufacturing of synthetic materials and purposes other than energy.

Envision the amazing initiatives we could embark upon if our national energy policy and research was freed from the control of the oil companies and their political puppets.

Imagine that the Interstate Highway System and most major streets and highways in America could be improved to provide a constant source of electro-magnetic energy sufficient to power a standard automobile, with comfortable seating for five adults, anywhere in America at no cost to the operator.

Think about triple-hybrid cars designed to operate primarily on electro-magnetic energy supplied through the surface of most highways and freeways, and which are equipped with small fuel efficient internal combustion engines to supplement rechargeable batteries for trips on local streets and byways.

We could travel for free throughout the United States as a matter of national privilege. We could get to our jobs without having to work for an hour each day just to pay the way. We would have more money to spend on vacations, and we would be able to tour this great nation, see the grand sights, and visit with our friends and relatives along the way.

Imagine the boon to tourism if foreign visitors could rent a car at the airport and drive around America for free, spending their excess cash at our small businesses along the way.

Is this a realistic dream? Where would we be today if we had wisely invested in unlimited space power, instead of wasting a trillion dollars on a stupid war in the Middle East to seize a few more barrels of oil? As a bonus, the development of space solar power would act as a tremendous boost to the economy.

Ultimately, the entire national economy could be powered by space solar power and other renewable sources of energy, such as surface solar, wind, and wave power systems.

The introduction of space solar energy into the United States economy and its ultimate adoption by other countries would do much to reverse the harm caused to our fragile planet by industrialization, and it could save all of us from the threatening effects of global warming. Shouldn't we at least think about it, and, if given a chance, vote on it?

Although there are substantial costs associated with the development of space solar power, it makes far more sense to spend the space exploration budget on developing an efficient and reliable power supply for the future, than upon stupid and ineffective missile defense systems. On the other hand, the development of space solar power would solve one of the last major stumbling blocks to space exploration—reducing the cost of moving material from Earth to orbit.

With funding for the space shuttle ending in 2012 and for the space station in 2017, America must decide on a realistic policy for space exploration, or else it will be left in the dust by other nations, such as Japan, China, and the European Union, which are rapidly developing futuristic space projects.

The first nation that captures and effectively makes use of space solar energy to provide low-cost transportation will dominate the world economy for generations to come and will become a much healthier and far more secure society.

Education

Although Xiomara often remained in the background when she was present for our roundtable discussions of social and political issues, she had more than a little to say about President Bush and his "no child left untested" program and President Obama's "race to the top." She insisted that no book on political philosophy could ever be complete without some consideration of the role of education in the making of a nation. Sam, who once dreamed of becoming a school teacher wholeheartedly agreed. He recounted an old Chinese proverb, "If you are planning for a year, sow rice; if you are planning for a decade, plant trees; if you are planning for a lifetime, educate people."

As the professional practitioner, we encouraged Xiomara to take the lead. She said, "We have to remember that it was President Bush who ignorantly said, 'Rarely is the question asked, Is our children learning?'" His program was designed by his corporate supporters and was equally brilliant. It was designed to impose the business plan on education in order to create better workers—not happy, creative, well-balanced, and questioning citizens."

> With the No Child Left Behind Act, the federal government imposed unattainable mandates on local public schools, yet refused to fund the effort required to give them any chance of meeting the standards. As is often the case, the federal

government got its priorities backwards. I spend far too much of my time dealing with testing—rather than the subjects that will help improve the future happiness and well-being of my students—who primary come from families living in poverty.

In 1998, President Clinton proposed voluntary national testing of all fourth graders in reading and all eighth graders in basic math. Instead of covering specific, detailed curriculum, the proposed tests were basic, reflecting a common set of expectations. The short 90-minute tests were intended to provide reliable data on how American children were mastering the basics, rather than to punish students, teachers, or schools for failure.

Clinton's Secretary of Education, Richard Riley, stated, "If all of our efforts to raise standards get reduced to one test, we've gotten it wrong. If we force our teachers to teach only to the test, we will lose their creativity. . . . If we are so consumed with making sure students pass a multiple-choice test that we throw out the arts and civics then we will be going backwards instead of forward." That quiet voice of reason was lost in the business model of education imposed by President Bush's No Child Left Behind Act.

The statistics tell part of the story. Coming into the Bush administration, local school districts raised about 43.8 percent of their budgets, the states contributed 46.8 percent, and the federal government chipped in less than seven percent. Although Congress, over the objection of President Bush—who wanted less—ultimately provided almost $18 billion in additional funding of the Act, it has been estimated that at least $84.5 billion to $148 billion would be required for the public schools to even come close to meeting the Act's mandates. Thus, the Bush administration threatened to come in and take over local schools if they failed to meet its unattainable goals, yet it refused to provide the funds to meet its standards! Most of us in education considered the law to be a failure.

We all had great hopes for President Obama and his call for an educational "Race to the Top." We should have been warned when he appointed his friend, Arne Duncan as the Secretary of Education. Duncan had served as the CEO of the Chicago Public Schools district, where he presided over the closing of neighborhood public schools and replacing them with private charter schools.

Although Obama secured some increase in federal funding, local and state jurisdictions continue to carry the greatest burden of paying for education. The financial crisis has reduced school budgets across the country resulting in massive layoffs of teachers, at the same time as the military budget has been increased and banks have been bailed out. Obama's overall goal of the education system was clear when he said "it's time to prepare every child, everywhere in America, to out-compete any worker, anywhere in the world."

Obama has essentially continued and intensified Bush's corporate policies. He has used student test scores, even in underfunded schools, to evaluate and dismiss teachers; he has shut down and "reconstituted" schools that failed federal testing standards; and he has expanded private, publically funded, charter schools. Teachers continue to be forced to concentrate on "test prep," rather than critical thinking. He has provided little "hope" and no "change."

Sam said, "It is true that public education is and should remain one of the most important tasks of our federal government. Indeed, our society can never achieve its true potential, and it will never have the collective strength to be all it can be, until every child has equal access to nutrition, education, and health care."

Education

Is the education of our children so critical to the future of our society that we should think of it in the same terms as national defense? What can we do to preserve public education—the very institution that set our nation on the path to greatness?

Let us envision for a moment that, as a matter of public policy, we decide that education is just as important as the military for the protection of our future. Imagine that the smart and simple tax allows the federal government to raise sufficient money to fully fund public education, even while it reduces individual federal taxes. Imagine that the federal government recognized that, while national standards may be beneficial, most education decisions should be made by local school boards in order to meet the specific needs of local communities. Imagine this!

If we valued public education as much as we value our military, we should establish a National Education Academy along the lines of the military service academies. With a mission to establish the highest standards for professional education administration, graduates would become officers in a National Education Corps.

Graduates of the Education Academy would agree to serve the same obligatory period as military officers. Officers should be required to spend at least two years teaching in low-income public school class rooms following graduation, before returning for a master's degree in education management. The purpose of these requirements would be to prepare a cadre of professional managers for the Education Corps and to inspire and improve the operation of public schools in every school district across the country.

Given the complexities of the world we live in, shouldn't we also improve the standard free public education to include a two-year academic or vocational college degree?

Moreover, shouldn't we provide a free four-year college education for young volunteers who provide a year of valuable public service at age 18, when they become adults? Perhaps we should also provide free public education through a master's degree for those who contribute a second full year of valuable public service? Students who want to participate in the public service program could voluntarily register with the Education Corps at age 16 to begin planning their public service offering to ensure that it provides the maximum value to our society.

Imagine the incredible boost to our economy if we forgave the repayment of all outstanding student loans and substantially increased the average education level of our populace!

The Education Corps would establish national educational standards and would administer national standardized testing of all students. However, testing should never include draconian punitive sanctions.

Xiomara said, "It is possible to establish effective national standards, without federal control. For example, the National Board for Professional Teaching Standards has proven to be a very successful, non-governmental program for administering and awarding national teaching credentials.

"The National Board is an independent, nonprofit, nonpartisan organization governed by a board of directors, most of whom are classroom teachers. It created a system of advanced certification based on high and rigorous standards and constructed a workable system to assess accomplished teaching. The Board issued its first national certifications in 1990, and there are now more than 100,000 board certified teachers."

Sam said, "Let us imagine that we could evolve our public education system to its fullest potential, one that truly outshines the efforts of all other nations. What about the private school system, the one relied upon by the wealthy, by those who prefer a religious education for their children, or by those who believe their local public schools to be unsafe or substandard? Clearly, in a free society, they should retain that right of choice."

It should not be difficult to determine the average annual cost, per student, for public education. Those parents who provide private education for their children, through two years of college, should receive a direct tax credit equal to the average value of the same public education.

Education

That, however, does not mean that the rest of us should subsidize private education through vouchers or publically-funded charter schools, as long as we provide a safe and beneficial public education system for all children.

Just as a baby bird must ultimately stand at the edge of its nest and either spread its wings and fly off into its future, or fall back into the nest and die, we stand trembling at the edge of our polluted nest, fearfully looking out into a peaceful universe. We shall find the courage and strength to fly away, but not until every child has equal access to nutrition, education and health care.

This then is our task—to create a government that nurtures us and thoughtfully provides for the future of our children. Otherwise, we shall fall back into chaos, ruin, and despair—a brief footnote in the annals of time.

Social Security and Retirement

The essays on education, transportation, and energy were delivered to the publisher by Thanksgiving for inclusion in the next printing of *Sam*. The holiday was spent at the beach house, as Sam's extended family gathered around the large antique dining table.

Aileana offered the blessing, "Divine One, who gave us life, thank you for the beauty that surrounds us and for the bounty of your earth. Bless our friends and family, give us strength on our journey, and guide us on our way."

At one-and-a-half years, Mei Lynn sat in her highchair feeding herself a mishmash of dressing, sweet potatoes, and green beans. She wore as much as she ate, but entertained everyone, especially herself. K.D. helped clean the floor around her.

Sam was almost entirely restricted to the wheelchair. Although it was becoming increasingly difficult for him to speak, he accepted his disability with good humor. He had enjoyed talking about the future of education with Xiomara and, especially, transportation and space solar energy with Heather and Tala, saying, their generation will have to implement new ideas—or live with the consequences of failure.

After an array of desserts and a short walk down the Strand, we built a roaring fire in the living room fireplace and talked about where we were going with our writing. Sam had been thinking about a number of subjects, but he was concerned about attacks on the soundness of social security, the ending of employer-provided retirement, and the failure to fund repairs and improvements in the national infrastructure. While the first two chapters had not been as long or detailed as earlier ones, having to produce two compositions during the past year had proved tiring for Sam, and he decided to be less ambitious during 2011.

Social Security

As a lifelong fan of Roosevelt's Labor Secretary Frances Perkins, Aileana had an interest in the history and background of Social Security.

On August 14, 1935, in the midst of the Great Depression, the American people entered into a contract with our government in which we collectively bartered a percentage of our wages to pay for an insurance policy to ensure that none of us would become destitute when we are no longer able to work.

The Depression was brought on by the 1929 crash of the Stock Market—when it suddenly lost 40 percent of its value and more than $26 billion in wealth disappeared from our economy. It took 25 years for the Market to regain its value at the time of the crash. In the meantime total wages fell by almost half, and millions of workers were unemployed and without any income.

By 1935, more than half of the elderly in America were dependent on others for support, and although a majority of the states had some form of old-age pensions, only three percent of the elderly received any benefits, which averaged only 65 cents a day.

Social Security immediately began to take care of the people, and with the addition of disability insurance in 1954, Medicare in 1965, and Supplemental Security Income (SSI) in 1972, we have contributed $4.5 trillion from our wages and have received more than $4.1 trillion back in benefits.

We have kept our side of the bargain, and each time we receive our paychecks most of us see that 6.2 percent of our wages has been withheld and deposited in the Social Security Trust Fund. Our employer is required by law to match our contribution with another 6.2 percent. Thus, were it not for Federal Insurance Contributions Act (FICA) taxes, we could receive an additional 12.4 percent in our salary. However, our employers might not be so generous in the absence of legal coercion, and we might not be so faithful in putting aside the increase for hard times.

It has been a good bargain, a win-win situation. For the oversight of our contributions, we pay only one-quarter of the amount paid by private pension funds to their money managers. Overall, more than 99 percent of our premiums go to benefits and less than one percent is spent on overhead.

Our Social Security Trust Funds have been wisely and conservatively invested in the interest-bearing obligations of federal government bonds (as required by law), which has benefitted the overall operation of our government. While we may have missed out a little bit on the booming stock market, we didn't see our trust funds reduced or wiped out by the Great Recession. Currently, $2.8 trillion of the nation's national debt of $18 trillion is owned to the Trust Fund.

Today, more than 90 percent of all employees and the self-employed are covered by Social Security, and one in seven Americans, or more than 44 million of us, are receiving a benefit. Most beneficiaries are receiving a return on their contributions that is far greater than they would have received if they had invested the same funds in the private financial markets.

All, however, is not rosy. While a one-earner couple who retired in 1980 generated Social Security benefits equal to a 7.7 percent (adjusted for inflation) return on their investment, the same couple retiring in 2010 may only earn a 3.6 return. The reduction in return is due to the aging of the population (the Baby Boomers),

Social Security and Retirement

the increase in benefits, and the requirement that trust funds be invested conservatively.

So, why doesn't the government just sell bonds at a low interest rate and invest the proceeds in the stock market? The reason is that higher returns are necessarily associated with higher risks, and if we are to count on having money to retire on and to avoid being dependent upon others, we have to minimize the risk of loss. This is why we have always wisely invested our Social Security trust funds in very conservative interest-bearing government bonds.

Since benefits are primarily paid out of current contributions and since the population is aging, there is a predicted shortfall of $3.5 trillion at some distant point in the future. However, there is a present surplus, and there are sufficient assets to pay 100% of benefits until 2042. Even then, without any further increases, the Fund could pay more than 70% of benefits for many decades after that. Other estimates, including that of the Congressional Budget Office, allow for sufficient existing reserves to pay full benefits through 2052, if not the 2080s.

Sam said the most important thing was not to mess with social security. As a conservatively invested insurance policy paid for by workers and employers, it provides an essential safety net. He did have a suggestion to ensure its continuing solvency.

One way to balance the Trust Fund beyond 2042, or 2052, or even 2082 is to simply raise or eliminate the annual cap on contributions, which is presently $106,000.

Currently, because of the cap, lower- and middle-income workers pay a higher FICA tax rate than those who earn over $106,000.

Since only 83 percent of all wages paid are subject to social security taxes, elimination of the cap would increase annual Social Security revenues by $100 billion per year, more than enough to take care of any future shortfall.

Since there is resistance to eliminating the cap altogether, perhaps the law could be changed to establish the cap at the President's salary—which is currently $400,000. Shouldn't we all share the burden to save social security?

Unquestionably, the lives of millions of American workers and our families will be devastated in the future by the thoughtless and selfish actions of our representatives if some of the politicians succeed in their cockamamie attack on Social Security. It is dangerous to think they might care more for us than for their wealthy friends, corporate sponsors, and Wall Street conspirators. They are the only ones guaranteed to benefit from the ill-conceived scheme to privatize Social Security. Just look what would have happened to the trust fund if it had been invested in the stock market when it failed in 2008.

There is a great risk that our Congress, presently controlled by the wealthy and large corporations, will enact changes by a simple majority vote that will abrogate the contract we made with our government 70 years ago and which we have faithfully kept. They have accumulated substantial fortunes during their years of public service, and they never have to worry about paying for food, shelter, or health care.

A National Retirement System

Sam had some thoughts about retirement, but first he asked for some background on the status of retirement plans in the United States.

In addition to Social Security, Congress established the Railroad Retirement Board in 1935 to cover railroad workers. Supported by New Deal legislation and regulations, most company pensions survived the Depression, as more businesses began to provide retirement plans with defined benefits. Under these plans, based on years of service, final income, and other factors, retired workers received a guaranteed amount until their deaths. In the 20 years between 1940 and 1960, coverage grew to include more than 30 percent of workers. By 1975, more than 40 million workers were covered.

In addition to plans offered by single employers, multi-employer pension funds commonly known as Taft-Hartley plans, were established by collective bargaining in the same or related industries and labor unions. These plans allow workers, such as those engaged in the building and construction trades, and truck drivers, to move between employers and maintain and build retirement benefits.

The bankruptcy of the Studebaker car manufacturer in 1963 caused 4,000 workers to lose their retirements and was the catalyst for the Employee Retirement Income Security Act of 1974 (ERISA). The Act requires adequate funding of pensions and contributions to an insurance fund maintained by the Pension Benefit Guaranty Corporation to pay benefits in case of inadequate funding. Within the maximum annual pension allowed by the law, the Guaranty Corporation is presently paying benefits to 1.3 million workers, and there is a deficit or $21 billion between assets and obligations.

Businesses are moving away from defined benefit retirement plans. From 175,143 plans in 1983, there are now only 46,926 plans. Those that continue to offer retirement benefits are moving in the direction of defined contribution plans, such as those allowed under section 401(k) of the Internal Revenue Code. These plans are not covered by the Pension Benefit Guaranty Corporation.

Defined contribution plans, such as 401(k), allow employers to reduce their obligations under defined benefit plans by shifting the burden of planning for retirement onto their workers. Originally intended as a supplement to defined benefit plans for corporate officers, 401(k) plans have become the standard retirement benefit offered to most employees.

Contributions are automatically withheld from employees' paychecks and placed in investment funds, as directed by employees. Taxes are not paid until money is withdrawn from the funds. Employers are not required to contribute money to the funds, but some do as an employee benefit and to receive a tax benefit for the employer. Depending on market conditions, the funds can increase or decrease. Subject to a 10 percent penalty, funds sometimes can be withdrawn and spent before retirement. Layoffs and loss of employment frequently trigger withdrawals and quickly leave unemployed workers without any retirement savings.

The average contribution by employees is three percent; however, 10 to 12 percent is required to adequately fund a retirement. Employees can begin to withdraw funds to live on following retirement; however, stock market crashes, such as occurred in 2008, can wipe out or severely diminish their capital base.

Unlike Social Security, where government management costs less than one percent, the fees paid to the companies that manage investments usually exceed one percent to account for the profit needs of investment companies. Investment managers have no fiduciary duty to the employees making contributions and can increase their profits through their buy and sell decisions and the commissions they earn on transactions.

More than half of all workers have less than $10,000 in retirement savings, and 75 million workers do not even have access to 401(k) plans.

Sam said that he believed Social Security should remain as a safety net and 401(k) investment plans should continue to allow workers to make their own investment decisions. "However, there should be another way to extend the ownership of personal retirement plans in a manner that is beneficial to society and is even more secure for workers."

We should seriously consider an alternative personal investment plan as a supplement to traditional Social Security, whereby employees make additional tax-free contributions to personal accounts in a National Bond Fund that invests its assets in the obligations of local and state governments and primarily used to repair and improve the infrastructure.

Looking at her laptop, Aileana noted that the national infrastructure was in desperate need of attention.

Social Security and Retirement

It appears that one-third of the roads in the U.S. are in poor condition and that many dams and levees are failing. Nearly a quarter of the 600,000 bridges in the United States are "structurally deficient" or "functionally obsolete," and ancient water and sewer systems in older cities pose substantial risks to public health.

Sam continued to explain his idea.

Employers could agree to match Bond Fund contributions as a job benefit; employees could take their accounts with them from job to job; workers could negotiate the level of each employer's contribution; retirees could decide for themselves whether to invest their savings in a lifetime annuity at retirement; they could choose to spend their entire nest egg as they please; they could leave it to their heirs; or they could invest in a small business.

The stability of investments in state and local bonds would require minimal management costs, increase the rate of returns, and allow the principal placed in personal accounts—which could be withdrawn at any time to meet emergencies—to be guaranteed by the federal government just as it does for bank deposits. Earned interest would also be guaranteed, but could not be withdrawn until maturity.

Bond Fund accounts could be established by parents at the birth of their children and grow throughout the children's lifetime until they choose to retire. There could be survivor benefits similar to those provided by traditional Social Security, and the personal accounts could mature as early as age 55, allowing workers to transition to other, and perhaps more interesting, secondary careers.

America would benefit as a whole from an alternative retirement savings plan by having a readily available, domestic source of investment funds to restore and improve its state and local infrastructure and public facilities.

Small business owners and other self-employed people would be able to more easily provide for their own retirement. Since these people often transition between being self employed or employed by others, the retirement could grow throughout their working years. Additionally, the fund might be a source of loans to small business owners to borrow against their investment principal in order to start or improve their businesses.

Many of us will never have the sophistication, discipline, or excess capital to consistently make good investments in a personal portfolio. For most workers, the social security bargain we made with our government back in 1935 remains the best deal we can hope for when we retire or if we become disabled. We do not have to worry that our retirement or a serious accident will coincide with an economic recession, when the stock market is in decline, or that we will outlive the value of our private investments. Quite simply, we are secure in our society.

We the people, the ones most affected, have the right to vote directly on any risky gamble with our money and future well-being. No other question is more amenable to a policy vote during a National Policy Referendum.

Let us dream of a society in which we are able to prosper and enjoy the full fruits of our labor. Let us imagine a society in which we can retire in comfort and security without worrying about shelter, food, and medicine, or that we will become a burden on our families or communities.

The Election of 2012

It was hard to believe four years had passed since we had begun to write Sam's political philosophy, but 2012 brought another presidential election. Barack Obama was running for reelection, and it appeared Mitt Romney was to be his Republican opponent.

Sam's ALS disease had progressed to the point where he could no longer travel, but the extreme popularity of his book and the additional chapters presented during subsequent printings had kept his thoughts before the public.

To many people, Sam had become a folk hero, saying in simple and direct language what many of them, of every political persuasion, thought. Bumper stickers and yard posters were available on the Internet proclaiming "President Sam in 2012." The beach neighbors were particularly supportive, and Sam enjoyed seeing their yard signs during his outings in his motorized wheelchair, accompanied by K.D.

Our contractual obligations to the publisher had been satisfied and there were no plans to deliver future additions. Occasionally, I was asked to present at a conference or special event, and I was pleased to do so whenever possible.

Tala had become an essential member of the family. She not only helped Aileana care for Sam and Mei Lynn, but her liveliness and good humor also brought light and laughter into the home. Heather was no longer employed full time in promoting *Sam,* and she enrolled to attend graduate school in the fall. The two young women were often out and about together. Neither had a steady boyfriend, but the affections of both were sought by many.

In spite of living under an imminent sentence of death, there was no room for dark thoughts or bad moods in the beach house. Xiomara and I visited as often as possible. Few things brought as much joy and fulfillment as sitting around the dining table or living room talking about the events of the day and watching the delightful antics of Mei Lynn, who was two years old on the first of May.

Sam was up early each morning reviewing the latest news on the election campaign and closely followed its progress on the Internet. He said there really wasn't a spit's worth of difference between the two major parties on the issues that really matter.

Because corporations have gained control over campaign financing and have been authorized by the Supreme Court to spend unlimited amounts of money as a form of political free speech, both parties pretty much follow the dictates of Corporate America in matters of diplomacy, war, defense spending, homeland security, energy production, education, and the environment. It doesn't matter which candidate wins the election, because the corporate position on these issues will continue to prevail.

It is almost as though there is a conspiracy to avoid talking about the critical issues that would involve compromises in the political process and both sides working together to make progress. If astrophysicists exactly predicted a massive asteroid was on a track to strike Earth in 10 years, the two parties would squabble about global warming, a woman's freedom of choice, same-sex marriage, and immigration.

It seems the art of politics can be found in the adroit ability of professional politicians to avoid taking positions or spelling out the details of proposed policies. Rather than attract supporters with well-thought-out proposals, they attack the positions of each other. In doing so, both sides lie with impunity.

The Election of 2012

In August, Naomi Washington called to report a contact from the CBS producers of *60 Minutes*. Bob Simon wanted to film a segment for an episode to be presented before the election in October. Sam had a lot of respect for the show and Simon as a journalist. We all agreed it would be an worthwhile experience.

A film crew arrived in September and set up in the living room of the beach house. The whole family participated. Since Sam was experiencing increased difficulty speaking, Aileana helped by repeating some of his comments. Mei Lynn was on her lap and K.D. was by his side. The rest of us watched from off camera.

Filming took several hours, but Sam's answers to Bob Simon's questions about the election and various issues were clear and concise.

The most important life and death issues facing humanity today are the environment, including the availability of clean water, the production of energy to sustain our civilization, and how we are going to feed and educate our children.

Our failure to aggressively and competently deal with these issues results from the efforts of the powerful corporations to avoid doing anything about any problems that might interfere with their short-term profits. Government decisions should be based on what is best for the most in the long term.

Primarily, we must do what we can to ensure the future happiness and well being of our children.

If we fail to believe the ninety-nine out of every hundred scientists who—relying on solid science—tell us that global warming is a result of human activities, we are fools for accepting corporate propaganda to the contrary. We are equally foolish if we fail to act on scientific recommendations that—unless we make changes in the manner in which we energize our society—warn of the destruction of the human race. We have a responsibility to our children not to be foolish.

By nature, the environment is interdependent and self limiting, while capitalism must continually expand or collapse. Only an enlightened government that is oriented to the society that creates it can reconcile these differences in a manner that benefits the People, rather than corporations.

We are not protecting our children if we allow corporations to privatize public water systems and to permit waterways and aquifers to be polluted by the unregulated discharge of industrial and commercial agricultural waste.

We are failing our children if we allow the business model to be imposed on our public school system, forcing our children to be relentlessly tested and made into failures. We are irresponsible if we allow the public education system that enabled the development of our society to be privatized into a corporate charter school system.

We are not only neglecting the future of our children by supporting the endless war against terrorism created by corporations for their eternal profit, but we are also guaranteeing that their futures will be filled with pain and suffering.

It is sad to see that the voters of every political party are not demanding that these matters be addressed by the candidates they vote for. The world we are leaving for our children is fraught with danger and it is up to our young people to step forward and take charge of their own futures. Of everything I survey, I have faith in this first generation to come of age in the new millennium.

Simon asked Sam what he thought about the candidates.

Mitt Romney is a corporate takeover financier, who is proud of the thousands of employees he has put out of work and the jobs he has caused to be shipped overseas. It is difficult for me to believe he has an ounce of empathy for ordinary hardworking men and women. He was born to privilege and has never known suffering. His answer to the economic woes is to allow the capitalist system to sort out the winners and losers and for people to take care of themselves.

Barack Obama was not born to privilege, but he took advantage of available opportunities to secure a privileged education and to secure a comfortable place among the intellectual and financial elite. Once elected as a U.S. senator, he quickly aligned himself with the corporate power structure, which rewarded him with generous campaign contributions during his elections. As President, he has turned off his message of hope and change. Instead, he has followed the politics of greed, the culture of militarism, and the pursuit of empire in betraying the people who elected him.

Obama was awarded the Nobel Peace Prize before he had settled into his office and has made a mockery of it. By continuing and expanding the drone warfare of Bush Junior, by prosecuting more whistle blowers under the espionage act than all previous presidents combined, and by endorsing and expanding the surveillance state, President Obama is more than a disappointment—he is a disgrace to his office. I have little or no respect for him and most of his administration.

What distresses me, indeed makes me angry, is the virtual absence of anti-war protests and demonstrations during the Obama administration. The progressive left has given him a free pass to expand the use of armed drones and Special Force killing teams beyond what Bush Junior thought he could get away with.

Dr. Jill Stein, the Green Party candidate is an interesting woman, and I certainly respect what the party stands for; however, I have failed to identify any concrete policy positions that could be the foundation for administering the Nation should she be elected. There is much to be said for an opposition party that offers a philosophy of ecological wisdom, social justice, grassroots democracy, and nonviolence. This is especially true as the New Democrats have essentially abandoned all of these principles, but you can't administer a massive government without a comprehensive plan and experienced managers.

The Libertarian Party's candidate, former New Mexico Governor Gary Johnson, offers an alternative to traditional republicanism. Minimum government and maximum freedom sounds good when talking about the failed War on Drugs, military imperialism, or government intrusion into personal decisions, such as abortions and same-sex marriage; however, it seems awfully cold-hearted when offering little or nothing to help the millions of unemployed and desperate people survive from one day to the next.

Bob Simon asked which candidate Sam would be voting for, "Unfortunately, not one of them is committed to outlawing war and the murder of innocent children." When asked what he would do, Sam said, "I will carefully write in the name of someone, perhaps my wife, Ana, whom I believe would act in the best interests of the children of the world. I will not waste my vote on the best of bad choices."

What can ordinary working people and small business owners do to change things? If you are offered only candidates who all stand for the same thing on major issues, or candidates who have no chance of being elected, then your vote is ineffective and without value—unless it is used as a protest against the system.

All of these parties and those who believe in and work for them have something to offer. What is needed is something to bring all of them together in creating a political system that allows every individual to have a real influence on the government they elect. As it is, unless drastic changes are made in the manner in which that government is elected, the corporations will continue to run the show and the people will be left in the cold.

After the film crew left, Xiomara hugged Sam and thanked him for his remarks on public education. She said it was the only hopeful comment on education she had heard during the campaign.

The 2012 presidential election was the most expensive in history, with both major candidates raising and spending more than a billion dollars each. More than 80 percent of the money was spent on negative advertising attacking the positions of the other candidate.

The election was uninspiring, with voter turnout dropping from 62.3 percent in 2008 to 57.5 percent. Almost half of American voters sat out the election, when they could have—at least—cast a protest vote. I wrote in Sam's name, as did thousands of other voters. Our votes were not counted, but they were not wasted.

The Election of 2012

Election day four years earlier had been a glorious occasion. Sam and Aileana were married and we celebrated by watching Barack Obama's acceptance speech in Chicago's Grant Park. There was no election party in 2012. The grim outlook for the nation during a second Obama administration was matched by the prognosis of Sam's disease.

Sam maintained good cheer and refused to give in to depression. He looked forward to 2013 and the happiness of his family.

The Power of Voting

New Year's resolutions for 2013 did not involve any more writing. Indeed, even though he remained mentally alert, it was becoming difficult for Sam even to dictate his thoughts, as talking had become difficult. Usually, Aileana or one of us familiar with his speech patterns helped interpret. We recorded what he wanted to say and read to him whenever he wanted. He maintained some movement of his arms and hands and had a limited ability to scroll through the Internet news using the arrows, but he became frustrated when he could not find something he was curious about.

Tala and Aileana administered an exercise program to maintain Sam's mobility and massages to relieve cramping and muscular pain. They also engaged him in speech therapy to extend his ability to communicate. A hospital bed had been installed in his large downstairs study, as he could no longer make it up the stair lift. Aileana or Tala slept on a large couch in the room, and someone was always available to assist his needs.

During the day, Sam often sat at the large plate glass window in the living room looking out at the ocean, with K.D. at his side. He didn't get out as much as he used to in his wheelchair, but he would return the waves of neighbors as they passed by on the Strand. His greatest joy was to hold Mei Lynn in his lap or watch her play around him. He loved to sit quietly as Aileana read Mei Lynn's favorite books

The Power of Voting

to her and smiled as she began to recognize and repeat the words and phrases.

A truly happy child, Mei Lynn celebrated her third birthday with a group of her play friends. There is nothing more enchanting than a group of happy and rambunctious children. The beach house and outside patio were filled with life and those who were living it to the fullest.

Mei Lynn got a stack of new picture books and a baby doll to care for. With Sam's diet of high-energy foods that are easy to swallow, he joked that he could finally have all the ice cream he wanted.

The new homeowners continued to make the beach house their own, as Aileana added more plants to her container garden in the front patio. She placed South American milkweed plants among the citrus trees to attract monarch butterflies, who winter in Southern California. Sam and Mei Lynn enjoyed watching the butterflies feed on the red and gold milkweed flowers and flit about the garden.

Heather started her graduate studies in the UCLA journalism department, with minors in political science and the environment. She continued to live at home and joined us on Sunday afternoons at the beach house whenever she could.

Sam had been thinking about the last presidential election and the upcoming 2014 congressional elections. He said it seemed that campaigns and the raising of money to conduct them never ceased. Sam wanted to talk about voting, and he asked if I would transcribe what he had to say into a readable form. Over the years, we had come to think alike and to anticipate each other's thoughts, and with Aileana's help, I was glad to help him express his ideas.

One of the most frustrating things about ALS is that it affects only the motor neurons, and the mind remains active and engaged. As Sam struggled to make his tongue, lips, and vocal cords express his complex and politically sophisticated thoughts, we began our most difficult writing project. Although the result is not lengthy, it was months in the making.

Voting is the essence of democracy, and republics are founded upon the ability of the people to vote for their representatives in government. Voting may take place in dictatorships and monarchies, but the votes are meaningless, unless the people are well-informed and free to vote as they chose.

Voting must be effective. In the United States, where both major political parties are controlled by the same corporate and wealthy interests, voting no longer makes a real difference. Unless candidates actually represent the interests of those who elect them, it doesn't really matter whom one votes for—the result will be the same.

Effective voting, as a form of free speech, is the most important right, for without it, as Madison said, all other rights are forfeit.

Short of a violent revolution, voting is the only real power ordinary people have over their government. To be effective, the power of voting must be physically demonstrated. In other words, voting and its results must be transparent, visible, and palpable. Voting on a computer touch screen is not the same as handwriting on a paper ballot. The ballot must be a physical expression of individual power and will.

Even with a paper ballot, if the choices presented do not represent the needs of the people, any vote is illusory. Choosing the best of two bad candidates is not effective voting.

Governments, even those that do not represent the will of the people, require voting in order to achieve a semblance of legitimacy. The only way for the people to regain control of their government is to creatively use the voting process to peacefully rebel against an unrepresentative government.

If the government does not provide paper ballots, people should create their own ballots and deposit them at the polling place—even if they are not counted.

If a voter does not want to vote for one of the candidates on a paper ballot, he or she should carefully write in the name of his or her choice, even if the vote is not counted.

The Power of Voting

If people are not allowed to vote, they should protest, loudly, in every way they can imagine to attract attention to the deprivation. They should take to the Internet, create their own elections, and encourage others to join them.

Gaining the right to cast effective votes is worth creating a ruckus. Empowerment of the voting experience is the key to freedom!

Aileana had been helping to get Sam's thoughts organized, but she had something to say on her own. "Speaking of voters' rights, can you believe that Americans do not have a constitutional right to vote?"

Of all the democracies in the world, the United States is one of the very few that does not include the right to vote in its constitution. As the Supreme Court said in Bush v. Gore, "...the individual citizen has no federal constitutional right to vote for electors for the President of the United States."

The Thirteenth Amendment prohibits discrimination in voting based on race, the Nineteenth Amendment prohibits voting discrimination against women, and the Twenty-Sixth Amendment prohibits age discrimination in voting, but nowhere in the Constitution is there an affirmative right to vote!

Because the regulation of voting, including registration and qualifications, is pretty much left up to the individual states, Congress has little power to regulate even federal elections. The result is that, in regard to elections, the United States looks like a "banana republic." In truth, however, because their constitutions guarantee the right to vote, elections in South and Central America are often more orderly and less subject to dispute.

As a journalist, I frequently observed how the overwhelming power of the wealthy elite, corporations, and other special interest groups managed to purchase the major benefits of government, while avoiding the burden of taxation. This is nothing new. The danger presented by the power of money has been a risk to democracy throughout American history.

Sam: A Political Philosophy

Thomas Jefferson hoped that "we shall crush in its birth the aristocracy of our monied corporations which dare already to challenge our government to a trial by strength, ..." Almost two hundred years later, Franklin Roosevelt said, "We know now that Government by organized money is just as dangerous as Government by organized mob."

Sam said, "Legalized bribery in the form of campaign contributions pollutes the entire political process."

Candidates avoid taking positions on critical issues and ignore the concerns of ordinary voters. Much like commercial ad campaigns, political parties enact policy platforms designed to attract voters and then ignore their promises once their candidates are elected. When the government, the media, and candidates lie to voters, they cast uninformed votes.

Is there any wonder that voters are turned off by elective politics and stay home on election day?

If they are to ever achieve true representative democracy and the freedom and opportunity inherent in its promise, the People of the United States must transform their government, rather than reform or restore it back to something which will not serve or protect their best interests.

Sam had been considering the various proposals for constitutional amendments to deal with corporate power over the election process when he discovered the United States Voters' Rights Amendment on the Internet. The website, usvra.us, incorporates the best proposals to terminate constitutional rights for corporations and to end the equation of money and free speech, but it goes much further.

First and foremost, the USVRA provides a constitutional right to vote, but it addresses other critical electoral issues, including corporate personhood, campaign financing, lobbying, and conflicts of interest in creating *the right to cast an effective vote*.

The USVRA goes beyond reformation to transformation. It proposes holding a national policy referendum coincident with presidential elections on national paid holidays to allow the People to make their own policy and to write in the names of the federal representatives they choose to implement their policy. The purpose of the USVRA is to transform the American government into an effective democratic republic that is oriented to the society which elects it.

Sam said the USVRA is a voters' bill of rights.

It would clearly establish that the right to cast an effective vote is an inherent right under the Constitution, and it allows the people to have a more direct role in the formulation of public policy.

The USVRA not only provides for a national paid voters' holiday, but it also requires a national hand-countable paper ballot and eliminates the electoral college.

The minor parties would gain greater political power, and there is a great likelihood that a multi-party system would result. Congress would necessarily become more issue oriented, and its members would be forced to collaborate and compromise in effectuating the People's policies.

One of the most important things about the Amendment is its requirement that "It shall be a primary function of the government to ensure that the People are supplied with truthful, unbiased, objective, and timely information regarding the political, economic, environmental, financial, and social issues that affect them, and that all students are educated in the nature and responsibilities of representative government."

Imagine that! Our government forced to tell us the truth about what we need to know in order to govern ourselves!

Those who founded the United States possessed an extraordinary breadth of vision in creating our representative democracy. The people of today, particularly those just coming of age, have to once again engage in big dreams about the way things ought to be, and to collaborate in compelling a renegotiation of our contract with our government. The Voters' Rights Amendment is a blueprint for transformation—a voters' Bill of Rights—but its effectiveness is in the doing. Making it happen is an essential part of the vision. Once the Amendment becomes a part of the Constitution, things will never again be the same.

Sam: A Political Philosophy

I am encouraged by the activities of Youth for the Voters' Rights Amendment—or Y4VRA. They are driving the nonpartisan movement to secure the right to vote, which is the only way it will ever be achieved. Older people are too divided and set in their ways. The future belongs to the young people—it is up to them to make it safe for themselves and their own children.

The Passage

Time seemed to slow down, as the days shortened in the winter and began to lengthen through spring and into the summer of 2014. We all knew the end was inevitable, but we wanted to stretch out our time with Sam for as long as possible.

The 4th of July fireworks show on the Manhattan Beach pier had become an annual celebration; however, Sam could no longer go out on the sand in his wheelchair. We sat on the large bricked-in front patio to watch the show and greet neighbors who passed along the Strand. Sam privately told me this would be his last 4th, but his goal was to be at Mei Lynn's fifth birthday party next May, "I want to live long enough for her to be able to remember me."

Mei Lynn continued to be fascinated with the orange and black monarch butterflies that gathered on the milkweed in the patio, and Tala showed her how to use a magnifying glass to find their eggs on the leaves. They watched as the tiny green and black striped caterpillars hatched and began to voraciously feed on the leaves and quickly grow larger. The adjacent citrus trees were a perfect place for the caterpillars to climb up and attach themselves in becoming beautiful jade and gold colored chrysalises. Mei Lynn was enchanted to see a butterfly emerge from its chrysalis and slowly unfold and wave its wings in the sun. She was delighted to hold it on a finger, before it flew away.

Tala and Mei Lynn rescued a small monarch with deformed wings that they named Flutter Butter. They fed the butterfly with sugar water in a netted terrarium for weeks, as it lived out its life. After he died peacefully, they decorated a small box and buried the butterfly in the side garden beneath the roses and wisteria vine. Speaking with the help of Aileana, Sam reassured Mei Lynn that Flutter Butter continued to live—whenever she thought about him. Sam asked her to shut her eyes and imagine him, and she said she could see him with perfect wings flying free outside his cage.

Heather attended the butterfly's funeral and asked Mei Lynn if she would like to make a book about the life of Flutter Butter. Using folded paper, they made an illustrated picture book showing the butterfly's life cycle. Mei Lynn made sure to get the black dot in just the right place on his wings, as she had learned, to show he had been a male.

I received a call late one evening at about this time from Aileana. She said there was no dire emergency, but hoped I could come down immediately. When I arrived, I found a police car parked in back of the house and a detective inside talking with Aileana. She said that earlier in the evening K.D. had begun to run from one part of the house to another barking furiously. Aileana called 911, and when the officers arrived they saw a man crouched down beside the house. He jumped the wall onto the beach and ran, but the officers were able to catch him. No shots were fired, but he was armed with a semi-automatic pistol and several clips of hollow-point ammunition.

A search of his van, which was found double parked in the alley, revealed a stash of other weapons, including an assault rifle. There were also articles about Sam and a copy of his book, which was filled with scribbles accusing Sam of being a "gun grabber," among other things. A record check revealed the man had a record of felony assault in Idaho, where he was associated with the Ayran Nation white supremacy movement. The man had refused to talk, but was being held on weapons and trespass charges.

The detective left and I spent the night. The next morning, Aileana and I talked with Sam about what had happened and discussed what should be done. Sam labored to tell us that he thought the man was probably a "lone wolf" and that it was unlikely he was part of a conspiracy. He tried to laugh and said all the man had to do was to just wait a little while. Sam said he wasn't afraid for himself, but was concerned about Aileana, Mei Lynn, and Tala.

They decided to upgrade their security, and over the next week a silent alarm system was installed along with security lights around the perimeter of the house. Sam said K.D. had proven she was all the alarm system they really needed.

During the fall, we learned through news reports that Sam was under consideration for the Nobel Peace Prize, but he discouraged any discussion. He was very pleased with the announcement in October that Kailash Satyarthi and Malala Yousafzai had received the award for "their struggle against the suppression of children and young people and for the right of all children to education."

Sam was disappointed by the November elections. He communicated that it was not so much that the Republicans made sweeping gains in the congressional, state, and local elections, because he was essentially nonpartisan as between the parties. Sam was, however, concerned that the campaigns did not actually address the critical economic and environmental issues that besieged the Nation. President Obama was blamed for all that was wrong, but the candidates offered no realistic solutions. Sam was discouraged that things probably will not be any better in two years when a new president is elected to replace Obama.

Xiomara, Heather, and I continued to visit most weekends, and I would drive down during the week whenever I could. Sam truly had become the brother I never had, and I looked forward to seeing his face light up when I entered his room.

Sam had little speech left, but his mind remained fully engaged. He indicated he had some final thoughts to be combined with his ideas on voting to be published in subsequent printings of *Sam*. Naomi

Sam: A Political Philosophy

Washington confirmed that the publisher would be glad to print anything Sam had to offer.

Ongoing book sales, worldwide, continued to produce large royalties, and Aileana had wisely and conservatively invested their income. The beach house was paid for and they had no debts—Mei Lynn's financial future was secure.

Sam wanted to talk about his underlying personal philosophy—the foundation of his political thinking. We had discussed the subject over the years and he had briefly touched on it in some of his writing. I was able to make sense of what he wanted to say and to transcribe it in a more complete manner than the few words he was able to manage. He was able to read and confirm what I wrote on my laptop.

Sam was a deeply spiritual man, who was comfortable with his beliefs and could express them in a commonsense manner. He supported the right of people to worship as they choose to believe, and he believed spirituality was important and diversity was valuable. Rather than seeking to define God for himself or others, he looked at scientific evolution, including the development of consciousness, as a continuing process that had brought us to this point in human history. Sam believed that while our bodily processes of eating, elimination, and reproduction were the same as other animals, our conscious mind produced the thoughts, emotions, and creativity that defined us as a species.

Like many people on Earth, Sam did not believe we are alone in the universe, nor that humanity is the first advanced civilization in all of eternity. He believed we are lovingly watched until such time as we learn to fly from our nest.

Rather than Mankind, Sam believed we are Mindkind, the progeny of evolution on Earth. As such, we are an integral part of universal creation wherever it has, or ever will occur. Sam believed that creativity was the essence of Mindkind, and that it was our creations—which are unique throughout the universe and eternity—which defines our kind.

The Passage

To become physically capable of joining the celestial family of Mindkind, however, we must, on our own, accomplish two things. We have to shed the heavy burden of deception, violence, and war that weighs down our progress. Equally important, we must ensure that every child on Earth has equal access to nutrition, health care, and education. Then and only then will humanity achieve the unimaginable ability, knowledge, wisdom, and power required to fly into the universe, into adjacent dimensions, and throughout eternity.

Knowing it was probably Sam's last, we made every effort to make Christmas as joyous and memorable as possible. I had conspired with Sam to obtain and assemble his present for Mei Lynn. Red was her favorite color, and red was the color of the little bicycle sitting beside the tree when she got up on Christmas morning.

Sam had secured presents for all of us, including an old-fashioned ink fountain pen for Heather, the fledgling writer, and one for me, the old columnist. We had continued the tradition of making ornaments for the tree, and Aileana discovered a beautiful little box hanging on one of the branches. Within, she found a pair of exquisite emerald earrings Xiomara had located on behalf of Sam. Emeralds are Mei Lynn's birthstone and are the symbol of love and rebirth. They also matched Aileana's Scottish green eyes.

Aileana and Sam generously gave Tala a homemade gift certificate, redeemable for her graduate school tuition. K.D., the guard dog, was pleased to unwrap a large meaty bone, which she carried to the side of the fireplace to gnaw on. Mei Lynn gave Sam a new pair of red silk pajamas, which Sam proclaimed to be the "cat's pajamas." Mei Lynn exclaimed, "We don't have a cat, we have a dog!"

The training wheels on Mei Lynn's bicycle were not needed for very long as she quickly began to race up and down the Strand in front of the beach house. As the weather warmed into the new year of 2015, Tala would bring Sam outside in his wheelchair to watch Mei Lynn zip by, peddling furiously, ringing the bell on her handlebars to warn pedestrians out of her way.

Sam was forced to make some decisions about the progress of his disease. The only medication available for ALS was Riluzole, which could only help prolong life for a few months. He decided to commence treatment, even though side effects included increased weakness and sedation. He traded alertness for time with those he loved.

His weight had been steadily dropping, and he was becoming dehydrated, as swallowing became almost impossible without choking. Sam agreed to a surgical procedure to place a permanent feeding tube through his abdominal wall to allow nutrition, water, and medications to be directly inserted into his stomach. He tolerated the procedure and returned home after a few days.

Sam's downstairs study resembled a hospital room, and supplemental part-time nurses were employed to help Tala and Aileana care for him around the clock.

Sam accepted the feeding tube, but made clear he did not want to be placed on a ventilator. He received positive-pressure pulmonary therapy several times a day to expand his lungs, and mucous had to be suctioned from his nose and throat.

Verbal communication was becoming almost impossible, but Sam had some last thoughts to share. He wanted to reassure Aileana and Mei Lynn that he would be with them throughout their lives—whenever they remembered him. He had earlier explained to me his theory of an electromagnetic or quantum physical basis for the soul. Sam believed that after we pass, our quantum soul is attracted to the physical energy whenever someone thinks about us in the future. We are either in heaven and hell, depending on the kind of thinking—love or hate—that compelled our presence. Given Sam's positive influence on the lives of millions of people, I had no doubt he would find a loving reception whenever or wherever his spirit traveled in response to the multitude of kind and loving thoughts around the world, and perhaps throughout the universe.

In March, the Army formally apologized for the manner in which the military had treated service members exposed to chemical agents during the first Gulf War and promised to provide improved medical support in the future. For years, the Department of Defense and CIA had covered up the fact that as many as 700,000 American troops were exposed to nerve gas and other chemical agents. Aileana said the apology was better than nothing, but wondered if history would hold the Reagan and Bush I administrations accountable for their encouragement of U.S. corporations to sell the chemical agents and equipment to produce mustard and nerve gas to Iraq in the first place.

Mei Lynn celebrated Easter by coloring eggs in the kitchen and rediscovering them magically hidden around the beach house. As her fifth birthday approached, Sam continued to listen eagerly to the Internet news, as it was read to him each morning. He could no longer use his computer, but he valued online reporting by *The Guardian*, *Reuters*, and independent Internet news sites. He had little regard for what the mainstream American corporate media, particularly television, had to offer.

Sam especially looked forward to the moment each morning when Mei Lynn, having dressed and finished her breakfast, bounded into his room.

Mei Lynn was a precocious and marvelously articulate child, who happily climbed into Sam's lap and carried on animated conversations with him—in which his responses were mainly smiles and head movements. She loved her father, he loved her, and they both knew it.

His present for her on her first of May birthday was an iPad, which she took to with a passion. She quickly worked her way through the menus and figured out things that even Tala and Heather hadn't discovered. She picked a photograph of herself, Sam and K.D. for the iPad's wallpaper.

It was in the middle of the night about a week later that Aileana called me and said I should come. Sam's respiratory system was exhausted, and the time when it could no longer sustain life was near.

Aileana and Tala were with Sam. He was receiving oxygen through a nasal cannula, and his breathing was laborious. Although he appeared to be sleeping, his eyes opened as I approached the bed, and he lifted his hand to me. Aileana and I sat on either side of the bed holding his mutilated hands—which had brought us together—as his life slipped away. K.D., sensing that something was different, lay near, but she would rise and pace from one side of the bed to the other.

Sam seemed to be trying to say something, and Aileana leaned in and quietly asked, "What is it Samuel?" He managed a weak smile and whispered, " My Ana."

Sam and I had once discussed whether it was possible at the moment of death to see what lay beyond. He had said that, while he wanted to cling to life as long as possible, he had no fear of the passage and was indeed curious of what, if anything, he would find on the other side.

As dawn approached, Sam pulled Aileana and me closer and with his last breath whispered what he saw: "Peace."

I telephoned the paper and, as an ending to the story I had started about Sam so many years before, I told the night editor to release on the wire service the obituary I had on file.

Epilogue

Aileana woke Mei Lynn as usual, helped her brush her teeth, dress, and eat breakfast. She and Mei Lynn went into the living room, and Aileana explained that her father had not had the strength to make it through the night, even though he had wanted to be there for her.

Mei Lynn had learned the meaning of death to the extent her young mind could understand it. She was led into Sam's room to be with him for the last time. He was clean and dressed in the red pajama's she had given him for Christmas; his face was calm, and he appeared to be peacefully sleeping. She climbed up beside her father for the last time, gave him a hug, told him goodbye, and asked if he was flying.

All arrangements had been made, and Sam's body was quietly taken away to be cremated. As planned, a memorial service was held on the UCLA campus in Royce Hall, which was filled to its 1,800 seat capacity. The magnificent pipe organ played Sam's favorites. Pursuant to his wishes, there were no public speakers, even though many—of every political and religious persuasion—including President Obama, had asked to participate.

Aileana, holding Mei Lynn and with K.D. at her side, welcomed everyone to the service and expressed the gratitude of Sam's family for their support. As Sam had asked me to do, I read his final thoughts on life's ultimate journey, and we all wished him well on his flights of mind, soul, and spirit.

On the 4th of July, we all gathered at the Redondo Beach Harbor and boarded a rented boat to motor up the coast and watch the Manhattan Beach fireworks. As the show reached its crescendo, Aileana and Mei Lynn released Sam's ashes over the side, so they could wash ashore in front of the beach house and mingle with the sand.

Tala continued to live in the beach house and started graduate school to become a physician assistant. In a step towards her own independence, Heather moved into one of the extra bedrooms. Aileana and Mei Lynn were surrounded with family—as they began to make their way into a future without the physical presence of Sam.

K.D. continues to protect the family and accompanies Mei Lynn wherever she goes, except to kindergarden, but can often be found in Sam's study lying next to his chair in front of the picture window.

I have often wondered what might have happened if Sam had not been forced to fight in the Gulf War. If his enlistment had expired and he had returned to college and become a teacher—if he had married and had a house full of children. Undoubtedly, he would have been a gifted teacher, a good husband, and wonderful father.

Or, given the tremendous courage and extraordinary intelligence he displayed during his ordeal and the aftermath, I wonder if he might have made a more traditional, yet significant, contribution to political scholarship and leadership.

What I do know is that Sam brought light into a darkening world, that he confronted the demons of war and injustice, and introduced the angels of peace and mercy.

He had far more to offer than the few words we were able to record. I was honored to be his scribe.

Author's Note

This is Sam's story, not mine; however, to the extent his fiction derives from my fact, a bit of history may help to understand how this book came to be written.

A new chief of police was appointed in Los Angeles in 1970, and his first order was that department policy—the principles, philosophy, and operational wisdom that guide the exercise of police discretion—be identified and written down. As a young police officer just starting law school, I was assigned the task.

Two years later, after the Police Commission approved publication of the *Policy Manual*, the chief was appointed to chair the Police Task Force of President Nixon's National Advisory Commission on Criminal Justice Standards and Goals. Chief Davis "loaned" me to the commission staff and gave me the job of researching and writing the role of the police in America. Retired Deputy Chief Jim Fisk graciously organized faculty seminars at UCLA to help me through the effort.

It was a time of great personal growth, and ever since then, the experience has greatly influenced my views on the manner in which a free people should protect and govern themselves.

Following graduation from law school, I spent a year in Washington, DC working with the Justice Department to implement national criminal justice standards.

Sam: A Political Philosophy

Returning to Los Angeles, I prosecuted criminal defendants for the District Attorney's Office for a few years. Having been a habitual runaway and ward of the court as a teenager, I became uncomfortable when I was assigned to the juvenile court to prosecute delinquents. I resigned and opened a small inner-city neighborhood practice primarily representing young people accused of serious crimes. Dr. William Vicary, a highly-qualified forensic attorney-psychiatrist, helped me with a number of my cases.

At the time, I also looked around and wondered if there was anything else I could do to make use of my education and experience for the public good.

On July 9, 1979, acting pursuant to the First Amendment right to petition our government for redress of grievances, I filed a class action lawsuit directly in the U.S. Supreme Court on behalf of every citizen of the United States seeking a *writ of mandamus* from the Court to the executive and legislative branches of government.

The petition alleged that "the Congress of the United States is in the grips of special interest groups and is no longer responsive to the needs of individual citizens."

As a remedy, the Court was asked to order the Congress and the President to hold a National Policy Referendum during the presidential election. The referendum was "to peaceably explore the will of the people necessary to ensure their survival and that of their common government."

Without comment, the Supreme Court declined to hear our petition; however, the *Los Angeles Times* did report it was one of the ten more interesting cases the Court choose *not* to hear that term.

Thus, in the presidential election of 1980, the people were forced to chose between the policies of Jimmy Carter or Ronald Reagan—instead of having the right to decide their own policies in a national referendum.

Given this lack of choice, I became a candidate for president to stir up publicity for a national policy referendum and to promote a

Author's Note

peaceful protest in which all voters write in the name of the person they select to exercise the policies of the people.

Moreover, I had come to believe the United States should renounce war against other nations and their people as a matter of public policy. Instead, my platform advocated adoption of a law enforcement model, whereby Congress declares the offender to be an "outlaw" and authorizes the "arrest" of petty dictators—and what they are doing to harm their own citizens and our national interest.

My campaign consisted of a midnight radio talk show on the local rock and roll station and a few sparsely attended press conferences, with generally favorable coverage.

When the results came in and Reagan was elected, I traveled to the Santa Barbara hotel where the world news media had gathered at the foot of the mountain below Reagan's ranch.

My final campaign press conference was held over drinks in the cocktail lounge, during which I conceded the election and did not demand a recount.

I also dropped off a hand-written letter addressed to the president-elect at the transition press office. In it, I urged Reagan to recognize that the USSR was undoubtedly lying about the extent of its military prowess, and I asked him to please kick a few tires before buying off on a needless expansion of the arms race. He must not have read my letter.

Reading and thinking about politics and the philosophy of government over the next 20 years, I mainly shared my thoughts with my journals. However, the options presented by the 2004 presidential race and the dangers of four more years of a Bush administration compelled me to write and publish a *Brief on the Bush Presidency* titled *You're Not Stupid! Get the Truth.*

With Bush's reelection, the growing power of large corporations and the neoconservative movement, the capitulation of the neoliberals, the endless war on terrorism, and the destruction of freedom in America, I decided to write a book on political philosophy.

Sam: A Political Philosophy

I published a series of articles on various political subjects on the Internet; however, something prevented me from completing the book. I just couldn't bring myself to publish another heavily footnoted nonfiction book on politics. I wanted to speak more freely and directly about war and justice in a commonsense manner.

One afternoon, I awoke from a nap in which I had been dreaming about a homeless Gulf War veteran named Sam who chewed off all of his fingers, one by one, in an attempt to focus attention on the war and to force President Bush to bring home the troops.

I wrote up a fictional story narrated by a syndicated newspaper columnist about Sam's ordeal and published it on the Internet.

The response to *The Man Who Ate His Fingers—A Story About the Stupidity of War and the Idiots Who Glorify It* was phenomenal. In just a couple of weeks, the title could be found at tens of thousands of websites around the world, and the reader response was overwhelmingly favorable.

I decided to complete the political philosophy project as a reality-based fiction. I found my writing voice with Sam, Aileana, the never-named newspaper columnist narrator, and his daughter, Heather. Several of the characters, including Dr. Vicary and my mentors Jim Fisk and Ed Davis are true-life participants in my life story, and the ideas presented by their characters are essentially the same as I recall.

Initially, I intended to publish the book in three parts, and the first part, *The Man Who Ate His Fingers: War and Justice*, was released electronically in 2012. I then hit a writer's block, and the remaining manuscript sat unfinished on my desk for more than two years. As a new year's resolution in 2015, I resolved to rewrite and complete the book.

I could not have kept my vow without the encouragement and professional assistance of my dear friend, Jacquie Gentry, who edited the manuscript—even though she didn't agree with all of my ideas. A teacher of English and Professor of Law, she taught potential attorneys how to write at a law school, until her retirement. She not only

Author's Note

corrected my grammar, but also improved the fictional narrative. (Her own legal fiction is published under the name of J.E. Gentry.)

Of course, my wife, Helen, is always my editor of last resort. A master artist, she also painted the image of Sam and K.D. for the cover.

The complete text of the United States Voters' Rights Amendment follows immediately after this note. Of everything I have ever accomplished in my life, I believe the USVRA is among the most important. Much like Sam, my dream is to live long enough to see it enacted.

Sam, who suffers in the book for peace and justice, lives on in the hearts and minds of all of us who yearn to be free of the stupidity of war, and who want our government to nurture our society, rather than to feed upon it.

The United States Voters' Rights Amendment (USVRA)

Section 1.
The right of all citizens of the United States, who are eighteen years of age or older, to cast effective votes in political elections is inherent under this Constitution and shall not be denied or abridged by the United States or by any State.

Section 2.
Equality of rights under the law shall not be denied or abridged by the United States or by any State on account of sex.

Section 3.
The States shall ensure that all citizens who are eligible to vote are registered to vote.

In balancing the public benefit of maximum voter participation with the prevention of voting fraud, Congress and the States shall not impose any unjustifiable restriction on registration or voting by citizens.

The intentional suppression of voting is hereby prohibited and, in addition to any other penalty imposed by law, any person convicted of the intentional suppression of voting shall be ineligible for public office for a period of five years following such conviction.

Section 4.
The rights protected by the Constitution of the United States are the rights of natural persons only.

Artificial entities established by the laws of any State, the United States, or any foreign state shall have no rights under this Constitution and are subject to regulation by the People, through Federal, State, or local law.

The privileges of artificial entities shall be determined by the People, through Federal, State, or local law, and shall not be construed to be inherent or inalienable.

Section 5.
Federal, State and local government shall regulate, limit, or prohibit contributions and expenditures, to ensure that all citizens, regardless of their economic status, have access to the political process, and that no person gains, as a result of their money, substantially more access or ability to influence in any way the election of any candidate for public office or any ballot measure.

Federal, State and local government shall require that any permissible contributions and expenditures be publicly disclosed.

The judiciary shall not construe the spending of money to influence elections to be speech under the First Amendment.

Section 6.
Nothing contained in this article shall be construed to abridge the freedom of the press, which includes electronic and digital publication.

Section 7.
In balancing the public benefits of corruption-free elections with allowing candidates to accept private campaign contributions,

The United States Voters' Rights Amendment (USVRA)

Congress and the States shall favor public financing over private contributions.

Broadcasters using the public airwaves shall provide free airtime for political campaign programming; ensure controversial issues of public importance are presented in an honest, equitable and balanced manner; and provide equal time to opposing candidates and political points of view.

No campaign for elective public office, including receipt of campaign contributions, shall commence prior to six months before such election.

Section 8.
Election districts represented by members of Congress, or by members of any State legislative body, shall be compact and composed of contiguous territory. The State shall have the burden of justifying any departures from this requirement by reference to neutral criteria such as natural, political, or historical boundaries or demographic changes. Enhancing or preserving the power of any political party or individual shall not be such a neutral criterion.

Congress shall apportion the number of representatives according to the decennial census to ensure the representation of a maximum of 250,000 Persons in each district.

Section 9.
It shall be a primary function of the government to ensure that the People are supplied with truthful, unbiased, objective, and timely information regarding the political, economic, environmental, financial, and social issues that affect them, and that all students are educated in the nature and responsibilities of representative democracy.

The University of the United States shall be established to incorporate all federal service academies and to provide education on the nature and responsibilities of representative democracy, the meaning of freedom, and the appropriate limitations on the use of coercion and force.

Section 10.
During the calendar year preceding a presidential election, Congress shall solicit public comment regarding the political issues that most concern the People.

Prior to the end of the calendar year preceding a presidential election, Congress shall adopt a joint resolution articulating questions regarding the twelve most critical policy issues to be addressed by the next president and Congress.

Failure of Congress to adopt such a joint resolution prior to the end of such calendar year shall result in the disqualification of all sitting members of Congress to be eligible for reelection.

Section 11.
Federal elections conducted every second year shall be held on a national voters' holiday, with full pay for all citizens who cast ballots.

Federal elections shall be conducted on uniform, hand-countable paper ballots and, for the presidential election, ballots shall include the twelve most critical policy questions articulated by Congress, each to be answered yes or no by the voters.

Paper ballots shall provide space allowing voters to handwrite in their choice for all elective federal offices, if they choose, and all such votes shall be counted.

Section 12.
Clauses Two and Three of Article Two, Section One and the Twelfth and Twenty-third articles of amendment to the Constitution of the United States are hereby repealed.

Clause Four of Article Two, Section One of the Constitution of the United States is amended to read as follows: "The Congress shall determine the dates of the primary and general elections of the president and vice president, which dates shall be the same throughout the United

The United States Voters' Rights Amendment (USVRA)

States. The presidential and vice presidential candidates receiving the most popular votes by all citizens of the United States shall be elected."

Section 13.
No person, having previously served as an official of the federal government, whether elected, appointed, employed, or serving in the military shall engage in any employment to advocate an interest or position to any Government official for a period of time following such service equal to the period of such service.

No person advocating an interest or position to any government official, whether or not for pay, shall offer or provide any campaign contribution, gifts, or things of value, including favors, services, travel, meals, entertainment, honoraria, and promises of future employment to such government official, nor shall such official accept any such proffering.

Restrictions imposed on such persons by this section shall not be deemed to violate the rights of free speech or petition for redress.

Section 14.
No member of Congress, federal judge, or federal official shall vote, or rule on any matter in which such person or their spouse, domestic partner, child, or contributor of more than minor amounts of campaign funds has a financial, legal, or beneficial interest.

Section 15.
This article shall be inoperative unless it shall have been ratified as an amendment to the Constitution by conventions in the several States, as provided in the Constitution.

Delegates to State conventions to ratify this amendment shall be selected by special elections held within three months of its being proposed by Congress to the States. The voters in each congressional district in the several States shall elect one delegate. All delegate candidates shall affirm under oath when filing as a candidate whether they will vote yes or not for ratification of the proposed amendment, and their position shall be printed with their names on the special election ballot. Delegates shall not have the power to vote differently than their stated intention.

Conventions shall be held in the capitals of each State within three months of the election of delegates, with the chief justice of the highest court in the State chairing the convention. Tie votes by delegates shall be considered a vote for ratification.

The power of delegates convened pursuant to this section shall be restricted to voting yes or no for ratification of the proposed amendment. Such conventions shall not have the power to make changes to the proposed amendment or to consider other constitutional amendments.

The costs of ratification pursuant to this section shall be an expense of the federal government.

William John Cox

For more than 45 years, William John Cox has written extensively on law, politics, philosophy, and the human condition. During that time, he vigorously pursued a career in law enforcement, public policy, and the law.

Cox was an early leader in the "New Breed" movement to professionalize law enforcement. He wrote the *Policy Manual* of the Los Angeles Police Department and the introductory chapters of the *Police Task Force Report* of the National Advisory Commission on Criminal Justice Standards and Goals, which continues to define the role of the police in America.

As an attorney, Cox worked for the U.S. Department of Justice to implement national standards and goals, prosecuted cases for the Los Angeles County District Attorney's Office, and operated a public interest law practice primarily dedicated to the defense of young people.

Cox volunteered *pro bono* services in several landmark legal cases. In 1979, he filed a class-action lawsuit on behalf of all citizens directly in the U.S. Supreme Court alleging that the government no longer represented the voters who elected it. As a remedy, Cox urged the Court to require national policy referendums to be held in conjunction with presidential elections.

In 1981, representing a Jewish survivor of Auschwitz, Cox investigated and successfully sued a group of radical right-wing organizations which denied the Holocaust. The case was the subject of the Turner Network Television motion picture, *Never Forget*.

Cox later represented a secret client and arranged the publication of almost 1,800 photographs of ancient manuscripts that had been kept from the public for more than 40 years. *A Facsimile Edition of the Dead Sea Scrolls* was published in November 1991.

He concluded his legal career as a Supervising Trial Counsel for the State Bar of California. There, Cox led a team of attorneys and investigators which prosecuted attorneys accused of serious misconduct and criminal gangs engaged in the illegal practice of law. He retired in 2007.

Continuing to write about political, philosophical, and social issues since his retirement, Cox's primary initiative has been the United States Voters' Rights Amendment (www.USVRA.us and www.Y4VRA.org). He can be contacted through his personal website at www.williamjohncox.com.

www.ingramcontent.com/pod-product-compliance
Lightning Source LLC
LaVergne TN
LVHW051108080426
835510LV00018B/1948